Commentaries

Commentaries

1 6 2   E S S A Y S   O N   W Y S U

―――

Tom Shipka

© 2018 Tom Shipka
All rights reserved.

ISBN: 1976046173
ISBN 13: 9781976046179
Library of Congress Control Number: 2017914754
CreateSpace Independent Publishing Platform
North Charleston, South Carolina

Dedication

To WYSU staff, volunteers, members, and listeners

Note to the Reader

THIS VOLUME CONTAINS THE ESSAYS which I aired on WYSU, the National Public Radio affiliate at Youngstown State University, from 2005 to 2015. They deal with a variety of topics but a recurring one is religion. I believe that most of them address issues or problems which remain central in American culture and politics today. Unless you were a WYSU listener who seldom missed morning broadcasts on weekdays, or faithfully read the commentaries posted on the WYSU website, there are many in this collection that you will encounter for the first time.

My allotted air time for these commentaries was a maximum of three minutes and forty-five seconds. Most have footnotes and, in some cases, these were part of the original body of the commentary which I shifted to footnotes to accommodate the time constraint. I urge you to read the footnotes for additional information on the topic of a given commentary.

WYSU aired each of my commentaries twice on a weekday, usually a Thursday, at 6:35 a.m. and 8:35 a.m. Of the 162 commentaries, 70% of them (113) aired from 2005 to 2009 and 30% (49) aired from 2010 to 2015. As a rule I taped the commentaries in a WYSU studio a day or two before they aired.

The commentaries appear here chronologically from the first in March 2005 to the last in December, 2015. Some cite information, usually from surveys, that was accurate at the time but may not be today.

You can find elaborations of many of the topics and historical figures in the commentaries in my previous books – *Philosophy: Paradox and Discovery*, Fifth Edition, 2004, and *Beliefs and Practices: Taking a Fresh Look*, 2016. Both are available at Amazon.com, as is this volume.

Tom Shipka
Emeritus Professor of Philosophy
Youngstown State University
tashipka@zoominternet.net

Acknowledgements

I AM GRATEFUL TO GARY Sexton, WYSU Director, and David Luscher, WYSU Associate Director, for their cooperation and help over the years. Gary screened all of my commentaries in draft stage and made constructive suggestions on some which I incorporated. He also approved their publication. David, a former student of mine, taped nearly all of them and scheduled them for broadcast.

Table of Contents

Note to the Reader · vii
Acknowledgements ·ix

On Toleration (March 10, 2005) · 1
On Experts (March 17, 2005) · 3
Emily Rosa (March 24, 2005) · 5
The Golden Rule (March 31, 2005) · 7
The Bible and Homosexuality (April 14, 2005) · · · · · · · · · · · · · · · · · 9
John Hick on God and Evil (April 21, 2005) · · · · · · · · · · · · · · · · · · 12
In the Name of God (April 28, 2005) · 15
Erudition or Gobbledygook? (May 5, 2005) · · · · · · · · · · · · · · · · · · · 17
The Right to Die (May 19, 2005) · 19
The Founders (June 3, 2005) · 21
The Skeptic and the Believer (June 16, 2005) · · · · · · · · · · · · · · · · · · 23
The Individual (June 30, 2005) · 25
Everything Happens for a Reason (July 14, 2005) · · · · · · · · · · · · · · · 27
The Law and Morality – the Mixed Legacy of Socrates and Plato
(July 28, 2005) · 29
Betting on God – Pascal's Wager (August 4, 2005) · · · · · · · · · · · · · · 31
Moral Rules: Clear as Mud (August 18, 2005) · · · · · · · · · · · · · · · · · · 33
Leopold and Loeb (August 25, 2005) · 35
A Lesson from the YSU Strike (September 8, 2005) · · · · · · · · · · · · · 37
Searching for the Soul (October 6, 2005) · 39

America's Philosophical Father (October 28, 2005) · · · · · · · · · · · · · · · · 41
Freedom – a Clarification (November 10, 2005) · · · · · · · · · · · · · · · · · · 44
Letter from Birmingham Jail (November 17, 2005) · · · · · · · · · · · · · · · · 46
Are You a Critical Thinker? (December 1, 2005) · · · · · · · · · · · · · · · · · · 48
Thomas Aquinas on God (December 15, 2005) · · · · · · · · · · · · · · · · · · · 51
George W. Bush on Surveillance – A Lockean Appraisal (December 29, 2005) · 54
When Bad Things Happen to Good People (January 12, 2006) · · · · · · · · 56
Bertrand Russell and the City College of New York (January 26, 2006) · · · 58
Sam Harris, *The End of Faith* (February 2, 2006) · · · · · · · · · · · · · · · · · 60
John Locke on the Separation of Church and State (February 9, 2006) · · · 62
Pragmatism (February 16, 2006) · 65
Tim Russert, *Big Russ and Me* (March 2, 2006) · · · · · · · · · · · · · · · · · · 68
Frank McCourt, *Teacher Man* (March 17, 2006) · · · · · · · · · · · · · · · · · 70
Jimmy Carter, *Our Endangered Values* (March 30, 2006) · · · · · · · · · · · 72
Miracles (April 13, 2006) · 74
So What Exactly Do Philosophers Do? (April 27, 2006) · · · · · · · · · · · · 76
Mill on Diversity (May 11, 2006) · 78
John Locke on Power (May 25, 2006) · 80
Gilbert Ryle on Mind (June 9, 2006) · 82
Self-Interest (June 22, 2006) · 84
James Rachels on Cultural Relativism (July 6, 2006) · · · · · · · · · · · · · · · 86
Thoreau on Civil Disobedience (July 20, 2006) · · · · · · · · · · · · · · · · · · · 89
Science and Intercessory Prayer – the STEP Study (August 3, 2006) · · · 92
Ayn Rand (August 17, 2006) · 95
The Freedom from Religion Foundation – Bucking the Trend (August 31, 2006) · 97
Funny Moments (September 14, 2006) · 100
Sam Harris – an Update (September 28, 2006) · · · · · · · · · · · · · · · · · · 102
Aayan Hirsi Ali – A Voice of Dissent in Islam (October 13, 2006) · · · · 105
Liberty or Security – a False Dilemma (October 26, 2006) · · · · · · · · · 107
Sam Harris, *Letter to a Christian Nation* (November 9, 2006) · · · · · · · 109
Garry Wills, *A Country Ruled by Faith* (November 30, 2006) · · · · · · · 112

Commentaries

David Kuo, *Tempting Faith* (December 14, 2006) 115
The Costs of College and Perceived Value (January 5, 2007) 117
Nora Ephron, *I Feel Bad About My Neck* (February 1, 2007) 120
Robert Green Ingersoll, *The Shakespeare of Oratory*
(February 16, 2007) 123
Bernard Rollin, A Dog's Best Friend (March 1, 2007) 125
James Randi (March 16, 2007) 127
Would You Vote for an Atheist or Agnostic? (April 5, 2007) 129
A Day with Ted Williams (April 19, 2007) 132
Suicide Isn't Always Bad (May 3, 2007) 134
A 1981 Warning about Religion and Politics (May 17, 2007) 136
Religion and Morality (June 14, 2007) 139
Hein v. Freedom from Religion Foundation, Inc. (July 19, 2007) 142
The Religious Right in the Post-Falwell Era (August 2, 2007) 144
The Christian Reconstructionists (August 16, 2007) 146
Paul Kurtz (August 30, 2007) 149
The Power of Belief (September 13, 2007) 152
Mark Lilla on the Great Separation (September 27, 2007) 154
World Religions in Modesto (October 25, 2007) 157
Kitzmiller v. Dover Area School District (November 8, 2007) 159
Thanksgiving Day – a Modest Proposal (November 29, 2007) 161
Judge John E. Jones III (December 13, 2007) 164
Government-Sponsored Nativity Scenes – a Prediction
(January 24, 2008) 167
Justice Brennan's Dissent (February 7, 2008) 170
The Gospel of Prosperity Under Fire (February 21, 2008) 173
Senator Obama on Religion (March 6, 2008) 176
Alan B. Krueger, *What Makes a Terrorist?* (March 20, 2008) 179
U.S. Religious Landscape Survey (April 24, 2008) 182
Confronting the Debt Culture (May 8, 2008) 185
So You Want to Be a Professor? (May 22, 2008) 188
The Costs of Family Fragmentation to Taxpayers (June 5, 2008) 191
Edward Filene, Father of the Credit Union (June 19, 2008) 194

For a New Thrift: Confronting the Debt Culture – Part 1 (July 3, 2008) · · · 197
For a New Thrift: Confronting the Debt Culture – Part 2 (July 17, 2008) · · · 200
Energy – the Turning Point (July 31, 2008) · 203
Whatever Happened to Jefferson and Madison? (August 14, 2008) · · · 206
The Faith-Based White House (August 29, 2008) · · · · · · · · · · · · · · · 210
Mistakes Were Made (but not by me) (September 11, 2008) · · · · · · · · · 213
Jim Tressel, Coach *and* Author (September 25, 2008) · · · · · · · · · · · · 216
Chris Hedges on the Radical Evangelicals (October 9, 2008) · · · · · · · · 219
Chris Hedges on the New Atheists (October 3, 2008) · · · · · · · · · · · · · 222
Are American Voters Stupid? (November 13, 2008) · · · · · · · · · · · · · · 225
A Lesson from Scandinavia (November 27, 2008) · · · · · · · · · · · · · · · 228
Galbraith on Global Warming and Planning (December 11, 2008) · · · 232
Religious Illiteracy (December 26, 2008) · 235
Charles Curran's Rocky Road (January 8, 2009) · · · · · · · · · · · · · · · · · 239
Sidney Poitier's Remarkable Journey (January 22, 2009) · · · · · · · · · · · 242
Rabbi Wolpe's Rebuttal (February 5, 2009) · 245
Faith Healing and Children (February 19, 2009) · · · · · · · · · · · · · · · · 248
John Haught and the New Atheists (March 5, 2009) · · · · · · · · · · · · · 251
Christopher Hitchens on Religion (March 19, 2009) · · · · · · · · · · · · · 254
Ted Kennedy's Legacy (April 9, 2009) · 257
American Religious Identification Survey 2008 (April 23, 2009) · · · · · · 260
Redemption at Starbucks (May 14, 2009) · 263
Suicide Terrorism (May 28, 2009) · 265
President Obama's U-Turn (June 11, 2009) · 268
Karl Rove (June 25, 2009) · 271
Carrie Fisher (July 9, 2009) · 273
Richard A. Clarke on National Security (July 23, 2009) · · · · · · · · · · · 276
Isaiah's Resilience (August 6, 2009) · 279
Cell Phones – A Moral Challenge (August 20, 2009) · · · · · · · · · · · · · 282
John Stuart Mill on Women's Rights (September 3, 2009) · · · · · · · · · · 285
Is Socialism Coming? (September 24, 2009) · · · · · · · · · · · · · · · · · · · 287
Religion in the Public Schools (October 15, 2009) · · · · · · · · · · · · · · · 289
Tiger's Two Lives (August 19, 2010) · 292

Chris Hedges on American Culture (September 16, 2010) · · · · · · · · · · 294
Ayaan Hirsi Ali's Jeremiad (October 14, 2010) · · · · · · · · · · · · · · · · · 297
Lou Holtz (November 18, 2010) · 300
Krista Tippett (January 6, 2011) · 303
Richard P. Stevens, Humanitarian and Globetrotter
(February 17, 2011) · 306
Marlo Thomas (March 17, 2011) · 309
James A. Haught, *Fading Faith* (April 14, 2011) · · · · · · · · · · · · · · · · 313
Nathan Leopold's Atonement (May 19, 2011) · · · · · · · · · · · · · · · · · · 316
The Class of '61 – Fifty Years Later (July 7, 2011) · · · · · · · · · · · · · · 319
Rob Bell on Hell (July 14, 2011) · 321
When Marriage Disappears (July 28, 2011) · · · · · · · · · · · · · · · · · · · 324
Michael Shermer, Skeptic (January 19, 2012) · · · · · · · · · · · · · · · · · · 327
John Dewey on Religion (February 9, 2012) · · · · · · · · · · · · · · · · · · · 331
Bertrand Russell - Prophet (March 8, 2012) · · · · · · · · · · · · · · · · · · · 334
Abundance (June 28, 2012) · 337
Free Will on Trial (July 19, 2012) · 340
Jim Abbott (September 13, 2012) · 343
Popular Beliefs: A Critique by Guy P. Harrison (October 18, 2012) · · · 346
The Invisible Gorilla (October 25, 2012) · 349
Guy P. Harrison on Religion (November 8, 2012) · · · · · · · · · · · · · · · 352
Eben Alexander's Journey into the Afterlife (November 15, 2012) · · · 355
Race One and Race Two (November 29, 2012) · · · · · · · · · · · · · · · · 358
John Stossel, Gadfly (December 13, 2012) · 361
Juan Williams – Part One (December 27, 2012) · · · · · · · · · · · · · · · · 364
Juan Williams – Part Two (December 28, 2012) · · · · · · · · · · · · · · · · 367
Sam Harris on Guns (January 3, 2013) · 370
Etiquette in Today's World (March 5, 2013) · · · · · · · · · · · · · · · · · · · 373
Elyn Saks (March 15, 2013) · 375
Religion – Can We Take a Fresh Look? (May 9, 2013) · · · · · · · · · · · · 378
Tom Flynn on the State of Religion in America (June 6, 2013) · · · · · · 381
Jim Haught on the State of Religion in America (June 13, 2013) · · · · · 384
Sylvia Browne, Psychic (June 27, 2013) · 387

Dr. Carl Hart (August 1, 2013) · 390
Academically Adrift (August 29, 2013) · 393
Alternative Medicine (October 31, 2013) · 396
Herbal Supplements: a New Study (November 7, 2013) · · · · · · · · · · · · 399
Jennifer Hecht on Suicide (December 5, 2013) · · · · · · · · · · · · · · · · · · 402
Religion and the Founders (December 19, 2013) · · · · · · · · · · · · · · · · 405
The Care and Feeding of the Brain (January 1, 2014) · · · · · · · · · · · · 408
Jerry DeWitt's Journey (January 9, 2014) · 412
The Odd Couple (January 16, 2014) · 415
Ted Williams (January 24, 2014) · 419
Larry Doby (March 6, 2014) · 422
Casinos and Seniors (March 13, 2014) · 424
The Cost of Higher Education: the Problem (March 27, 2014) · · · · · · · 427
The Cost of Higher Education: the Solution (April 3, 2014) · · · · · · · · 430
Domestic or Foreign? (May 8, 2014) · 434
Faith (December 17, 2015) · 437

About the Author · 441

On Toleration (March 10, 2005)

SUPPOSE SOMEONE SAYS SOMETHING THAT rubs you the wrong way.

You might be a Christian whose blood pressure spikes when people object to the Ten Commandments in a government building or to the phrase "one nation under God" in the pledge of allegiance. Or you might be a pro-life advocate who cringes at the comments of a spokesperson for the National Organization of Women. Or you might be a teacher who is angry at hearing attacks on public education. Or you might be a welfare recipient who bristles at criticisms of the welfare system by a multi-millionaire U.S. Senator.

None of us enjoys hearing from people who strike at the core of our deeply held beliefs. So, why tolerate them?

There are historically two main justifications, one based on rights, the other on utility.

The 17th century British political theorist, John Locke, argued in the *Second Treatise of Government* and other writings that the Law of Nature – his phrase for the moral law – confers on all human beings the rights to life, liberty, and estate and that the purpose of government is to protect and defend these rights. Liberty entails freedom of expression. Locke had a powerful influence on the founders. This is seen in the First Amendment to the Constitution which affirms:

> Congress shall make no law respecting an establishment of religion, or prohibiting the free exercise thereof; or abridging the freedom of speech, or of the press; or the right of the people peaceably to assemble, and to petition Government for a redress of grievances.

The implication here is clear. If you have a right to speak or write, I have a duty to allow you to do so. Of course I retain the right to sue at court if I believe that you are guilty of libel.

The other justification of toleration focuses on social utility. This approach was championed by the 19th century Utilitarian philosopher, John Stuart Mill. In his famous essay, *On Liberty*, Mill wrote:

> ...(T)he peculiar evil of silencing the expression of an opinion is, that it is robbing the human race; posterity as well as the existing generation; those who dissent from the opinion, still more than those who hold it. If the opinion is right, they are deprived of the opportunity of exchanging error for truth: if wrong, they lose, what is almost as great a benefit, the clearer perception and livelier impression of truth, produced by its collision with error.

For Mill toleration must be permanent, not sporadic. Why? In Mill's words, "Complete liberty of contradicting and disproving our opinion is the very condition which justifies us in assuming its truth for purposes of action." To do otherwise, he argues, is to impute infallibility to oneself, a foolish stance given the fact that all humans are fallible.

The next time you're tempted to censor or ignore or punish a person or group whose views rub you the wrong way, pick up a copy of Locke's *Second Treatise* and his *Letter Concerning Toleration* or Mill's *On Liberty*. These two intellectual pillars of modern democratic society have much to say that is relevant to American today.

On Experts (March 17, 2005)

WE LIVE IN A WORLD of specialization in knowledge and skills. We depend daily on experts to fix our cars, diagnose and treat our ailments, repair our computers, and represent us in legal proceedings.

Reliance on experts comes with risks, however, that we shouldn't forget.

In the first place, there's the issue of whether a self-declared expert really has any special knowledge or skill. I have in mind psychics, channelers, tarot card readers, astrologers, and practitioners of therapeutic touch, among others. Therapeutic touch practitioners, for instance, assure us that they can detect and manipulate the human energy field to help cure sick people. Some nursing organizations approve of therapeutic touch and there are even schools that award certificates in this field. But there's a slight problem. There's simply no evidence of a human energy field. Practitioners who have been tested to see if they can detect such a field have all failed. Patients who say they feel better after therapeutic touch therapy are exhibiting the placebo effect.

In the second place, even where a person's expertise is authentic, he or she may be mistaken. Experts remain fallible human beings. Here's a few examples.

1. Respected Harvard theologian Harvey Cox wrote a book in 1965 called *The Secular City* in which he chronicled the collapse of traditional religion in America. As one looks at the vitality of traditional tradition forty years later, it is painfully obvious that Cox gave us a premature obituary for religion.

2. Scientists in Nazi Germany thought that they could see nonexistent physical differences between blood particles of Jews and Aryans.
3. Astronomers Giovanni Schiaparelli and Percival Lowell claimed to see canals on mars; later photos from the Mariner 9 spacecraft showed no such canals.
4. French scientist Rene Blondlot believed he had discovered another form of radiation soon after X rays had been discovered. He called them N rays. American physicist Robert Wood showed that Blondlot and his associates had been victims of perceptual construction.
5. When Galileo's experiments and observations furnished support for Copernicus's theory that the earth moves and that the sun is the center of the universe, experts – both ecclesiastical and academic – attacked him.
6. And let us not forget the failures of intelligence and security experts in the terrorist attack of 9/11, of ship designers in the Titanic disaster, and of NASA officials in the Challenger space shuttle explosion. (1)

So what can you and I do to protect ourselves when we deal with experts?

- We can check out the credentials of a supposed expert and the legitimacy of his or her field.
- We can ask our expert to furnish evidence to us to support his or her conclusions and recommendations.
- We can seek a second opinion.
- We can strive to be well-informed on a continuing basis.
- Finally, we can discuss the opinions of experts with family and friends whose own experience may prove helpful.

These steps will not insulate us completely from risk but they will diminish it.

---

1. Many of the examples here are taken from Theodore Schick, Jr., and Lewis Vaughn, *How to Think About Weird Things*, Third Edition, McGraw-Hill, 2002.

Emily Rosa (March 24, 2005)

WHERE DO YOU LOOK FOR groundbreaking research? Universities, research institutes, corporate R&D departments? All good guesses, certainly. But how about the fourth grade?

Ten years ago a fourth grader, Emily Rosa, asked her mom, a nurse, about an idea for her class science project. Mom was skeptical about a popular fad among nurses – therapeutic touch or TT. The daughter made TT the focus of her project.

Advocates of TT say that the human body has an energy field that sometimes becomes blocked or out of balance, causing various illnesses. This energy field, they say, extends beyond the skin where trained practitioners can detect it and massage it so that sick people can recover. TT practitioners never actually touch a patient. They wave their open hands palms down over the patient.

Emily decided to test whether TT therapists can really detect the human energy field. If a practitioner plans to message the human energy field, she reasoned, he or she must first be able to detect it.

Emily set up a card table with two chairs on opposite sides and a piece of cardboard anchored on the table at its midpoint. She cut two holes in the cardboard. TT practitioners would insert both hands palms up through the holes. Emily would hold one of her hand palms down above one of the practitioner's hands and ask the practitioner whether her hand was over the practitioner's right or left hand.

Emily tested twenty-one practitioners. Collectively they had 280 chances. They had 123 hits and 157 misses for a 44% average, less than chance. The cost of this project? Less than $10.00.

After completion of the project, Emily was persuaded to share her test with a wider audience. Initially her study was reported in *Skeptic* magazine. Later, with the help of adults, she submitted it to one of the most famous science journals in the world, *The Journal of the American Medical Association*, or JAMA, where it was published on April 1, 1998.

Suddenly Emily Rosa became a celebrity. Over 100 stories about her appeared in the press and she was interviewed on network TV news programs. Emily was also featured in John Stossel's ABC News special, *The Power of Belief*, which showed how stubbornly people cling to their beliefs, facts notwithstanding. The Skeptics Society bestowed the Skeptic of the Year Award on Emily and the Guinness Book of World Records listed her as the youngest author to be published in a major science journal.

Technically Emily didn't prove that therapeutic touch does not facilitate healing. But she did show that the claim of practitioners that they can detect a human energy field is suspect. Her research was creative, simple, inexpensive, and important.

A fourth grader taught us that not all worthwhile research costs a fortune and that science is not exclusively a man's game. Look around. There may be an Emily Rosa in your family or neighborhood or school. If there is, support and encourage her.

The Golden Rule (March 31, 2005)

RELIGION ROUTINELY FIGURES INTO CONFLICT and violence. One thinks, for instance, of Hindus and Muslims in South Asia, Muslims and Christians in the Sudan, Catholics and Protestants in Northern Ireland, Sunni and Shia Muslims in Iraq, and Islamic extremists, among others.

British philosopher John Locke understood the tendency of religious groups to be intolerant of outsiders and this prompted him to make a case for toleration in the 1680s in his famous *A Letter Concerning Toleration*. Locke wrote that all churches should "lay down toleration as the foundation of their own liberty, and teach that liberty of conscience is every man's natural right, equally belonging to dissenters as to themselves." Locke said that the only legitimate tools are "exhortations, admonitions, and advices." Locke's *Letter* influenced the founders of our nation and helps to explain the First Amendment to the Constitution which says in part that "Congress shall make no law respecting an establishment of religion, or prohibiting the free exercise thereof…"

One way to promote tolerance among our religions is to emphasize what they have in common instead of what separates them.

Consider these statements:

1. "Treat not others in ways that you yourself would find hurtful." (*Udana-Varga 5:18*)
2. "Do not do to others what you do not want done to yourself." (Confucius, *Analects 15:23*)

3. "Regard your neighbor's gain as your gain, and your neighbor's loss as your loss." (*T'ai Shang Kan Ying, P'ien, 213-218*)
4. "In everything, do to others as you would have them do to you." (Jesus, *Matthew 7:12*)
5. "Do not do to others whatever is injurious to yourself." (*Shayast-na-Shayast 13:29*)
6. "One should treat all creatures in the world as one would like to be treated." (*Mahavira*, Sutrakritanga)
7. "What is hateful to you, do not do to your neighbor." (*Hillel*, Talmud, Shabbat 31a)
8. "Not one of you truly believes until you wish for others what you wish for yourself." (The Prophet Muhammad, *Hadith*)
9. "Lay not on any soul a load that you would not wish to be laid upon you, and desire not for anyone the things you would not desire for yourself." (Baha'u'llah, *Gleanings*)
10. "This is the sum of duty: do not do to others what would cause pain if done to you." (*Mahabharata* 5:1517)
11. "I am a stranger to no one; and no one is a stranger to me. Indeed I am a friend to all." (Guru Granth Sahib, p. 1299)

I have just quoted verbatim from the sacred teachings, respectively, of Buddhism, Confucianism, Taoism, Christianity, Zoroastrianism, Jainism, Judaism, Islam, Baha'i, Hinduism, and Sikhism.

The great religions offer us the same basic rule to guide our conduct – the Golden Rule.

So often we become immersed in the doctrines, scriptures, rituals, and traditions of our own church or sect. Meanwhile, we forget what the world's religions teach in common and we forget what unites 6.2 billion of us across the planet as members of the human family.

To promote toleration, mutual respect, and collaboration among religious groups in a troubled world, we can start by renewing our own commitment to the Golden Rule.

The Bible and Homosexuality
(April 14, 2005)

I OFTEN HEAR THE CLAIM that homosexuality is wrong because it is condemned in the Bible. This claim raises two fundamental questions: Does the Bible actually condemn homosexuality? And if it does, should the Bible dictate public policy?

Many devoted Christians and qualified interpreters of the Bible deny that it condemns homosexuality, among them Reverend Peter Gomes, preacher to Harvard University. Gomes writes in his book entitled *The Good Book*:

> ...(N)o credible case against homosexuality or homosexuals can be made from the Bible unless one chooses to read scripture in a way that simply sustains the existing prejudice against homosexuality and homosexuals. (p. 147)

Gomes points out that there is no mention of homosexuality in the Ten Commandments, in the Summary of the Law, in the teachings of the prophets, or in the teachings of Jesus. He argues that those who say that the fact that Genesis talks about Adam and Eve, not Adam and Steve, implicitly outlaws homosexuality, ignore the fact that Genesis also fails to mention friendship or the single state, both of which Christians approve. He examines virtually all the other passages in the Bible usually cited to attack homosexuality (e.g., Leviticus 20:13) to show that they do not say what many Christians believe they do. I invite you to read Gomes's *The Good Book* to appreciate the scope and depth of his analysis.

But perhaps Gomes is self-serving. After all, he came out of the closet a few years ago. Perhaps this gay clergyman put a homosexual spin on scripture.

How then do we account for legions of other informed interpreters of the Bible, mostly heterosexuals, who agree with Gomes? How about historian James Boswell and theologians Hilmut Thielicke, Victor Furnish, Jeffrey Siker, and Charles Hefling, to mention only a few.

But suppose that Gomes and the others are wrong. Suppose the Bible condemns homosexuality. As Gomes and others point out, the Bible also authorizes a father and other members of a community to stone a disobedient child to death (Exodus: 21:15, Exodus 21:17); the Bible declares that women who are not virgins when they marry shall be put to death (Deuteronomy 22:20-21); the Bible proclaims that adulterers - men and women – shall be put to death (Deuteronomy 22: 22-24); and the Bible prohibits tattoos (Leviticus 19:28).

And how about slavery? The Reverend Richard Furman of South Carolina wrote in 1823:

> ...(T)he right of holding slaves is clearly established in the Holy Scriptures both by precept and example... Had the holding of slaves been a moral evil, it cannot be Supposed that the inspired apostles...would have tolerated it for a moment in the Christian Church. (See Leviticus 25: 44-46 and Ephesians 6:5)

Moreover, there seems to be no explicit approval in the Bible of human rights, democracy, capitalism, toilets, or televisions, and no explicit disapproval in the Bible of rape. Should we then dispense with the former and legalize the latter?

If segments of the Christian community opposed to homosexuality can alter their understanding of the Bible on slavery, as they have, why can't they also alter their understanding of persons who are attracted to persons of the same sex? If we can look past Biblical passages sentencing disobedient children and non-virgin brides and adulterers of both sexes to a brutal death and prohibiting tattoos, why can't we look beyond the passages that purportedly outlaw homosexuality so that consenting adults of the same sex who wish to share love and life on a monogamous basis may do so? Whatever happened to "Love thy neighbor as thyself?"

John Hick on God and Evil (April 21, 2005)

———

CASE 1. MICHAEL HAS TOO much to drink at a tavern. Impaired, he drives home but swerves left of center, causing a horrific two-car crash. Michael is hospitalized, near death, but eventually recovers. A mother and father in the car that Michael hit die at the scene. Their children, ages three and five, survive, but their recovery takes months.

Case 2. An earthquake beneath the Indian Ocean causes a tidal wave hundreds of miles wide which drowns 180,000 people and destroys billions of dollars of property in a dozen countries.

Case 1 is an example of moral evil, suffering caused by humans. Case 2 is an example of natural evil, suffering caused by nature. Both cases raise a fundamental question in the philosophy of religion: Why would an all-powerful and all-good God permit this suffering?

Dr. John Hick, a British theologian who teaches at the Claremont Graduate School in the United States, attempts to solve this mystery from a Christian perspective with four arguments.

Firstly, Hick reasons, a great deal of suffering is an unavoidable side effect of free will, a precious gift that God gave humans to direct the course of our own lives. God could have programmed Michael never to drink and drive, thus averting the tragedy, but then Michael would be a mere puppet doing God's bidding, not an autonomous agent.

Next, Hick argues that suffering prompts a person to grow in virtue and merit salvation. In the aftermath of the crash in Case 1, Michael, an impudent man, comes to value his nurses and doctors, and pledges to help the surviving children for the rest of his life. Michael has learned humility and compassion. In the aftermath of the tsunami in Case 2, millions of people around the world rally around the survivors with money and services to help them rebuild their lives.

Thirdly, Hick says that suffering caused by nature is perpetuated needlessly by humans because we have failed to gain the knowledge and skill to alleviate it by squandering our time, talent, and resources. Suffering that we associate with nature would have been significantly reduced or eliminated by now had we humans had a greater sense of urgency about it all along. We are culpably incompetent, that is, we can be justifiably blamed for a lack of knowledge and skill that we could have acquired had we tried more aggressively.

Fourthly, Hick argues that the constant interventions of God to prevent suffering would disrupt the laws of nature and destabilize the environment, making human planning and action impossible. Sometimes gravity would work; other times it wouldn't.

Does Hick exonerate God? Consider these points as you form your judgment:

Is it logically possible for God to be all-powerful, as tradition affirms, **and** for humans to possess power to direct their own lives?

In the wake of the Holocaust, terrorism, murder, rape, and child molesting, is free will really such a precious gift?

Does suffering always result in moral development?

On an objective cost-benefit analysis, does the benefit produced by suffering justify the cost?

If humans are chronically lazy by nature, shouldn't the creator receive at least some of the blame?

If suffering is necessary to trigger moral development, do we really need the thousands of diseases and ailments which afflict humankind? Wouldn't a dozen or so serve the purpose adequately?

And couldn't God quietly incapacitate the Hitlers and Osama bin Ladens of the world to forestall massive suffering without disrupting the laws of nature?

These are basic questions that we should answer honestly and satisfactorily before we let God off the hook.

In the Name of God (April 28, 2005)

THE TERRORISTS RESPONSIBLE FOR 9/11 told the world that they were martyrs in a *jihad*, a holy war against the infidels. They believed that the slaughter of innocent people was a holy act because they, the terrorists, had acted in the name of God. Does this strike you as odd? It shouldn't. History is replete with stories of religion being used to justify atrocities.

Consider slavery. For generations prior to the Civil War, Americans were assured by Christian leaders such as the Reverend Richard Furman that:

> …(T)he right of holding slaves is clearly established in the Holy Scriptures, both by precept and example. In the Old Testament, the Israelites were directed to purchase their bondmen and bondmaids of the heathen nations; except they were Canaanites, for these were to be destroyed. And it is declared that the persons purchased were to be their 'bondmen forever,' and an 'inheritance for them and their children.' Had the holding of slaves been a moral evil, it cannot be supposed that the inspired apostles, who feared not the faces of men and were ready to lay down their lives in the cause of their God would have tolerated it for a moment in the Christian Church. (1)

This prevailing sentiment caused many opponents of slavery, such as Charlotte Forten, a young free African-American student from Philadelphia, to condemn the Church as a "bulwark of slavery" and "a great obstacle to the removal of slavery from our land." (2)

Those who invoke the name of God to justify moral outrages such as terrorism and slavery teach us a lesson - the moral compass of religion is far from perfect.

On the one hand, religion can inspire the Zakat, a sharing of wealth by Muslims with the less fortunate, and the heroic devotion of Mother Teresa to the poor and the sick, and the courageous fight for social justice of Mohandas Gandhi and Dr. Martin Luther King, Jr.

On the other hand, religion can inspire the madness of the Crusades, the Inquisition, the witch hunts, the persecution of the Jews, the denial of life-saving medical care to children by faith-healer parents, and the suppression of human rights of girls and women (3), and religion can fuel hatred and violence between Protestants and Catholics in Ireland, Hindus and Muslims in India and Sri Lanka, Christians and Muslims in the Sudan, and Sunni and Shia Muslims in Iraq.

Let us remember, then, when it comes to moral issues today, including stem cell research, the right to die, homosexuality, abortion, casino gambling, and many others, those who claim to speak or act in the name of God may be wrong.

---

1. *The Annals of America*, Volume 5, Encyclopaedia Britannica, Inc., 1968, p. 38.
2. *The Annals of America*, Volume 8, Encyclopaedia Britannica, Inc., 1968, p. 273.
3. Fast forward to December 28, 2011. In the blog of the Freedom from Religion Foundation, Co-President Annie Laurie Gaylor reviews a series of stories in today's *New York Times* in which women are victimized by religion. One reports on Somalia where a teenager was stoned to death for refusing to marry a jihadi commander and countless Somali girls and women are raped by jihadis who proclaim boldly that any resistance is "a crime against Islam, punishable by death." Another describes the plight of an eight-year old second-grade student in Israel who, as she walks to school, has been spat upon and called a "whore" by gangs of ultra-Orthodox men who object to her style of dress (which is conservative and customary).

Erudition or Gobbledygook? (May 5, 2005)

Is it erudition or gobbledygook? How often I asked myself that question during graduate school as I poured over the esoteric writings of philosophers Kant, Hegel, Heidegger, and Sartre, and social theorist Talcott Parsons. How refreshing it was to encounter the clear, simple, and accessible prose of Descartes, James, and Russell.

Today, when I read the obscure, technical, polysyllabic narratives of postmodern philosophers, such as Derrida, Foucault, and Levinas, I find myself asking again, "Is this erudition or gobbledygook?" A popular sticker spoofs postmodernism well. It says "Eschew obfuscation."

Let's say that Sam decides to propose marriage to his significant other. Sam might say:

I love you, and I would like to spend the rest of my life with you. Will you marry me?

The significant other might reply:

Yes, of course. But let's negotiate a pre-nuptial agreement to protect both of us.

By contrast, a postmodern philosopher's proposal of marriage would go something like this:

Given that there is a traditional transcendence of social antinomy and polarity in a variety of culturally sanctioned paradigms of persisting mutuality and reciprocation, and given that a multiplicity of precedents in our interactions predispose one to envision the practicality and workability, and indeed the durability, of our acquiescing in an appropriate mode of combating social antinomy and polarity, it seems prudent that you and I launch the culturally sanctioned paradigmatic transcendence of antinomy and polarity such that the overall consequence will be a maximization of multiple utilities and benefits that are beyond the reach of the isolated and not uncommonly forlorn individual.

And how would the postmodernist significant other reply?

In respect to the foregoing hypothesized possible future, the proffer is deemed meritorious but only contingently, the contingency being that the implementation be predicated on a mutually satisfactory and culturally sanctioned agreement assuring that the proposed paradigmatic transcendence is non-hegemonic and liberating.

Now isn't that touching?

I remember interviewing Talcott Parsons at Harvard University as part of my doctoral dissertation research when I was a graduate philosophy student at Boston College. Based on his writings, I fully expected him to be formal, stiff, and pompous. I found him to be a charming, plain-spoken, disheveled, cigar-chomping look-alike for an ex-boxer. What a wonderful surprise! But why, when he turned to his typewriter or pen, did he turn into a manufacturer of jawbreakers in sentences that run half a page or longer?

I fully understand that a shared technical vocabulary is part of the world of highly educated and trained people, particularly when they deal with their peers. But all of us should remember that language is a tool to enable us to understand one another, not a weapon to impress or confuse or intimidate. Join the movement to reduce linguistic pollution. Give brevity, clarity, and simplicity a try.

The Right to Die (May 19, 2005)

THE TERRY SCHIAVO CASE IN Florida catapulted the issue of right to die into national prominence in an unprecedented way. Millions of Americans are asking "Does a person have a right to die?" I believe that the answer is yes.

Two main arguments support the right of a person to die, one from autonomy, the other from compassion.

The argument from autonomy, or self-determination, holds that a person has the right to determine as much as possible the course of his or her life, dying is the last chapter in a person's life, and therefore a person has the right to determine as much as possible the circumstances of his or her dying.

The argument from compassion holds that a person is entitled to be spared suffering, protracted dying often involves considerable suffering, and therefore a dying person is entitled to hasten his or her death in order to end this suffering.

Those who propose such arguments almost always offer them in the context of several assumptions. These include the requirement that the person has been diagnosed as dying, that the person is a competent adult, that the person expresses his or her wishes about death in writing or verbally, and that the person is not under any pressure to hasten death by family members or others who may benefit in some way from the death.

There are many counter-arguments to the arguments supporting the right to die. I will mention two common ones.

Some say that only God has the right to terminate the life of a human being and that those who choose to die sooner rather than later are "playing

God." But this point is not particularly helpful. In the case of Terry Schiavo, for instance, was keeping her alive in a persistent vegetative state assisting God's will or defying it? If your interpretation is that it was assisting God's will, that's fine, for you! Write your living will soon if you haven't already done so expressing your wish to be kept alive indefinitely by medical technology when there is no realistic prospect of recovery. But you do not have the right to speak for others who do not share your interpretation.

Others say that improvements in pain relief – palliation – enable doctors and organizations such as Hospice to take the sting out of dying. With morphine and other drugs they can substantially reduce pain so that a dying patient is spared the suffering and agony that we used to associate with many causes of death. Palliation will give the patient additional weeks or months of life relatively free of pain. The problem with this argument is two-fold. In the first place, palliation often diminishes mental acuity. I remember members of my own family whose morphine injections relieved pain but put them in a permanent fog for the rest of their days. In the second place, palliation does not alter the typical course of deterioration in which a dying person loses mobility, becomes confined to a bed permanently, loses control of his or her bowels, and becomes ever more dependent upon others and ever less dependent upon self. In other words, the side effect of palliation can be loss of self-reliance, pride, and dignity.

Debate over the right to die will continue in America, as it should. As it does, all of us should read, listen, and reflect. The stakes for each of us individually and for the nation as a whole are high. Meanwhile, if you don't have a living will, it's time to prepare one.

The Founders (June 3, 2005)

A LETTER TO THE EDITOR which I read recently recited a litany of America's moral shortcomings and proposed that the only way to restore a moral compass is to rediscover our Christian roots and practice the faith of our founders.

I am not sure if America has lost its moral bearings. I am sure that the writer needs to spend some time studying revolutionary history and the writings and speeches of the founders.

Most of the founders were not traditional Christians, although all remained nominal Christians. The founders were deeply influenced by Deism, a religion of reason which originated in Europe during the Enlightenment, and many of them openly embraced Deism.

Deists believed in a God because of a rational argument — the design argument. They had great confidence in reason and the capacity of humans to understand and control nature; they sought beliefs based on facts, not faith.

Deists rejected the divinity of Jesus. Jefferson said: "(Jesus) ascribed to himself every *human* excellence" but "never claimed any other."

Deists rejected prayer. Ethan Allen wrote: "Prayer to God is no part of a rational religion… The only way to procure food, raiment, or the necessities of life, is by natural means: we do not get them by wishing or praying."

Deists rejected miracles because they required suspension of the laws of nature.

Deists acknowledged the Bible as a purely human product. In fact, one of them, Thomas Paine, author of the highly influential revolutionary pamphlet *Common Sense*, wrote a book length indictment of the Bible called *The Age of Reason*. It was so caustic that Benjamin Franklin implored Paine, unsuccessfully, not to publish it.

Deists had little respect for clergy. Jefferson said that the clergy thrust abstruse theology on the simple moral message of Jesus to guarantee themselves jobs, power, and prestige.

Deists found little to applaud in the Bible with the exception of the Sermon on the Mount and the Golden Rule. Jefferson extracted these moral prescriptions and recast them in a document called *The Jefferson Bible*.

As to the source of our understanding of right and wrong, Jefferson said that all human beings are born with a moral instinct which disposes us to care about one another. He wrote:

> …(G)ood acts give us pleasure, but how happens it that they give us pleasure? Because nature hath implanted in our breasts a love of others, a sense of duty to them, a moral instinct, in short, which prompts us irresistibly to feel and to succor their distress… The Creator would indeed have been a bungling artist, had He intended for man to be a social animal, without planting in him a social disposition… If we did a good act merely from the love of God and a belief that it is pleasing to Him, when arise the morality of the Atheist?

What's this? Morality flows from human dispositions? And atheists are moral? It's no wonder that Jefferson was attacked by his political adversaries as a "champion of atheism." Can you imagine what would happen to Jefferson if he were a candidate for office in today's political climate?

I agree in principle with the writer of the letter I referred to that taking a fresh look at our founders can be illuminating and perhaps inspiring. I differ with him, however, as to why this is so.

The Skeptic and the Believer
(June 16, 2005)

IN 1876 W. K. CLIFFORD, a British mathematician and philosopher, gave a talk entitled *The Ethics of Belief* that symbolizes the modern skeptical and scientific outlook. "…(I)t is wrong always, everywhere, and for anyone, to believe anything upon insufficient evidence," he said. Central to Clifford's position, called "Evidentialism," is the issue of the origin of the belief – how we came to endorse it. The responsible way to form a belief, according to Clifford, is through patient investigation that shows that the belief rests on a firm foundation of evidence. Too often, he felt, we adopt beliefs without appropriate scrutiny due to custom, the urgings of our parents or teachers or friends, or the consolations that the beliefs afford. Too often we exempt ourselves from the duty to inquire and evaluate, even when nagging doubts warn us of a possible defect in a belief.

Also, in those cases when a belief that we support on insufficient evidence turns out to be true, we are still guilty of wrongdoing, Clifford insists, because our commitment was premature. Clifford viewed embracing and transmitting unfounded beliefs as a cause of serious social harm because this fosters ignorance and gullibility and, sometimes, actions with disastrous consequences. Given this, it is not at all surprising that Clifford's personal intellectual journey took him from Catholicism to agnosticism.

Clifford's talk was later published and American philosopher and psychologist William James read it. He immediately decided to craft a rebuttal which he titled *The Will to Believe*. James argued that there are some beliefs which a person may embrace in the absence of sufficient evidence, such as the existence of God. As a philosophical Pragmatist, James treated claims as hypotheses which must be put into practice to determine if they are true. If a belief, when acted upon, produces expected results, it's true; if not, it's false. James also said "(F)aith in a fact can help create the fact." For instance, your belief that you have the willpower to lose weight prompts you to try and hopefully to succeed. Time will tell. But absent the hypothesis that you can lose weight, there is neither verification nor falsification.

On the question of God, James argued that people may believe if they wish because what they believe has not been shown false, what they believe gives them happiness, and what they believe in time may turn out to be true.

Clifford died of tuberculosis before he could answer James. Had he lived, no doubt he would offer several counter-arguments, including this one:

> Mr. James, I fully agree that we often need to treat a hypothesis as provisionally true and act upon it to see if we're right. Scientists do it all the time. You do indeed need to embrace the hypothesis that you have the willpower to lose weight when you go on a diet. As you weigh yourself daily, you know what evidence counts **for** and what evidence counts **against** the hypothesis. But this isn't the case with religious beliefs. Believers don't explain what evidence counts for and what evidence counts against belief in God. Indeed, they are unlikely to acknowledge that any evidence counts against their hypothesis.

And further, Clifford would say, "Mr. James, while surely religion brings consolation to millions, it also brings harm, sometimes on a massive scale. You ignore the dark side of religion."

In these two intellectual giants we see our society and perhaps our species in microcosm. Some of us, like W. K. Clifford, are tough-minded skeptics; others, like William James, are tender-minder believers. Which are you?

The Individual (June 30, 2005)

HAS THE INDIVIDUAL BEEN ECLIPSED in today's world of powerful nation-states, huge conglomerates, and other complex and hierarchical organizations? Is the individual adrift in a sea of bureaucracy? Not at all. The individual is as important and valuable today as ever.

Nearly eighty years ago sociologist C. Warren Brown observed in his book *Social Groups* that:

> As the group has no energy or force in itself independent of its members, it is evident that this group force is an expression of the combined spirit and energy of <u>individuals</u>.

Brown recognized that organizations large and small are simply collections of individuals performing different roles. Behind the scenes of a successful organization are hard-working, creative, skilled, and knowledgeable individuals without whom the organization would fail and collapse.

French Existential philosopher, Jean-Paul Sartre, spoke about organizations as "parasitical" because they draw their energy, insight, and skill from individuals. American Pragmatist philosopher, John Dewey, and British Utilitarian philosopher, John Stuart Mill, noted that organizations depend on individuals for insights that can spark timely reform in beliefs, habits, and practices. This is one reason that both stressed the need for toleration of dissent.

Civil rights leader Dr. Martin Luther King, Jr., criticized the myth of progress. Progress is not assured with the mere passage of time, he said.

Time is neutral; we can squander it or use it to build a better future for ourselves and others. In his famous *Letter from Birmingham Jail*, Dr. King wrote:

> Human progress never rolls in on wheels of inevitability; it comes through the tireless efforts of men and women willing to be co-workers with God, and without this hard work, time itself becomes an ally of the forces of stagnation.

King understood that insightful, brave, ethical, and resourceful individuals are the beacons of progress.

Why did Youngstown become the site of Ohio's first park district in 1891? Why did renowned landscape architects converge on Youngstown to create plans for trees, trails, and lakes through a gorge along Mill Creek? Why has Mill Creek Park become an outdoor treasure of Ohio and the nation? Because Volney Rogers dedicated thirty years of his life to founding, developing, and protecting it.

Why did a recent surgery of a friend or family member go smoothly? Because well-trained and caring health care providers did their jobs well.

Why did YSU have a phenomenal string of football victories during the 1990s? Because a remarkable coach surrounded himself with competent and dedicated colleagues who together recruited gifted young student-athletes and motivated them to perform beyond their expectations.

Why do we have penicillin, social security, computers, skyscrapers, jet planes, television, compact discs, cell phones, and hundreds of life-saving and life-enhancing drugs? Because imaginative and knowledgeable individuals working alone or with others came up with fresh ideas.

In the corporate world, CEOs frequently get too much credit for the success of their corporations. While CEOs are important, so too are the staff who solved problems, introduced innovations, and met other challenges in the workplace day after day. Wouldn't it be refreshing if a corporate board of directors remembers this the next time they are tempted to hand out a bonus of millions of dollars to a CEO?

Everything Happens for a Reason
(July 14, 2005)

"Everything happens for a reason." How often I hear this popular saying. But what exactly does it mean? And is it true?

"Everything happens for a reason" can mean six quite different things. Let's call them versions 1, 2, 3, and so on.

Version 1 is: Events in the present flow out of events in the past. This version is reflected in statements such as "Alexis failed her history exam because she didn't study" or "Ralph has lung cancer due to thirty years of smoking."

Version 2 is: All events are part of a grand plan which humans cannot change. One form of this version, predestination, attributes this grand plan to God. Another form, fatalism, attributes it to a mysterious force called Fate. A predestinationist might say "George died yesterday because he had finished all the work on earth that God had assigned to him" and a fatalist might say "George died yesterday because his number was up."

Version 3 is: All events, even unfortunate or tragic ones, have a beneficial effect which explains or justifies these events. This version is seen in statements such as "Stephanie has stopped drinking since her DUI" and "The South Asia tsunami brought together a divided world in sympathy and compassion for the victims."

Version 4 is: The actual causes of events are not the apparent causes but surprising and inconspicuous ones. This version, a favorite of conspiracy theorists, is seen in statements such as "FDR knew about the Japanese plan to attack Pearl Harbor in 1941 but he chose not to repel it because he wanted the attack to draw America into the war."

Version 5 is: The events which occur in a person's current life are determined by the moral quality of a previous life. A Hindu or Buddhist who believes in karma might observe: "Fred must have done awful things in his last incarnation to suffer so many painful afflictions the past few years."

Version 6 is: The causes of some natural events are non-natural or supernatural. This version is found in statements such as "AIDS is God's way to punish homosexuals" or "Amy's recovery shows that God has answered our prayers."

So, "Everything happens for a reason" can mean different things to different people.

Our next task, of course, is to figure out which of these versions, if any, is true. Unfortunately, this task requires far more time than this forum allows.

For now, I will say only that version 1 – *Events in the present flow out of events in the past* – gets my vote for three reasons: it has strong support in ordinary experience and in scientific investigation, it makes fewer assumptions than the other versions, and it complies with Ockham's Razor, the principle that one should always seek the simplest adequate solution or explanation.

OK, that's where I stand. How about you? What do you take "Everything happens for a reason" to mean and why do you believe that your version is true?

The Law and Morality – the Mixed Legacy of Socrates and Plato (July 28, 2005)

THE SCENE IS A JAIL in Athens, Greece, twenty-five centuries ago, one day before the scheduled execution of Socrates. Crito pays a visit to his friend Socrates to inform him that sympathetic benefactors have bribed law enforcement officials and arranged an escape so that Socrates can leave Athens and flee to a safe haven in a distant land where he can live in exile on a pension which the benefactors have raised for him until he dies of natural causes.

Despite the urgings of Crito, Socrates declines the offer. The main reason that he offers for his refusal to escape is that defying the sentence of the court would require him to break a promise that he had made as a young adult when he agreed to remain in Athens as a full-fledged citizen. In a mock conversation with the laws as reported in Plato's dialogue entitled *The Crito*, the laws say to Socrates:

> If he (a citizen) does not like us when he has become of age and has seen the ways of the city, and made our acquaintance, he may go where he pleases and take his goods with him. None of us laws will forbid him or interfere with him… But he who has experience of the manner in which we order justice and administer the state, and still remains, has entered into an implied contract that he will do as we command him unless he convinces us through gentle and reverent persuasion that our commands are unjust.

In this implied contract the citizen pledges to obey the government and the government pledges to serve and protect the citizen. It is clear from several passages in *The Crito* that Socrates sees the citizen's duty to obey the law under this contract as unconditional. No conditions could possibly arise which would excuse a citizen from compliance.

Why did Socrates not anticipate that government could become corrupt or incompetent or both, or enact evil laws, or unreasonably resist rational persuasion by citizens? Why did he not value the role of civil disobedience in the pursuit of social justice?

The answer is found in another dialogue of Plato, *The Republic*, in which Socrates outlines the structure of an ideal society. In this society the leaders would be a class of philosophically trained models of knowledge and virtue. They would grasp the *Forms*, transcendent and stable non-physical realities of which physical realities are flawed copies. Their perfect knowledge would enable them to craft perfect laws, obviating the need for reform.

Thus, Socrates and Plato have bestowed upon the modern world a mixed legacy. The ideas that a person needs to consent voluntarily to government before he or she becomes a citizen, and that there is a contract between the government and the governed, are part of the foundation of modern democracy. On the other hand, the ideas that the citizen has an absolute duty to obey the law and that rule by a gifted few is superior to democracy have become part of the foundation of modern authoritarianism, including twentieth-century fascism.

Perhaps this explains why Plato's dialogues find an audience generation after generation. There is something in them for everyone.

Betting on God – Pascal's Wager
(August 4, 2005)

People love to bet. Blaise Pascal understood this. Three and a half centuries ago in France, Pascal, a scientist and mathematician, framed the question of the existence of God as a wager.

It was in the *Pensees*, or *Thoughts*, a collection of fragmentary writings which editors assembled and published after Pascal died, that Pascal proposed the wager argument. It was not Pascal's intention to convert atheists to theism. Rather, he aimed at fence sitters, agnostics who remained uncommitted about the existence of God. He appealed to their common sense, that is, their long-term self-interest. His hope was to lure them initially to a commitment to God to pave the way for the infusion of grace in their souls by God and a rich life of faith which he expected would eventually follow. Pascal's wager states in part:

> Let us weigh the gain and the loss in wagering that God is. Let us estimate these two chances. If you gain, you gain all; if you lose, you lose nothing.
> Wager, then, without hesitation that he is.

Let's elaborate on this brief argument. Pascal sees two possible wagers: 1) There is a God, and 2) There is no God. One of these two bets will pay off. If you bet that there is a God, you can win or lose. If you win, you win eternal happiness. If you lose, you lose nothing. Similarly, if you bet that there is no God, you can win or lose. If you win, you win nothing. If you lose, you lose eternal happiness. Thus, there is only one wager that holds out any hope of a gain for you, the wager that there is a God.

Pascal's wager has been criticized by believers and non-believers alike. Some say that his wager offers no advice as to which religion is the true religion. If one wagers that there is a God but fails to embrace the religion ordained by God, one will likely lose eternal happiness. Next, critics say that Pascal promotes a faith of expedience, not honest conviction. Perhaps God will be offended by such rank opportunism. Further, critics say that Pascal assumes that God will reward believers and punish non-believers. But will a just God, they ask, punish honest skeptics who found insufficient evidence to support belief in God? Why, after all, they ask, did God endow human beings with reason and curiosity if God intended us to follow blind faith?

Beyond this, other critics say that Pascal errs in saying that a life of faith entails no loss if it turns out that there is no God. Doesn't diverting some of one's financial resources to a religion involve a loss? Doesn't obediently following religious authorities at the cost of personal autonomy involve a loss? Doesn't the practice of mortification in this life for the sake of gaining happiness in an illusory future life divert one's time and attention from achieving happiness in this life?

Pascal died in 1662 at the age of 39 due to chronic ill health, denying him the opportunity to hear his critics and to craft rebuttals to them. Nevertheless, his wager is a unique chapter in the history of thought about religion and it will continue to spark controversy in the future as it has in the past.

Moral Rules: Clear as Mud
(August 18, 2005)

SO YOU WANT TO BE an ethicist. Fine. First, you need to familiarize yourself with the major theories in general ethics. These include Religious Morality, Aristotelianism, Kantianism, Utilitarianism, Ethical Egoism, Intuitionism, the Ethics of Care, Cultural Relativism, and Emotivism. Each one of these theories has a vast literature that you must read and absorb. But once you've done that, there's still a lot of work ahead of you. Your next job is to investigate how various proposed moral rules apply to specific cases. This is the domain of applied and professional ethics, arguably the most controversial and confusing part of ethics.

Even when a group, large or small, settles on a moral rule either as binding on all human beings or as binding on a particular profession or occupation, there are often honest disagreements as to the way the rule applies to a case at hand. The Terry Schiavo case demonstrated that.

The French Existential philosopher, Jean-Paul Sartre, reported an experience of a young student of his during the German occupation of France in World War II to show how confusing the application of a moral rule can be. The student faced this dilemma. Should he stay in Paris to comfort his ailing mother or leave his mother to join the French resistance movement? Sartre wrote:

> Who could help him choose? Christian doctrine? No, Christian doctrine says 'Be charitable, love your neighbor, take the more

rugged path…' But which is the more rugged path? Whom should he love as a brother? The fighting man or his mother? Which does the greater good, the vague act of fighting in a group, or the concrete one of helping a particular human being to go on living? Who can decide *a priori*? Nobody. No book of ethics can tell him. The Kantian ethics says, 'Never treat any person as a means, but as an end. Very well, if I stay with my mother, I'll treat her as an end and not as a means; but by virtue of this very fact, I'm running the risk of treating people around me who are fighting, as a means; and, conversely, if I go to join those who are fighting, I'll be treating them as an end, and, by doing that, I run the risk of treating my mother as a means.

Another example of the difficulty of applying moral rules comes to us from 19th century pre-civil war America. Wouldn't you assume that the Golden Rule clearly outlaws slavery? Just as I would not wish to be another person's property, so I should not try to make another person my property. But the Reverend Richard Furman, a Baptist official in South Carolina, didn't see it this way at all. He argued in 1823 that the Golden Rule poses no threat to the basic master-slave relationship. Instead, he insisted, the Golden Rule simply requires the master to treat the slave as the master would wish to be treated if the master were a slave, and likewise, it requires the slave to treat the master as the slave would wish to be treated if the slave were the master. Fascinating, isn't it?

Striving to reach agreement on general ethical principles is certainly an important and necessary goal. But once we reach that goal, we still have a lot of work ahead of us. If you want to be an ethicist, visit a good library about ten hours a week for the next couple of years to read all the relevant literature and work on the virtue of patience. You're going to need a lot of it in the thicket of ethics.

Leopold and Loeb (August 25, 2005)

CLARENCE DARROW, A WORLD FAMOUS defense attorney who grew up in Farmington and Kinsman, Ohio, in Trumbull County, took a case late in his career in Chicago in 1924 involving Nathan Leopold, Jr., and Richard Loeb, two brilliant Chicago teen-agers from wealthy families. Leopold and Loeb were fascinated with philosopher Friedrich Nietzsche's doctrine of *ubermensch* or superman, a self-directed and defiant person who spurns the values, customs, and laws of the herd. They decided to demonstrate that they were *ubermenschen* by committing a perfect crime.

But it wasn't so perfect after all. Within days after they kidnapped and murdered fourteen-year-old Bobby Franks, they were arrested by Chicago detectives and they confessed. The case against them was so formidable that Darrow abandoned any hope of acquittal, pleaded them guilty at the start of the trial, and fought to save their lives.

Clarence Darrow brought his deeply held philosophical belief in determinism, hard determinism specifically, to the courtroom. Hard determinism is the view that nature and nurture shape individuals to think and act as they do. To the hard determinist, the individual is neither free nor responsible. The saint deserves no applause; the sinner deserves no blame. Neither could possibly avoid doing what they had done given their past.

This was the first time in his career that Darrow applied determinism to the elite because he was accustomed to representing political radicals and the underprivileged. He said in summation:

...Your Honor, it is just as often a great misfortune to be the child of the rich as it is to be the child of the poor. Wealth has its misfortunes. Too much, too great opportunity and advantage, given to a child has its misfortunes...

To the shock and amazement of virtually everyone, the judge sentenced the boys to life in prison instead of death. People shouldn't have been so surprised. During his career Darrow represented over 100 clients accused of murder and not one got the death penalty.

Richard Loeb was murdered in prison and Nathan Leopold, Jr., eventually won parole after more than thirty years as a model prisoner.

Today we continue to agonize over the issues at the heart of the Leopold-Loeb case – personal responsibility and punishment of wrongdoers. Are criminals helpless pawns of nature and nurture, compelled by causes in their past beyond their control to commit crimes, as Darrow argued? If so, punishment, particularly the death penalty, is suspect. Or, on the other hand, are criminals free agents who have the power to obey or disobey the law? If so, punishment, perhaps including the death penalty, is a mandate of justice

Long after the Leopold-Loeb trial, American philosopher Sidney Hook challenged Darrow's position on punishment. Conceding for the sake of argument that hard determinism is true, Hook reasoned that civilization requires rules, and that punishment of those who violate such rules is indispensable to ensure compliance with them. Hook expected that the effective threat of punishment will deter rationally self-interested persons from crime because they believe that their loss is likely to outstrip their gain. This was Hook's justification for punishment in a determined world.

A Lesson from the YSU Strike (September 8, 2005)

There are many lessons that we can learn from the strike at YSU this year, among them that YSU is a collaboration. The success of YSU depends on the knowledge, skill, energy, and dedication of 2,200 YSU employees spread across dozens of academic, administrative, and support units, and another 150 employees of private sector food service, janitorial, and vending companies. Take a segment or two of this work force out of the picture and the enterprise grinds to a halt.

Frequently faculty get the spotlight in university publications, news stories, and advertising. As vital as faculty are, however, faculty alone do not a university make.

It is tempting for an individual or department to inflate their own value to the university and to minimize or ignore or disparage that of others. All YSU employees from the president to the locksmith to the dean to the grounds worker to the professor to the advisor need to remind ourselves of our dependence on hundreds of others, most of whom we do not know personally, to accomplish the mission of the university.

Consider the following:

In 2004-2005 the staff in Financial Aid and Scholarships received 6,451 visits and 112,000 phone calls.

At the request of faculty in the last school year, the staff in Maag Library provided 349 information literacy classes which served 7,543 students.

The Center for Student Progress, the backbone of the university's retention strategy, served 5,844 students in 2003-2004 and more than 80% of those students who used the Center's services consistently stayed in school.

Materials Management purchased $25 million in goods and services for the university community last year.

Sudexho Food Service provides approximately 5,500 meals on campus in a typical week.

In one week last year, the staff in Undergraduate Admissions had 558 contacts with prospective students.

In a recent week this year, the Tech Desk in Computer Services, formerly called the Help Desk, received 103 requests for help.

Kilcawley Room Scheduling books roughly 150 events in Kilcawley Center a week.

Media and Academic Computing, in addition to servicing 23 permanent multimedia equipped classrooms as of fall 2005, picks up and delivers equipment for 60 to 75 classes a day.

In a typical week last spring, the Development Office processed 241 donations totaling more than $95,000.

During peak periods such as SOAR, registration, and the week before commencement, an academic advisor counsels hundreds of advisees and clears dozens more for graduation.

The Mail Room processes about a ton of mail a week.

And in a recent month, the YSU Police Department handled 1,498 service calls of all types.

These examples can be duplicated dozens of times across the campus in facilities, network services, athletics, payroll, WYSU, student services, alumni relations, the bookstore, career services, and all the other units that make up YSU.

As we strive in the weeks and months ahead to restore institutional equilibrium and to heal the wounds of labor-management strife, let us YSU employees remind ourselves regularly that we're part of a huge team of dedicated men and women across campus and that we need and deserve one another's respect, gratitude, and encouragement. Despite the fact that we may play quite different institutional roles, we are literally one another's support group.

Searching for the Soul (October 6, 2005)

MOST AMERICANS BELIEVE THAT A human being is a composite of two substances – a physical and observable one called the body and a non-physical and unobservable one called the soul or mind. A great many of those who embrace this view find support for it in their religious faith.

Putting faith aside for the moment, do reason and science offer any support for the soul?

In his *Meditations*, published in 1641, French philosopher Rene Descartes reasoned that because his sense experience often deceived him, he could successfully doubt not only the reliability of his sense experience but also the existence of the physical realm, including his own body, reported to him by his senses. On the other hand, he reasoned, even if he is plagued with doubt, he could not successfully doubt that he exists as a being which thinks, that is, as a soul or mind.

Later in the *Meditations*, Descartes established to his satisfaction two additional certainties. He used a version of the ontological argument to prove that there is a perfect being, God, and he reasoned that he, Descartes, could be certain of the existence of a physical realm, including his body, because God, a perfect being, is necessarily incapable of deceit and would not predispose Descartes to believe so strongly that there is a physical realm if indeed there is none.

The upshot is that for Descartes a human being consists of a non-physical soul and a physical body. Critics charged, among other things, that Descartes erred in believing that he could think independently of the perceptual data drawn from his surroundings, that the ontological argument is fatally flawed, and that he failed to explain how his non-physical soul or mind interacts with his physical body.

As for science, the key evidence for the soul is near-death experiences and past-life recollections.

Researchers into near-death experiences report that at times the body seems to shut down completely so that a person is clinically dead but yet undergoes experiences such as perceiving his or her body from a distance or seeing a bright light. They argue that if a person consciously experiences without reliance on his or her body, then the person must possess a non-physical component with which the experiencing occurs. Dr. Melvin Morse and Dr. Raymond Moody are among the authors who chronicle such experiences. But research by Dr. James Whinnery, a U.S. Navy aerospace scientist, involving pilots in a centrifuge, suggests that so-called near-death experiences may be simply dreams or hallucinations caused by oxygen deprivation in the brain.

Next, Dr. Ian Stephenson, in *Twenty Cases Suggestive of Reincarnation* and other books, reports dozens of cases of young children, mainly in India, who describe past events and persons in places that they had never visited since they were born, to show that a component of the personality had to live formerly and survived death as a receptacle and preserver of these memories. But skeptics such as Dr. John Hick, a Christian philosopher of religion, point out that these alleged past-life memories emanate from a culture where belief in reincarnation is strong and where the publicity attendant upon a claimed case of past-life memory brings celebrity status to a family. Hick cautions that these children may have been coached or gathered their information through normal sources unknown to their parents, and he recommends the investigation of other hypotheses to explain the phenomenon.

The next time you hear or read the terms soul or mind, ask yourself what they mean. Do they refer to something for which there is solid evidence? Or are they examples, as British philosopher Gilbert Ryle insists, of culturally sanctioned myths?

America's Philosophical Father
(October 28, 2005)

QUESTION: WHO IS THE BRITISH philosopher who died long before the American revolution but whose writings about government had a powerful influence on the founders of the United States of America?

This philosopher was part of a movement in late 17th century England to curtail the powers of the monarch which culminated in the so-called Glorious Revolution of 1688. At this time William of Orange was invited by Parliament to assume the British throne but only if he accepted reduced powers and granted other concessions that are landmarks in the development of limited government. Our mystery author's *Second Treatise of Government*, published in 1690, was both the theoretical justification for the Glorious Revolution and a primary source of the core principles of the American system of government, including human rights, government by consent, limited government, majority rule, the division of powers, and private property.

In the *Second Treatise* the author searches for the rationale for government by imagining people living together without government. He calls such a society a "State of Nature." He explains that though this society without government is a state of liberty, it is not a state of license, for there is a moral law, a "Law of Nature," which people can discover through reason. The Law of Nature provides that no person may destroy himself, no person may harm another person except in self-defense, and all humans possess entitlements (i.e., rights) to life, liberty, and estate. Estate means material possessions which are acquired, the author says, through one's labor. Note that these rights grow out of our status as human persons and precede the formation of government.

The author tells us further that in the State of Nature a person is granted the authority to protect his or her own rights by resisting, punishing, and taking reparation from criminals, but that this is difficult to do successfully. Why? For three reasons. Firstly, there are significant numbers of people who violate the rights of others due to malice or due to ignorance of their duties under the Law of Nature with the result that crime is rampant. Secondly, some victims of crime fail to be fair and impartial in determining guilt and punishment with the result that innocent persons are sometimes punished for crimes which they did not commit. And thirdly, some victims of crime cannot counter the superior force of criminals with the result that many criminals face no punishment at all for their crimes. Thus, in a society without government, the rights granted by the Law of Nature are in constant jeopardy.

The *Second Treatise* suggests that this prompts the law-abiding members of the community to form government to protect their rights. They agree to a pact, a social contract, with several provisions, including a permanent departure from the State of Nature, a permanent transfer to society of their authority to protect their own rights, a commitment to the "Lex Majoris Partis," the Law of the Greater Part, commonly called majority rule, and finally the selection of a specific type of government approved by the majority. The author refers to a society with government as "Political Society" or "Civil Society."

Finally, the *Second Treatise* provides that the authority granted to government by the people to protect their rights must be exercised responsibly so that government remains the agent of the people and not their master. Accordingly, the powers of government must be limited and divided, and the people must retain the authority to dismiss an illegitimate government, one which violates human rights or thwarts the will of the majority.

Who is our mystery philosopher? He is John Locke. If you don't already have a copy of Locke's *Second Treatise* in your personal library, it's time to buy one. By reading it from time to time, you can rediscover America's original guiding principles.

Freedom – a Clarification
(November 10, 2005)

It seems that everyone in our culture praises "freedom" but few take the time to clarify exactly what freedom is.

Freedom has two basic meanings, one dealing with the relationship between a citizen and his or her government and other social institutions, the other dealing with a person's choices.

The first meaning of freedom refers to the extent of a citizen's opportunity to live in society as he or she wishes. This type of freedom, often called "liberty" because it is derived from the Latin term *liber* which means free, exists in abundance if you can choose your occupation, your religion (if any), your significant other, your circle of friends, your reading material, your style of dress, and so on. On the other hand, if your government or other social institutions decide such issues for you, then you have little or no freedom or liberty. The system of government called democracy prioritizes liberty over other values, including order, while the system of government called dictatorship prioritizes order over other values, including liberty.

The second meaning of freedom refers to the relationship of causes from a person's past to his or her present choices. Every human being drags his or her past into the present. Our past includes the genetic code transmitted to us by our biological parents, our life experiences since we were born, and the influences on us of other forces, if any, such as God. Indeterminists, those who say that choices are "free," argue that causes from the past are compatible with at least two possible courses of action in a present choice, while determinists, those who say that choices are "not free," argue that causes from the past compel a person to a single course of action when he or she makes a choice now, such that the person could not possibly have chosen otherwise.

The debate between indeterminists and determinists rests on an agreement between them that a choice is free if any only if a person could have chosen otherwise than he or she chose. Indeterminists say that a person can often choose otherwise than he or she chose while determinists deny this.

But a school of thought developed in modern philosophy which denies that a free choice implies the power to choose otherwise than one has chosen. This school of thought, called *soft determinism* to distinguish it from the older form of determinism, which we now call *hard determinism*, asserts that your choice is free despite the fact that it is determined, as long as you choose the course of action that you *want* to choose. Since soft determinists see no incompatibility in the same choice being both determined and free, soft determinism is also called *compatibilism*.

For example, if you had oatmeal for breakfast today, an indeterminist would say that your choice was free because your past allows you to choose oatmeal, French toast, bacon and eggs, or other items today. Meanwhile, a hard determinist would say that your choice is not free because your past compels you to select only oatmeal today. Finally, a soft determinist would say that your choice of oatmeal is both determined and free, determined because given your past you could not possibly have chosen anything except oatmeal, but free because you wanted to choose oatmeal and no one prevented you from doing so.

Two things follow from the above. Firstly, when we talk about freedom we need to make clear whether we're talking about the relationship of a citizen to government and other social institutions, or the relationship of a person's past to his or her present choices. Secondly, we need to remember that our views as to whether liberty is good or bad, and whether choices are free or determined or both, are only as sound as the arguments that we can muster to support them. Simply holding a view with conviction isn't enough.

Letter from Birmingham Jail
(November 17, 2005)

Dr. Martin Luther King, Jr.'s *Letter from Birmingham Jail* states clearly and effectively the fundamental principles that guided his life and the civil rights struggle of the fifties and sixties.

The *Letter* was Dr. King's reply to clergy in Birmingham, Alabama, who had objected in a full-page newspaper ad to his presence in that city in 1963 to demonstrate against segregation. In their ad the clergy attacked Dr. King as a hypocrite because he urged obeying some laws but not others. This prompted Dr. King to remind his critics of the long-recognized distinction between a just and an unjust law. A just law, he says, squares with the moral law; an unjust law does not. "I would be the first to advocate obeying just laws," he wrote. "One has not only a legal but a moral responsibility to obey just laws." But, "Conversely," he adds, "one has a moral responsibility to disobey unjust laws." "Everything Adolf Hitler did in Germany was 'legal'…" and in Hitler's Germany, "(I)t was 'illegal' to aid and comfort a Jew…" Dr. King noted.

What made Dr. King's form of civil resistance unique was its repudiation of violence and its respect for the humanity of the oppressor. For Dr. King a citizen must never resort to guns, knives, or bombs as a means to reform society. Initially one should use rational persuasion. If that fails, one moves next to active, non-violent, non-cooperation. Dr. King wrote:

> One who breaks an unjust law must do so openly, lovingly, and with a willingness to accept the penalty. ...(A)n individual who breaks a law that conscience tells him is unjust, and who willingly accepts the penalty of imprisonment in order to arouse the conscience of the community over its injustice, is in reality expressing the highest respect for the law.

Dr. King's *Letter* shows his roots in the tradition of non-violent disobedience practiced by leaders such as Mohandas Gandhi. Dr. King rejects the divisive and violent tactics of militant black nationalists, on the one hand, and the do-nothingism of white moderates, on the other, who believe, foolishly, that time itself will miraculously cure all ills in society. Dr. King stakes out a strategy for social reform that only a disciplined and courageous person can practice. And Dr. King tells civil resisters that they must demonstrate that they are not criminals. Criminals violate laws, whether just or not, for the sake of personal gain, in secret, often resorting to violence, and always striving to avoid identification, capture, and punishment. Dr. King insists that civil resisters, by contrast, may violate only unjust laws, that their motive must be to improve the community, and that they must violate unjust laws openly, non-violently, and with a willingness to suffer for their actions. King understood that reform requires sacrifices of the reformer and that reform must educate and change the oppressor if there is to be long-term peace and civility in society.

If you haven't read Dr. King's *Letter* in a while, take a fresh look at it. In an era when love, sacrifice, and non-violence are endangered species on our planet, it is as relevant and inspiring as ever.

Are You a Critical Thinker? (December 1, 2005)

THINKING IS LIKE PLAYING TENNIS, driving a car, or dieting. It can be done well or badly. In modern education jargon, good thinkers are called critical thinkers. Critical thinkers have a mix of attitudes, skills, and habits that set them apart from sloppy thinkers. Are you a critical thinker? Test yourself by answering these questions.

1. Are you a successful problem-solver?
2. When you face a problem or a mystery, do you always seek the simplest adequate solution or explanation instead of a needlessly complex one?
3. Before you make a decision, do you first gather as many relevant facts as time permits?
4. Do you embrace a belief because it is supported by compelling evidence and sound arguments and not merely because it is popular or consoling?
5. Can you explain and defend your beliefs and practices capably?
6. Are your beliefs coherent so that some of them don't contradict others?
7. Do you use language with precision and clarity?
8. Are you a good listener?

9. Do you strive to be objective and even-handed in your evaluation of people, products, services, and organizations?
10. Are you aware that your perceptions can be distorted by your beliefs, expectations, biases, and state of mind?
11. Are you aware that your memory is selective and constructive and seldom provides a literal report of the past?
12. Are you willing to hear or read an elaboration or defense of a position that strikes you initially as weird, foolish, far-fetched, or immoral?
13. Do you have the courage to reevaluate a long-cherished belief and to acknowledge that it may be mistaken?
14. Do you successfully detect bias, special pleading, code words, propaganda, and exaggeration in what you hear or read?
15. Do you scrupulously avoid lying, exaggerating, and treating speculation, gossip, or rumor as fact, in order to influence or persuade others?
16. Are you aware that many TV programs, films, and publications deviate from the historical record and contradict well-established scientific laws and theories?
17. Do you regularly read books, newspapers, magazines, and other publications?
18. Do you balance your reading to expose yourself to a variety of views and perspectives?
19. Do you participate in serious, civil conversations about significant issues in the news?
20. Do you detect common fallacies in reasoning such as stereotyping, hasty generalization, *ad hominem*, the slippery slope, and others?
21. Do you strive to avoid the use of such fallacies in your own reasoning?

You have now completed the *self-evaluation* stage of the critical thinking test. Hopefully you answered "yes" to every question. To complete the critical thinking test, you need to move now to *peer evaluation*. Ask a person who knows you well and whom you consider to be a critical thinker to evaluate you using these same questions. Then, compare the two sets of answers. If there is a discrepancy between your answer and your peer evaluator's answer to a particular question, ask your peer evaluator for an explanation. Oops! I forgot one important question in the critical thinking test: "Do you welcome and act upon constructive criticism?"

Thomas Aquinas on God
(December 15, 2005)

MANY INFLUENTIAL WRITINGS OR SPEECHES are quite short. One thinks, for instance, of the Sermon on the Mount, the Declaration of Independence, President Lincoln's Gettysburg Address, and Dr. Martin Luther King, Jr.'s "I have a Dream" speech. In the world of philosophy, one brief passage that is among the most widely read, discussed, and debated in history is Thomas Aquinas's five proofs for the existence of God, which take up a mere two pages in his famous *Summa Theologica*, written in the thirteenth century.

Aquinas rejected the ontological argument for the existence of God formulated two centuries earlier by Anselm of Canterbury. Anselm, relying on reason alone, argued that we can form an idea of a perfect being, a being greater than which none can be thought, and that this idea entails the actual independent existence of this perfect being. Aquinas observed, however, that all of our ideas originate in sense experience – what we see, taste, hear, touch, and smell – and that we never encounter God directly in our sense experience, thus ruling out any possibility of our conceiving a literal idea of God.

Instead, Aquinas proposed that we look for clues to the existence of God in the world that we inhabit and observe with the aid of our senses. His five arguments, based on the work of the pagan and polytheistic Greek philosopher Aristotle, are called *cosmological* arguments because they aim to demonstrate the existence of God from God's effects in the world – motion, causality, contingency, gradation, and design. We can consolidate the five arguments into a single formulation this way:

> Events such as an auto accident, processes such as rusting, and entities such as a cell phone, did not cause themselves but were caused by previous events, processes, and entities.
>
> These previous events, processes, and entities did not cause themselves but were caused in turn by previous events, processes, and entities.
>
> The series of causes and effects cannot go on into the past indefinitely but had to have started through a First Cause, itself uncaused, that we call God.

Critics pose several objections to Aquinas's cosmological proofs. Why, they ask, must the series of cause and effect have a start? If matter-energy existed indefinitely into the past, we can easily imagine causes reaching back indefinitely. Next, why is God exempt from the need for a cause? If the reply is that God is self-caused, why, critics ask, cannot the cosmos be self-caused? Thirdly, even if we grant that the argument works, critics point out that it gives us a physical First Cause and not the spiritual, personal God whom billions of religious people pray to and worship. This is because a physical effect (e.g., a house) requires no more than a physical cause (e.g., carpenters, masons, electricians, plumbers). Since the cosmos is a physical system, it requires only a physical cause. Finally, critics say that the argument does not even provide that the First Cause exists today. This is because an effect (e.g., a century house) can remain in existence after the cause (e.g., carpenters, masons, electricians, plumbers) has ceased to exist. Even if the cosmos had a First Cause, the cosmos can persist without that Cause.

Whether these objections are valid or not, the famous two pages in which Aquinas states them rank among the most influential and studied passages in history. Moreover, his fifth proof, the argument for the existence of God based on design in the universe, became popular in the seventeenth and eighteenth centuries and remains popular today among the advocates of "intelligent design" who are lobbying for inclusion of this concept in the curriculum of our schools alongside biological evolution.

As is so often the case, the roots of controversies in popular culture are found in the dusty pages of a philosopher's reflections.

George W. Bush on Surveillance – A Lockean Appraisal (December 29, 2005)

THE MOST RECENT CONTROVERSY IN Washington is whether George W. Bush exceeded his authority as President by authorizing telephone wiretaps and interception of e-mail messages of suspected terrorists in the aftermath of 9/11 without prior judicial consent. The President defends his actions by saying that his role as commander in chief under the U. S. Constitution implies that he has the authority to order this eavesdropping for the sake of national security. The President's critics reply that such eavesdropping is explicitly disallowed by law, that it violates the Fourth Amendment to the Constitution which prohibits unreasonable searches and seizures, that it breaches the principle of the separation of powers, and that it borders on tyranny.

The system of government in America is founded largely on the ideas of British philosopher, John Locke, whose writings, including the *First Treatise on Government*, the *Second Treatise on Government*, and *A Letter Concerning Toleration*, had great influence on our founders. It seems sensible, therefore, to turn to Locke to see if he offers us any guidance on this controversy over surveillance.

As a matter of fact, Locke's *Second Treatise on Government* has an entire chapter entitled "Of Prerogative." Let's remember that Locke is an architect of limited government, the idea that the powers of government should be no greater than necessary to protect the rights and liberties of the citizens, and that he was clearly a deadly enemy of tyranny. Nevertheless, Locke recognized the need for a sovereign occasionally, in special circumstances, to take unusual steps to promote public safety and well-being. Locke said that in a well-managed society "several things should be left to the discretion of him that has the executive power...to be ordered by him as the public good and advantage shall require..." The foundational principle for allowing discretion to the executive, Locke says, is *salus populi supreme lex*, the health of the people is the highest law, that is, "that as much as may be, all the members of a society are to be preserved."

Thus, for Locke, an executive such as President Bush has the prerogative "...to act according to (his) discretion for the public good, without the prescription of the law and sometimes event against it." Locke says that as long as the executive uses prerogative for its intended purpose, the good of the people, it is legitimate and should be tolerated and supported. Should prerogative be used to harm the people, however, as when executives use it to promote "private ends of their own and not for the public good...", it is an abuse of power and is not to be tolerated and supported. The people, Locke says, should strictly limit prerogative through explicit law in cases which they find offensive or harmful to them, that is, when they believe the executive is promoting his or her own "pleasure or profit" instead of the public good. Prerogative, Locke insists, is certainly not "an arbitrary power to do things hurtful to the people." Locke reminds us that the executive and others in government are our servants, not our masters. Their sole purpose is to protect our rights and to do our bidding, not their own.

So, back to Washington. Did President George W. Bush act responsibly in the matter of suspected terrorists? Did the President seek to do public good without or against a law? That is certainly what the President and his supporters say. Although I believe that President Bush could have secured judicial approval for the wiretaps and the interception of e-mails of suspected terrorists quickly and quietly, and that he should have done so, it seems to me, nevertheless, that he met Locke's test of prerogative. What do you think?

When Bad Things Happen to Good People (January 12, 2006)

2006 MARKS THE 25ᵀᴴ ANNIVERSARY of the publication of *When Bad Things Happen to Good People* by Rabbi Harold S. Kushner who serves a congregation near Boston. Rabbi Kushner had a crisis of faith in the 60s and 70s when his son, Aaron, suffered and died from progeria, a disorder which accelerates the aging process. Rabbi Kushner agonized: "I believed that I was following God's ways and doing His work. How could this be happening to my family? If God existed, if He was minimally fair, let alone loving and forgiving, how could He do this to me?"

Kushner found standard religious explanations of suffering unacceptable.

- To those who say that God inflicts suffering on us because of our sins, Kushner says this ignores the fact that millions of innocent and virtuous people are victims.
- To say that God has reasons for inflicting suffering upon us that we don't understand, Kushner replies that this explanation turns God into an inscrutable monster who uses human beings as play things.
- To say that suffering produces benefits, Kushner cites cases from his professional experience where suffering either produced no benefit at all or a modest benefit at an enormous cost.

- To those who say that suffering is a test of our loyalty to God and the strength of our faith, Kushner answers that only a cruel and insensitive God could design such tests.
- Finally, to those who say that victims of suffering will be compensated in the afterlife, Kushner replies that we can say very little about the afterlife with confidence and that this explanation diminishes the importance of our duty to reduce suffering in the here and now.

All these traditional explanations, according to the Rabbi, "assume that God is the cause of our suffering, and try to understand why God would want us to suffer." He suggests instead that "Maybe God does not cause our suffering. Maybe (our suffering) happens for some reason other than the will of God." Kushner's God, though good and just, deals with an intractable creation, a creation with random events by the thousands every day, which He cannot fully control." "God wants the righteous to live peaceful, happy lives," he writes, "but sometimes even He can't bring that about. It is too difficult even for God to keep cruelty and chaos from claiming innocent victims." Creation, he says, did not conclude in the six days of Genesis but continues even today as a slow, evolutionary process. Here his views are quite similar to scientist Kenneth Miller's in his book *Finding Darwin's God*. When we suffer, Kushner advises, we shouldn't condemn God for our fate but instead turn to God, our family, our friends, and others for comfort, help, and consolation.

Kushner's book offends many orthodox believers who view Kushner's God as a powerful but not all-powerful God, a heresy in their eyes. Further, critics claim that his book offers ammunition to religious skeptics who welcome Kushner's admission that the traditional explanations of suffering by believers are problematical. Nevertheless, this little book will continue to console and inspire millions of people in the future as it has in the past as they struggle to understand and cope with physical and psychological pain.

Bertrand Russell and the City College of New York (January 26, 2006)

IN 1940 BERTRAND RUSSELL, BRITISH philosopher and mathematician, was offered a one-year appointment to the faculty of the City College of New York. As soon as the appointment was publicized, religious conservatives launched a campaign to nullify it because of Russell's writings which supported easy divorce by childless married couples, contraception, and sex education for children, and his reflections on the dark side of religion. The attacks on Russell demonized him, frequently quoting his writings out of context and branding him a "Communist" despite his long record of opposition to Soviet Communism.

Support for Russell's appointment to City College came from many quarters. Intellectuals such as John Dewey, Albert Einstein, Sidney Hook, and Alfred North Whitehead endorsed Russell's appointment, as did legions of other well-known political, religious, and academic leaders, and publishers. Supporters included the presidents of the University of California, where Russell was then teaching, and the University of Chicago, where Russell had taught previously, as well as the presidents of other colleges and universities and the presidents of dozens of learned societies. Also, the Parent Association of City College voted unanimously to endorse Russell's appointment despite the fact that Russell's opponents "paraded as spokesmen of 'offended parents.'"(1)

When the trustees of City College refused to cave into the pressure to withdraw the offer to Russell, the complainants turned to the courts. A taxpayer's lawsuit was filed that eventually reached Judge McGeehan who ruled swiftly that Russell's appointment was null and void on the grounds that he was not a U. S. citizen and that he had not taken a competitive examination. The Judge's opinion was curious in several respects.

- The statute which he cited in his ruling applied to public school teachers and not university professors.
- Distinguished foreign scholars had already received appointments at public colleges and universities in New York.
- A competitive examination was not legally required of professors as a condition of employment and no university instructor in memory had ever been required to take one; and
- In his opinion the Judge repeatedly characterized Bertrand Russell as a person of "immoral character" without once providing evidence to support such a claim.

John Dewey, reflecting on the Russell episode in New York, said that contrary to Russell's critics there is simply no filth or obscenity to be found in his writings and that all Americans should feel a sense of "shame for this scar on our reputation for fair play."

Some ten years later Russell was chosen to deliver the prestigious Machette Lectures at Columbia University in New York City and to receive the Nobel Prize for Literature.

What can we learn from all this that is relevant today? One important lesson, I think, is that neither the law nor fair play counts when a judge has a moralistic agenda and allows his or her court to be politicized.

---

1. The source of the quotations in this commentary, as well as much of the information about the Russell case, is taken from Paul Edwards in the Appendix to Bertrand Russell, *Why I am Not a Christian*, edited by Edwards.

Sam Harris, *The End of Faith*
(February 2, 2006)

IN *LETTERS FROM EARTH* MARK Twain wrote: "…(human beings) have the reasoning faculty, but no one uses it in religious matters." There is a new star among religious skeptics – Sam Harris - who echoes Twain's sentiment in a book entitled *The End of Faith: Religion, Terror, and the Future of Reason*. Harris was very angry over the terrorist attack upon the United States on September 11, 2001, and he began writing this book the very next day. He was angry not only at the terrorists but at faith-based religion. Harris writes:

> Tell a devout Christian that his wife is cheating on him, or that frozen yogurt can make a man invisible, and he is likely to require as much evidence as anyone else… (But) tell him that the book that he keeps by his bed was written by an invisible deity who will punish him with fire for eternity if he fails to accept its every incredible claim about the universe, and he seems to require no evidence whatsoever. (p. 19)

Harris cites passages in the Bible and the Quran that condone and command killing. For instance, in Deuteronomy 13: 7-11, God instructs believers how to deal with a heretic: "…(You) must kill him, your hand must strike the first blow in putting him to death (with) the hands of the rest of the people following (yours)." The Quran 9:73, similarly, teaches believers to "…(M)ake war on the unbelievers and the hypocrites and deal rigorously with them. Hell shall be their home…"

Harris argues that the utility of religion has ended with modern tools of war. He writes:

> Our technical advances in the art of war have finally rendered our religious differences – and hence our religious beliefs – antithetical to our survival. We can no longer ignore the fact that billions of our neighbors believe in the metaphysics of martyrdom, or in the literal truth of the of the book of Revelation, or any of the other fantastical notions that have lurked in the minds of the faithful for millennia – because our neighbors are now armed with chemical, biological, and nuclear weapons. (p. 14)

One of Harris's surprising targets is religious moderates. Harris concedes that moderates "do not want to kill anyone in the name of God." (p. 22) But moderates, he says, refuse to acknowledge that the Bible and the Quran "both contain mountains of life-destroying gibberish" (p. 23) which literalists *"really believe"* (p. 22) and they continue using the word "God" as though they know what they are talking about. (p. 22)

Harris's thesis is that the future of the human race is at risk unless words like God and Allah "slide into obsolescence" (p. 14) like Zeus and Apollo and faith-based beliefs go the way of alchemy and the flat earth. For Harris, religion is a luxury that rational and responsible people can no longer afford.

Harris expected that his book would earn him many enemies because, he says, "criticizing a person's faith is currently taboo in every corner of our culture." (p. 13) He's right. And that's the very reason that *The End of Faith* deserves to be read and discussed by religious and non-religious alike.

John Locke on the Separation of Church and State (February 9, 2006)

ONE KEY WRITING OF BRITISH philosopher John Locke (1632-1704) which had a powerful impact on our founders, is his *Letter Concerning Toleration*. The *Letter*, which was first published in Latin in 1685, then later in English in 1680, addresses the issue of the proper relationship between church and state. Locke wrote the *Letter* because of his reservations about the Anglican church's extensive political power in England and his fears about "the ranting sectarianism of (various groups) of Dissenters, their dogmatic insistence that they alone held the key to salvation," and the likelihood of civil strife if they gained political ascendancy. (1)

In his *Letter* Locke lays down the framework for the separation of church and state. According to Locke, the state is a voluntary association of human beings whose purpose is to protect and promote their human rights and liberties while the church is a voluntary association of human beings whose purpose is to promote the salvation of their souls. The state passes and enforces laws and punishes lawbreakers as necessary by depriving them of their treasure or freedom or life. The church, by contrast, Locke argues, may not use coercion. Its only legitimate tools are "exhortations, admonitions, and advices." In other words, the state may use force but the church may use only arguments.

The key to understanding Locke lies in his insistence that religious beliefs are based on faith and that there is no way to demonstrate that one set of faith-based beliefs is true while another is false. Believers are entitled to embrace with devotion their own set of religious beliefs but they must respect and tolerate the right of others in or out of their own sect to disagree. Coercion may never be used by church or state to assure compliance with or dissent from any given religious belief system. Locke observed, "For every church is orthodox to itself, to others, erroneous or heretical." From this Locke concludes "And therefore peace, equity, and friendship are always mutually to be observed by particular churches, in the same manner as by private persons, without any pretense of superiority or jurisdiction over one another."

Locke laid down several rules of toleration.

- The state is required to tolerate churches as long as they tolerate one another and do nothing to jeopardize the human rights and liberties of citizens, including their own members.
- Since religious faith is voluntary and inward, Locke said that neither a political nor an ecclesiastical authority may attempt to compel the individual citizen in matters of faith. If a church takes umbrage with one of its members, it may excommunicate him or her – period. And a church member may withdraw at any time from his or her congregation without penalty or prejudice.
- Further, no church may force or attempt to force its beliefs upon the state or upon society generally.
- And no state may attempt to coerce citizens based on the religious beliefs of its leaders or of church groups in society. In all religious matters the individual must be guided by his or her conscience alone.
- Further, the leaders of government, Locke says, may not command that certain forms of worship be used or not used by the churches and the churches may not have practices which deny the civil rights of their members.
- Civil authorities may punish only civil offenses but not sins.
- Civil authorities may not impede the expression of opinions generally or in a particular church.

- Civil authorities should not tolerate intolerant churches. All churches should "lay down toleration as the foundation of their own liberty, and teach that liberty of conscience is every man's natural right, equally belonging to dissenters as to themselves…"

Locke held, though, that there are exceptions to the rule of toleration. For instance, these groups are not to be tolerated: churches teaching against civil interests, any church which insists on intolerance, Papists, that is, Roman Catholics, and atheists. In the case of Catholics, Locke feared that they recognized the Pope as both an ecclesiastical and political sovereign. As for atheists, Locke believed that they lacked the foundation of morality which, in his judgment, requires belief in God as an authoritative law-giver.

Although the United States of America eventually went beyond Locke in extending tolerance to Roman Catholics and atheists, Locke remains the architect of the principle of the separation of church and state in our nation. I leave to your judgment whether our nation is faithful to the spirit and letter of Locke's famous treatise on toleration.

---

1. Howard R. Penniman, Editor, *John Locke on Politics and Education*, p. 17.

Pragmatism (February 16, 2006)

IN THE MIDDLE OF THE 19th century, in an oration entitled *The American Scholar*, Ralph Waldo Emerson chided American writers and intellectuals for their lack of originality and their willingness to continue to import the essentials of culture from Europe. As if on cue, three home-grown scholars – Charles Sanders Peirce, William James, and John Dewey – launched a new movement in philosophy called Pragmatism which crossed the oceans and transformed America to a cultural exporter for the first time. Peirce focused on the logical dimensions of Pragmatism, James the psychological dimensions, and Dewey the social dimensions.

Pragmatism "determines the meaning and truth of all concepts, and tests their validity, by their practical results."(1) It blends several components – acceptance of the theory of evolution and its non-static view of humans and nature, a confidence that the experimental method of modern science is the most powerful tool available to discover truth, and a theory of intelligence as primarily practical. Pragmatism rejects the spectator view of knowledge in which humans observe the world in order to ascertain a hoped-for objective truth. Instead, it views humans as actors within nature who construct ideas to solve problems and adopt specific habits and social arrangements to promote survival and happiness. The implication here is that beliefs need to be modified when they no longer solve problems, and habits and social arrangements need to be modified when they no longer enhance individual and social growth.

Although Pragmatism is complex and its three main figures sometimes differed on key issues, we can gain some insight into the Pragmatic approach to philosophy if we focus on the test of truth which Pragmatism bestowed upon the philosophical world.

The pragmatic test of truth says that a statement is true if, when you act upon the statement, you encounter anticipated or predicted results. To test a statement pragmatically, you conceive of an action that you can take and a result that such an action will cause if the statement that you are testing is true. For instance, take the statement "Sarah has an outstanding vocabulary." To test it, a Pragmatist would recast the statement into an if-then format as follows: "If I ask Sarah to define homophobic, then she will say 'having a fear of homosexuals.'" Or, "If I ask Sarah to work the Sunday *New York Times* crossword puzzle and she agrees, then she will successfully complete it within two hours." If you perform the actions in the "if" clauses, and the results predicted in the "then" clauses follow, then pragmatically the statement "Sarah has an outstanding vocabulary" is true; if not, it is false.

Obviously, the more tests, the better. The more times that your tests produce the predicted results, the more confidence you are entitled to have in the truth of the statement being tested. An ideal test is one that is simple and that you can initiate and control. As we've seen, the pragmatic test of truth focuses on a statements relation to *predicted experiences.* This test supplements two other tests of truth, the correspondence test which focuses on a statement's relation to *facts,* and the coherence test which focuses on a statement's relation to *other statements* already widely embraced.

Most Pragmatists hold the view that all meaningful statements should be testable pragmatically. You should be able to come up with actions and predicted results which enable you to judge whether the statement at issue is true or false. If you cannot project a test and a predicted result for a given statement, Pragmatists say that the statement may be meaningless.

Technical issues aside, Peirce, James, and Dewey put the United States on the world map of philosophy so that even today every serious student of philosophy on the planet investigates their ideas. All Americans can be proud of the impact that these native intellectual giants have had around the world.

---

1. *New World Dictionary*, Second College Edition, p. 1118.

Tim Russert, *Big Russ and Me* (March 2, 2006)

―――――

TIM RUSSERT HAS PUBLISHED AN autobiographical tribute to his father entitled *Big Russ and Me – Father and Son: Lessons of Life*. Tim Russert, you recall, is moderator of "Meet the Press" and senior vice president and Washington Bureau Chief of NBC News. Russert has a deserved reputation as a tough but fair interviewer who prepares extensively for every interview and who knows how to disagree agreeably. In *Big Russ and Me* Russert recounts his father's dedication to providing for his working class family in South Buffalo, New York, by holding down two jobs at the same time for many years. He reminisces about the down-to-earth advice that his father gave him as he grew up and as he became a celebrity journalist. He applauds his father's quiet dignity and humility and he brags about his military service in World War II. He paints his father as a firm but loving disciplinarian and acknowledges that the older he got, the smarter Big Russ got. He regales the reader with anecdotes of father and son, among them drives from Buffalo to Cleveland to see their beloved Yankees play the Indians, annual family trips over the Peace Bridge to the amusement park at Crystal Beach in Ontario, frequent trips to Buffalo Bills games, and visits to the gravesites of veterans on Memorial Day with his hero, Big Russ, Commander of American Legion Post 721.

As much as I enjoyed Tim Russert's nostalgic journey, two things struck me as odd.

The first is that he said next to nothing about his mother, despite the fact that he includes her in the book's dedication. While Dad was busy working two jobs, who ran the house and raised Tim and his three sisters? Who cooked the meals and nursed the kids back to health when they were sick? Who helped the kids with their school work and mediated the conflicts among Russert and his siblings? Russert admits he was shocked when his parents dissolved their marriage when they were empty-nesters. Although we get very little information about his mother in the book, I cannot help but wonder if she felt underappreciated by her husband and perhaps her celebrity son.

The second is that although Russert talks about his Catholicism extensively in *Big Russ and Me*, he ducks the issues that have caused so much anxiety among American Catholics. We learn about the importance of religion in his home. We learn about his experiences in Catholic schools and his admiration for Sister Mary Lucille, his 7th grade teacher at St. Bonaventure School, and Father John Sturm, Prefect for Discipline at Canisius High School. We learn about his years at John Carroll University, a Jesuit institution in suburban Cleveland. We learn about his admiration for Pope John Paul II and his excitement over an audience with the Pope at the Vatican. Yet Russert takes a vow of silence when it comes to the clergy sex scandal, the capture of the hierarchy by conservatives, the critical decline in vocations in the United States, the appointment by the Pope of Cardinal Law of Boston to a high Vatican post after he systematically covered up hundreds of cases of sexual abuse of children by priests for years, and the gap between many American Catholics and the Vatican on contraception, women's reproductive rights, homosexuality, end-of-life issues, and the status of women in the Church.

Despite this, the book is an enjoyable read and I recommend it to you. Nevertheless, I would like to have Tim Russert's job for a day. My guest on "Meet the Press" would be Tim Russert and I would grill him about his mom and his religion.*

---

* Tim Russert died in 2008 at age 58 from a coronary thrombosis.

Frank McCourt, *Teacher Man* (March 17, 2006)

AT AGE SIXTY-SIX, FRANK MCCOURT, a retired New York City high school English teacher, published his first book, *Angela's Ashes*, a memoir of his childhood in Ireland. It won the Pulitzer Prize and catapulted McCourt into national prominence, transforming him, he says, from a nobody to "mick of the moment." His latest book, *Teacher Man*, is a memoir of the agony and the ecstasy of his thirty-year teaching career.

In *Teacher Man* McCourt tells us about his struggle to cope with teenagers, many of whom were recent immigrants who spoke and wrote English poorly, and who wanted to be anywhere but in school. With wit and honesty he describes his heroic efforts to find a classroom management style somewhere between the extremes of a tyrant and a wimp. He agonizes over how little his teacher education program at New York University prepared him for the challenges of the real-life classroom. He writes about his run-ins with the hall roamers, principals and assistant principals, who chose so often to belittle classroom innovation and to placate parents with petty gripes. He tells about fits of anger which led him to say or do things to students that he regretted and for which he asked forgiveness. And he tells about the special moment when his students came alive as creative writers and surprised themselves, their classmates, and him.

McCourt's stubborn persistence enabled him to survive four different New York City high schools and end up, remarkably, in the most selective and prestigious school in the city – Stuyvesant. Here he came into his own as he crafted unusual but successful strategies to lure his students into writing. Having discovered that his students wrote most of the excuse notes for their absences, he challenged them to write better excuses. He had his students play the role of Adam or Eve in writing an excuse note to God for their mischief in the Garden of Eden. He had class singalongs of recipes from cook books. He took students on field trips on the subway to see films or plays. He challenged his students to imitate Mimi Sheraton, restaurant reviewer of *The New York Times*, by writing critical reviews of the food and service in the school cafeteria and neighborhood restaurants. He assigned his students to interview their grandmothers and grandfathers to get first hand insights into the past, a strategy that resulted both in learning and closer relationships. Through trial-and-error, he found ways to win respect and to inspire.

Honest to a fault, McCourt divulges his marital infidelities as his first marriage deteriorated, his procrastination as a graduate student at Trinity College in Dublin which cost him his doctorate, his heavy drinking, his visits to a therapist, his revulsions to grading huge stacks of papers day after day, proposals of romance from mothers of some of his students, his embarrassment as a writing teacher who published next to nothing during his entire teaching career, his amazement that he ever lasted thirty years amid thousands of teenagers fixated on sex and food, and his recurring sense of failure and inadequacy.

Teacher Man is a must read for anyone with a serious interest in public education – parents, current and future teachers, administrators, boards of education, legislators, and taxpayers.

On the day of his retirement, one of McCourt's students cried out to him, "Mr. McCourt, you should write a book." Indeed, he has – three of them. Hopefully *Teacher Man* won't be his last.

Jimmy Carter, *Our Endangered Values* (March 30, 2006)

THERE'S YET ANOTHER EXPRESSION OF concern about the political activism of religious conservatives in the United States, this one from Southern Baptist and Sunday School teacher, Jimmy Carter, thirty-ninth President of the United States, in his recent book *Our Endangered Values: America's Moral Crisis*.

President Carter argues in *Endangered Values* that "narrowly defined theological beliefs have been adopted as the rigid agenda" (p. 3) of the Republican Party. He traces the threat to mainstream values in America to a union twenty-five years ago between some Christian leaders and the conservative wing of the Republican Party. This collaboration has reached a point, he says, that "intensely committed (religious) hardliners" are "imposing their minority views on a more moderate majority" (p. 4) on a very broad set of domestic and foreign policy issues ranging from stem cell research to abortion to tax law to civil liberties reform. (p. 2)

Carter argues that mainstream views count for little in the political arena today. For example, he points out that "a majority of Americans think that abortions should be legal in all or most cases, and only one in six believes that all abortions should be illegal." (p. 11) Concerning gun control, he notes that "an overwhelming majority believe in the right to own weapons, but four of five Americans prefer modest restraints on handguns, including a background check, mandatory registration, and a brief waiting period before one is purchased." (p. 11) On same-sex relationships, he observes that there has been a reversal of public opinion in the past twenty years. Now a majority of Americans "believe it is acceptable for gays and lesbians to engage in same-sex behavior." (p. 14) And on the death penalty, Carter sees another dramatic shift in the mainstream such that today half of Americans support "life without parole" and only one-third believe that the death penalty deters crime. (p. 14) Yet actual or emerging consensus among the general public is systematically ignored, Carter says, by "true believers… (who are) convinced that they are right" and that "anyone who contradicts them is ignorant and…evil." (p. 34)

Carter charges that contemporary "fundamentalist" movements are led by "authoritarian males who consider themselves to be superior to others and… (who) have an overwhelming commitment to subjugate women and to dominate their fellow believers." (p. 34) It was this new and dangerous fundamentalism, Carter writes, that prompted him and his wife Rosalynn to sever ties with the Southern Baptist Convention while retaining their commitment to Baptist traditions. (p. 42) Carter is especially angry that the principle of the separation of church and state has been compromised by new laws and policies which, he says, channel "taxpayers' dollars to churches and other religion-based providers of social services under contrived rules that allow proselytizing, putting religious tests on hiring employees," and even subsidizing the renovation or construction of churches. (p. 61)

Coming from a principled and reflective man who has set the standard for service by former Presidents, and who values both his religion and his nation's unique democratic traditions, *Endangered Values* is a deadly serious warning of a tyranny of the minority, a threat to our way of life which deserves the serious attention of every American concerned about the direction of our nation at home and abroad.

Miracles (April 13, 2006)

MOST RELIGIONS AFFIRM THE EXISTENCE of events called miracles. The popular view is that miracles are anomalies, deviations from the routine in nature, that are caused by God, on some occasions in response to a supplicant's prayer. Let's call this type of miracle a *standard miracle*. Examples of a standard miracle would be if, in defiance of gravitation, a person suddenly rose from the ground and sailed effortlessly through the air without the aid of a propulsion device, or if a double amputee, contrary to our understanding of the human body, suddenly grew new limbs.

There is another category of miracles that gets less attention than standard miracles. This type of miracle is called a *coincidence miracle*. R. F. Holland gives us this example of a coincidence miracle. (1) Imagine a child driving a toy car near his house along a railroad track. A wheel becomes stuck under one of the rails and the child tries to pedal it free to no avail. A train approaches at high speed and the child's life hangs in the balance. The child's mother watches helplessly from a distance. Suddenly the train brakes and comes to a complete stop just a few feet from the child. The engineer, it turns out, had fainted in the locomotive due to a slight stroke, the most recent in a series of signs of his deteriorating health. When the engineer's hand fell from the control lever, the brakes engaged automatically. The mother surely believes that divine intervention took place here but there is no violation of any law of nature as seems to be the case in standard miracles. Ronald Nash observes that "What is crucial to the notion of a coincidence miracle is the *timing* or coming together of several events, each of which by itself is quite unexceptional." (2)

Not all who believe in God recognize miracles of any type. For instance, Deists such as Thomas Jefferson and many others of scientific temperament, hold that the cosmic designer imbued the cosmos with laws of nature that function inexorably and without exception. Further, religious skeptics in the tradition of David Hume look for mundane explanations of so-called miracles, applying the rule called Ockham's Razor – Always seek the simplest adequate solution or explanation. They look for fraud, trickery, or misperception and demand that extraordinary claims require extraordinary evidence.

If we assume for the sake of discussion that there are miracles, they remain vulnerable in my opinion to a strong persisting objection: Why does God work miracles in some cases but not others? Why does God intervene to help the child on the railroad track but not thousands of other children or adults at risk who are injured or killed such as the victims of the holocaust or the 9/11 terrorist attack or the South Asian tsunami or hurricane Katrina or famine and AIDS in Africa? Why do some patients, young and old, who are prayed for, leave the hospital on foot and others in a hearse? The failure of God to intervene so often when intervention would reduce or eliminate suffering raises questions about whether God is really all-powerful or all-good or both? This, of course, is the classic problem of evil.

---

1. R. F. Holland, "The Miraculous," in *Readings in the Philosophy of Religion: An Analytic Approach*, ed. By Baruch A. Brody, Prentice-Hall, 1974, p. 451.
2. Ronald Nash, *Faith and Reason: Searching for a Rational Faith*, Zondervan, 1988, pp. 245-246.

So What Exactly Do Philosophers Do?
(April 27, 2006)

ROBERT NOZICK, A PHILOSOPHER WHO taught for many years at Harvard University, told a story about a woman sitting next to him on an airplane who asked him "What do you do for a living?" When he answered, "I'm a philosopher," she said, "How exciting! What are some of your sayings?" The stranger on Professor Nozick's airplane is not alone in being unsure of what philosophers do. So let's ask today, "What exactly do philosophers do?"

The answer to this question begins with a reflection on the complex and systematic shaping of a human being from the moment that he or she is born to make that individual a functioning member of his or her culture. Social scientists refer to this as enculturation or acculturation. When a baby is born, it is neither religious nor secular. It prefers neither democracy nor dictatorship. It speaks neither Arabic nor French nor English. It prefers no particular mode of dress or hairstyle. It has a penchant neither for ice hockey nor football nor soccer. It holds no stance on when government may incarcerate a citizen, whether there is an afterlife, whether humans should eat other species of animals, whether a dying person may hasten death, whether there should be honor killings, or where government may draw the line between prudent security measures and overzealous infringement of liberties. As the baby becomes a child, the child an adolescent, and the adolescent an adult, conditioning by family, teachers, peers, religion, the media, and many other influences will change all this. Enculturated individuals will embrace the dominant views on all sorts of issues and the routine patterns of behavior in the mainstream of their culture or in their subculture.

The fact that a belief enjoys widespread support in a culture or subculture, even over an extended period, however, does not guarantee that it is true. History is replete with examples of beliefs, once popular, that have been abandoned. Lo and behold, the earth is not flat after all. And the cosmos is billions, not thousands of years old. And germs, not the evil eye, cause sickness and death. Similarly, the fact that a practice is widespread in a culture or subculture does not guarantee that it is sensible or ethical. Slavery, for instance, was commonplace for thousands of years.

So what does all this have to do with philosophy? *Philosophy is simply the evaluation of beliefs to determine whether they are true and the evaluation of practices to determine whether they are sensible and ethical.* Philosophers, both professionals and amateurs, take a fresh look at beliefs and practices to see whether they are supported by strong arguments and impressive evidence. Philosophizing requires skepticism – a willingness to doubt – and an atmosphere of intellectual freedom.

Unfortunately, in many parts of the world, very little serious philosophy takes place because young and old are shielded from debate and discussion by authorities in government or religion who prize conformity over self-determination and who declare that skepticism toward the received dogmas or changing one's mind is heresy deserving of punishment. When terrorists actually believe that a deity has written a book commanding them to kill infidels across the planet, as they do, we need two weapons to defeat them – an effective international military and intelligence strategy, on the one hand, and an infusion of philosophy in their cultures, on the other.

Mill on Diversity (May 11, 2006)

In *On Liberty* John Stuart Mill makes a persuasive case for individual freedom. The type of freedom that he discusses which has received the most attention is what he calls "liberty of thought and expression." On this score, Mill understood that knowledge is cumulative, acquired gradually with the passage of time. Given this fact, there is important social utility in allowing individuals the freedom to think and to express their thoughts, namely, this enables us to learn truth for the first time or to gain a deeper appreciation of a truth that we already know. In his words,

> (T)he peculiar evil of silencing the expression of an opinion is, that it is robbing the human race; posterity as well as the existing generation; those who dissent from the opinion, still more than those who hold it. If the opinion is right, they are deprived of the opportunity of exchanging error for truth; if wrong, they lose, what is almost as great a benefit, the clearer perception and livelier impression of truth, produced by its collision with error…

Yet Mill addresses other important freedoms in *On Liberty*, including what he calls "liberty of tastes and pursuits." Liberty of tastes and pursuits, he writes, is the freedom of…

> …framing the plan of our life to suit our own character, of doing as we like, subject to such consequences as may follow: without

impediment from our fellow-creatures, so long as what we do does not harm them, even though they should think our conduct foolish, perverse, or wrong.

Here, as in liberty of thought and expression, Mill emphasizes social utility. Just as ideas need to be injected into the marketplace of ideas in society to enable us to sort good ideas from bad ones, so too, he argues, different life styles, or as he calls them, "different experiments in living," need to be tried out to enable people to learn which life styles promote their fulfillment and which do not. Mindless conformity deprives both the individual and society of fresh paths to happiness. Mill writes:

> He who lets the world, or his own portion of it, choose his plan of life for him, has no need of any other faculty than the ape-like one of imitation. He who chooses his plan for himself, employs all his faculties. He must use observation to see, reasoning and judgment to foresee, activity to gather materials for decision, discrimination to decide, and when he has decided, firmness and self-control to hold to his deliberate decision... Human nature is not a machine to be built after a model, and set to do exactly the work prescribed for it, but a tree, which requires to grow and develop itself on all sides according to the tendency of the inward forces which make it a living thing... Among the works of man, which human life is rightly employed in perfecting and beautifying, the first in importance is surely man himself.

For Mill, in choosing your occupation, your style of dress, your social circle, your significant other, your domicile, your hobbies, your forms of entertainment, your religious or secular perspective, and your own beliefs and habits generally, you literally design what you are, and you illuminate for others the roads to take or to avoid in the quest for their own happiness. This is why Mill insists that all of us should welcome and promote self-determination and the diversity that it entails.

John Locke on Power (May 25, 2006)

ALTHOUGH JOHN LOCKE DIED SEVENTY years before the American Revolution, he has long been recognized by scholars as the key source of the system of government adopted by the founders.

Locke's most important writing is the *Second Treatise of Government* and arguably the core of the *Second Treatise* is Chapter XV. In this passage Locke discusses three types of power in society – parental, political, and despotical. (Although Locke uses the term "power" here, he really means "authority," morally justified power, as opposed to "force" or "coercion," morally unjustified power, but I'll defer here to his usage.)

On parental power, Locke makes three key points.

1. The power of parents over their children is *shared* by mother and father and not held by one or the other as had been the practice in many cultures for generations.
2. Parenting is a *temporary* custodial right and duty. Parents have the right to govern their children and the duty to help, instruct, and preserve them. The right and the duty dissolve when the children become adults and are able to govern themselves. Thus, parents neither own their children nor have any authority over them once they are grown. Adult children owe their parents respect, gratitude, and support during the remainder of their lives, *provided that the parents carried out their parental duties conscientiously,* but they no longer owe their parents obedience.

3. The job of parents is to teach their children to become *self-reliant, rational, and responsible*. The adult offspring of successful parents direct their own lives and manage their own resources intelligently, and they understand the rights and duties of human beings under the moral law, and of citizens under the civil law.

As to political power, Locke tells us that this is a *limited* power which the citizens grant to government in a social contract. The purpose of political power is to "preserve the members of…society in their lives, liberties, and possessions" by making and enforcing laws. In other parts of the *Second Treatise* Locke fills in details about political power. To avoid tyranny, the power to make laws should be placed in separate hands from the power to administer laws. He refers to government as the agent or deputy of the people which is answerable to them. Should a government alienate the people, meaning in practice the majority, those in government must step down; should they refuse, they have declared war on the people, Locke says, and the people may defend themselves against this illegitimate government just as they may defend themselves against criminals. This, of course, is Locke's doctrine of just revolution or rebellion.

Finally, Locke speaks of despotical power. This is the authority of the victims or intended victims of crimes or wars of aggression to protect themselves from those who have opted for the tool of beasts – force – and abandoned the tool of humans – reason. The criminal or aggressor who acts as a beast surrenders or forfeits his or her rights and authorizes actual victims or intended victims, or society acting through government on their behalf, to defend themselves by any means necessary, even killing. Here, paradoxically, Locke, an architect of the doctrine of human rights, endorses the death penalty.

These ideas on power in Chapter XV of the *Second Treatise*, a treatise written over three centuries ago, have had a lasting impact on our world. In Chapter XV Locke bestows an enduring gift on modern civilization. And, remarkably, he does this in a mere three pages!

Gilbert Ryle on Mind (June 9, 2006)

THE TRADITIONAL VIEW OF MIND in the West since the time of Plato, which was defended famously by Descartes in his *Meditations* of 1641, is that the mind is a non-physical and unobservable entity distinct from the body such that a human being is a composite of two substances, one incorporeal, the other corporeal, which interact mysteriously. This traditional view – dualism – has been the target of growing skepticism in the modern era by many scientists and philosophers, including Gilbert Ryle.

Ryle was a twentieth-century British analytic philosopher who held that most traditional philosophical puzzles are really pseudo-problems due to misuses of language and confusion over concepts. In his 1949 *Concept of the Mind*, Ryle tried to point out the flaws in the traditional view of mind and body which he referred to derisively as "the dogma of the Ghost in the Machine." The main culprit, Ryle says, is language. When we use terms, we assume that they refer to entities. For instance, when we speak about a computer, car, or sofa, we take these terms as pointers to objects that we observe. Similarly, when we speak about a person as intelligent, witty, passionate, angry, or optimistic, we are tempted to see these terms as pointers to an object, a mind, that we do not observe. This is a mistake, Ryle insists, because mental terms refer not to a mysterious, hidden chamber but to a variety of observable human behaviors. Here Ryle reflects the post-Darwinian perspective that a human being is a highly developed biological organism with a complex and unique nervous system that enable humans to exhibit a wide variety of behaviors, many quite remarkable.

Ryle uses an analogy between a university and a human being to show that the traditional view of mind is due to what he calls a "category mistake." He refers to a British institution but let's refer to one that we're more familiar with – YSU. If a visitor to YSU goes to Kilcawley Center, Maag Library, DeBartolo Hall, restaurants, classrooms and laboratories, and the bookstore, and meets faculty, staff, students, and alumni, but then asks to see YSU, he or she wrongly assumes that what we call YSU is something distinct from the facilities and people which taken together are YSU. Similarly, Ryle argues, a person who sees you send an e-mail, work a crossword puzzle, hang up on a telemarketer, or write a poem, but then asks to see your "mind," wrongly assumes that what we call your "mind" is something distinct from the observable acts which you perform.

Has Ryle succeeded in dispatching the traditional view of mind and body to the trash heap of history? Hardly. Firstly, the traditional view is sustained by most religions and skeptics such as Ryle aren't even a blip on the radar screen of most religious people. Secondly, even if consciousness is brain-based, as neuroscientists say, they have not yet fully explained it on naturalistic grounds. This gives aid and comfort to traditional dualists who treat the incompleteness of the scientific explanation of consciousness much like intelligent design advocates treat gaps in the fossil record supporting evolution. And thirdly, there is an ever-growing literature in the field of consciousness studies about near-death experiences and past-life memories that is fundamentally at odds with Ryle's viewpoint on several grounds. Thus, the merits of Ryle's critique aside, the traditional paradigm survives.

Self-Interest (June 22, 2006)

MANY SAY THAT TO BE moral a person must be an altruist, one who puts the interests of others ahead of one's own. A philosophical movement in the twentieth-century called Objectivism, led by novelist-philosopher Ayn Rand, challenged this and proposed that to be moral a person should put the interests of self ahead of the interests of others. Her position, called ethical egoism, affirms that human beings have a duty to promote their own long-term self-interest (or self-fulfillment or happiness). Rand's new proposal evoked strong criticism from many philosophers and religious leaders who accused Rand of abandoning ethics altogether.

While there may be shortcomings in ethical egoism, the idea that it prioritizes self-interest, is, in my view, not one of them. The critics of ethical egoism, I believe, have a superficial and simplistic understanding of what self-interest entails. It certainly does not entail a self-indulgent hedonism, living solely for the pleasures of the moment. And it certainly does not isolate the individual from others or authorize the individual to manipulate others or to ignore their right to their own happiness. Let's reflect on these points.

Genuine self-interest rules out self-indulgent hedonism. A person who seeks his or her own happiness in life is required to exercise self-restraint and moderation, to defer gratification, and to take into account long-term and not merely short-term consequences. Imagine, if you will, two people. Let's call them Jack and Jill. Jack is obese and never exercises while Jill has a balanced diet and goes to the gym three times a week. Jack routinely drinks himself into a near coma and lost his driver's license after a third DUI while Jill drinks moderately. Jack dropped out of high school, works sporadically, and has filed bankruptcy twice while Jill worked her way through college, eventually completed a master's degree in accounting and now leads her own solvent and growing CPA firm. Which individual is more genuinely self-interested? Is it the self-indulgent, undisciplined Jack or the self-restrained, disciplined Jill? I would argue that it is Jill.

Next, ethical egoists recognize that their own happiness is contingent on successful, mutually beneficial relationships with family, friends, business associates, and others. They recognize that their own happiness is served by earning and preserving friendship, trust, respect, and even love. Back to Jack and Jill. Jack is a loner who has few friends and a history of short-lived romances. On the other hand, Jill has a large circle of friends and has been with the same partner for a dozen years. Jack routinely stretches the truth and breaks promises, and seldom helps others, while Jill strives to tell the truth and to keep her promises, and her friends know that they can count on her in a pinch. Again, which individual is more genuinely self-interested? I would argue that it is Jill. Jill understands that her psychological, social, and economic well-being are linked to enduring relationships with people who come to value her. Indeed, one key source of her own happiness is being valued by others.

To the traditionally religious who speak disparagingly of self-interest, and demonize ethical egoists, I pose this question: Doesn't religion itself promote self-interest? Doesn't religion entreat people to save their souls so that they will enjoy eternal happiness?

James Rachels on Cultural Relativism
(July 6, 2006)

IN ONE SOCIETY, WE FIND sexual promiscuity; in another, a stern, ascetic, puritanical attitude toward sex. In one society, the aged are abandoned and left to die; in another, they are protected and cared for. Obviously, different societies have different routine practices. This fact has prompted some philosophers and social scientists to conclude that calling an action "right" or "good" or "moral" simply means that it is customary in a given culture and that "the idea of universal truth in ethics…is a myth." (1) For instance, anthropologist Ruth Benedict wrote in her *Patterns of Culture* that "Morality differs in every society, and is a convenient term for socially approved habits." (p. 254) This view that there is no objective, transcultural standard of right and wrong is called Cultural Relativism.

Philosopher James Rachels, a critic of Cultural Relativism, correctly notes in his *Elements of Moral Philosophy* that Cultural Relativism is supported by an argument which Rachels calls the cultural differences argument. This argument infers from the fact that "Different cultures have different moral codes" to the conclusion that "…there is no objective 'truth' in morality. Right and wrong are only matters of opinion, and opinions vary from culture to culture." (p. 257)

Is this a sound argument? No, it isn't. The conclusion does not follow from the premise. The fact that people in two different cultures disagree on an issue does not rule out that one or both of them may be wrong. Rachels uses this example. Imagine that one society believes that the earth is flat while another holds that it is round. The fact that they disagree does not rule out the possibility of objective truth as to the shape of the earth. As Rachels notes, "There is no reason to think that if the world is round everyone must know it. Similarly, there is no reason to think that if there is moral truth everyone must know it." (p. 258)

On the other hand, the fact that the cultural differences argument is flawed does not establish that there is objectivity in morals. Rachels attempts to make a case for objectivity in morals based on the desire and need for survival and happiness. He argues that "There are some moral rules that all societies will have in common, because those rules are necessary for society to exist... Rules against lying and murder are two examples." (p. 262) Regular communication, which is essential in society, is possible only within a framework of truth-telling; and security, which is also essential in society, is possible only if there is a strict rule against murder. (p. 262)

Further, Rachels argues that if Cultural Relativism were taken seriously, there would be unfortunate consequences which seem to make the theory implausible on its face. Among these consequences is that we could no longer say that the customs of one society are morally inferior to those of another. (p. 258) If one society condones slavery while another prohibits it, we could not say that one is better or worse than the other. Indeed Cultural Relativism, Rachels says, calls into doubt the very idea of moral progress, a position which few support. (p. 259)

Despite his many misgivings about Cultural Relativism, Rachels does find at least one redeeming feature. It teaches us, he says, "that many of the practices and attitudes we think so natural are really only cultural products." (p. 264) Cultural Relativism, "by stressing that our moral views can reflect the prejudices of our society, provides an antidote for...dogmatism." (p. 264)

For more about James Rachels's reflections on Cultural Relativism and other ethical doctrines, take a look at his *The Elements of Moral Theory*.

---

1. From James Rachels, *The Elements of Moral Theory*, as excerpted in Shipka and Minton, *Philosophy: Paradox and Discovery*, Fifth Edition, McGraw-Hill, 2004, p. 256. All references and quotations to Rachels here are by page number in the Shipka and Minton volume.

Thoreau on Civil Disobedience
(July 20, 2006)

———

IN 1907 A YOUNG LAWYER in India discovered an essay written by an American which helped to crystallize his own thoughts about social change. Eventually, this lawyer, Mohandas Gandhi, would become the leader of India's struggle for independence from Great Britain.

The essay which transformed Gandhi was Henry David Thoreau's "On the Duty of Civil Disobedience" which Thoreau published in 1849. Thoreau's essay inspired not only Gandhi but also Dr. Martin Luther King, Jr.

Thoreau's "On the Duty of Civil Disobedience" is brief, only thirteen pages. But its message will continue to influence generations. And what is this message?

Arguably the central message is that human beings are rational and moral creatures who are responsible for their own lives and for the society in which they live. If and when evil surfaces in society, Thoreau says, a human being ought to object publicly and non-violently. To do nothing, to wait patiently for reform, is to acquiesce in the evil. A person of conscience must act. Thoreau wrote:

> There are thousands who are in opinion opposed to slavery and to the war (against) Mexico, who yet in effect do nothing to put an

end to them… Must the citizen ever for a moment, or in the least degree, resign his conscience to the legislator? Why has every man a conscience then? I think that we should be men first, and subjects afterward. It is not desirable to cultivate a respect for the law, as much as for the right. Any man more right than his neighbors constitutes a majority of one already.

Thoreau's passion was to end slavery. To this end he refused for years to pay taxes and was jailed. He wrote: "I cannot for an instant recognize that political organization as my government which is the slave's government also." But Thoreau's objective was not to overturn government. It was, in his words, to produce "at once a better government."

Thoreau understood that social reform does not always win the reformer praise and respect. He observes that society chose to "crucify Christ and excommunicate Copernicus and Luther, and pronounce Washington and Franklin rebels."

Thoreau was convinced that living a good life is incompatible with wealth. The more assets you have, he reasoned, the less likely you are to resist your government when you should for you will fear that government will seize your assets. The moral life for Thoreau is a simple life of self-reliance and courage. For this reason he worked only occasionally as a surveyor and pencil-maker to earn a modest income.

Perhaps more than anything else, Thoreau sought to embolden the individual in an era of ever-increasing State power. He wrote:

> There will never be a really free and enlightened State until the State comes to recognize the individual as a higher and independent power, from which all its own power and authority are derived, and treats him accordingly.

Thoreau reminds us that the State exists to serve the people, not the reverse, and that moral progress is not automatic but comes on the backs of courageous, morally sensitive individuals who stick out their necks. Although tuberculosis took Thoreau at a young age, his ideas in "On the Duty of Civil Disobedience" guarantee him a permanent place in the minds and hearts of all who value individuality.

Science and Intercessory Prayer – the STEP Study (August 3, 2006)

THERE ARE SEVERAL TYPES OF prayer. One type praises God, another thanks God, and yet another requests God's help for oneself or others. Seeking God's help for others is called *intercessory* prayer as it asks God to intercede on their behalf. This particular form of prayer, it turns out, was the focus of a recent comprehensive study entitled the *Study of the Therapeutic Effects of Intercessory Prayer*, or STEP, the results of which were published in the March 30 online edition of *The American Heart Journal*.

STEP was supported by a $2.4 million grant from the John Templeton Foundation whose mission is to build bridges between science and religion, and it was directed by Dr. Herbert Benson, a cardiologist on the staff of Harvard University Medical School and Beth Israel Hospital in Boston. At Beth Israel Dr. Benson directs The Mind-Body Medical Institute. He first came to prominence in 1975 with the publication of a book entitled *Relaxation Response* which promoted relaxation techniques such as meditation to promote good mental and physical health. He is one of the central figures in contemporary medicine who recommends prayer as a component of a religious patient's healing.

The STEP study involved 1,802 patients undergoing coronary bypass surgery in six different hospitals. STEP was designed

...to study the effect of intercessory prayer (on these patients) and whether (their) knowledge that (they were) receiving prayer made a difference... Results were measured in terms of the number of medical complications encountered by each patient after surgery. (1)

The patients were divided into three groups. One group was prayed for and was told that it was prayed for, a second group was prayed for but was told that it might or might not be prayed for, and a third group – the control group – was not prayed for but was told that it might or might not be prayed for. Prayers were offered by three different groups – Silent Unity, a Protestant prayer ministry in Kansas City, Missouri; the Community of Teresian Carmelites in Worcester, Massachusetts; and the congregation of St. Paul's monastery in St. Paul, Minnesota. Those offering prayers were permitted to craft their own prayers but all prayers were required to request "a successful surgery with a quick, healthy recovery and no complications." Prayers began the night before surgery and continued daily for two week after surgery. Researchers monitored patients for a month after surgery.

And what were the results? The study showed that "intercessory prayer...had no effect on recovery from bypass surgery." (2) Oddly, the group which knew that it was being prayed for had a higher rate of postsurgical complications than the other two groups. The authors of the study hypothesize that the patients who knew that they were being prayed for may have suffered additional anxiety based on their assumption that they received prayers because their condition was especially serious. (3)

The STEP study is particularly important because it is the most rigorous and comprehensive study of the link between intercessory prayer and health ever conducted, it was carefully designed to correct for flaws in previous research on the subject, (4) and, given the reputation of its director, Dr. Benson, the conclusion that intercessory prayer is ineffective cannot be attributed to investigator bias.

In the wake of the STEP study, here's my advice. If you're going to have surgery soon and your relatives and friends offer to pray for you, feel free to accept the offer, but in the meanwhile, make sure your surgeon is board-certified and that your hospital is accredited.

---

1. Gregory Lamb, Online *Christian Science Monitor*, April 3, 2006.
2. David G. Myers, *Arm Twisting with the Almighty*, Online Edition, *Science and Theology News*, June 27, 2006.
3. Lamb, *op. cit.*
4. Lamb, *op. cit.*

Ayn Rand (August 17, 2006)

ONE OF THE MOST INTRIGUING figures in twentieth-century philosophy and literature is Ayn Rand. Born in Russia in 1905 as Alice Rosenbaum, she left Russia for the United States at age 21 to escape communism. She took a variety of odd jobs in America as she worked to master the English language so that she could pursue the career which she said she chose at the age of nine – a writer. Along the way she changed her name to Ayn Rand.

Although she spoke English with a Russian accent throughout her life, her English prose is polished and subtle. She sealed her reputation as a writer and intellectual with two novels – *The Fountainhead*, in 1943, which runs for 700 pages, and *Atlas Shrugged*, her *magnum opus*, in 1957, which runs for more than 1,000 pages. A film version of *The Fountainhead* was released in 1948 starring Gary Cooper and Patricia Neal, and a film version of *Atlas Shrugged* is planned for later this decade. A 1991 survey of its patrons by the Library of Congress placed *Atlas Shrugged* second behind the Bible as the most influential book in the United States. Rand's protagonists in her two novels – Howard Roark and John Galt – are archetypes, moral models, whom Rand uses to illustrate how to live rational, happy, and productive lives.

Rand summarized her philosophy in these words:

> My philosophy, in essence, is the concept of man as a heroic being, with his own happiness as the moral purpose of his life, with productive achievement as his noblest activity, and reason his only absolute. (1)

Rand was an unrepentant advocate of individual liberty and laissez-faire capitalism, a life-long enemy of altruism and collectivism, and a stern critic of faith-based worldviews, including religion. Although she championed capitalism all her life as the only economic system compatible with liberty, she irked many in corporate America because she argued that a free market is incompatible with tariffs, subsidies, and other forms of protectionism that so many businesses and industries covet.

In addition to her novels, Rand published her ideas in dozens of essays which appeared in *The Objectivist*, a newsletter named after her philosophical system – Objectivism. Although Rand died in 1982, all of her publications continue to sell tens of thousands of copies year after year, and scholars such as Tara Smith, Leonard Peikoff, Harry Binswanger, David Kelley, Nathaniel Branden, and others, continue to explain and interpret her ideas in a variety of forums. Indeed, if you do an internet search of Ayn Rand, you'll turn up dozens of active websites, including a dating service for disciples of Rand. Ayn Rand is more than a writer or an intellectual. She is an industry.

Ayn Rand certainly had her faults and shortcomings. She trucked with no dissent among the acolytes who made up her inner circle. Though married, she carried on an affair for years. And she read very little of the history of philosophy beyond Aristotle, whom she admired, and Kant, whom she disdained. Nevertheless, through her novels she brought drama, mystery, and romance to philosophy, a discipline that is so often dryasdust, and for this we should all be grateful.

---

1. *Atlas Shrugged*, 35th Anniversary Edition, p. 1075.

The Freedom from Religion Foundation – Bucking the Trend (August 31, 2006)

THE FIRST AMENDMENT TO THE Constitution of the United States says in part: "Congress shall make no law respecting an establishment of religion, or prohibiting the free exercise thereof…" This passage supposedly establishes the principle of the separation of church and state and the duty of government to remain neutral toward religion. The facts suggest, however, that there is a long-standing and growing gap between theory and practice in America on this score. Consider this:

- "In God We Trust" supplanted *E Pluribus Unum* (From Many, One), the original national motto, on our currency over half a century ago.
- The original Pledge of Allegiance was amended to add the phrase "under God."
- The Ten Commandments are on display in many public buildings, including the City Hall of Youngstown.
- There is ever-expanding tax support of church-related schools and their students.
- In violation of federal laws granting tax exemptions to churches, many pastors endorse candidates and seek passage of laws forbidding abortion, marriage by same-sex partners, and civil unions.

- Atheists and agnostics who hope to run for office are doomed if they publicly acknowledge their stance.
- Office holders and candidates flock to prayer breakfasts and close virtually every speech with a "God Bless You" and "God Bless America."
- Prisoners are urged by many prison officials to participate in tax-supported prison ministry programs.
- Efforts continue in many school districts to teach religious accounts of the origin and development of the universe in science classes in lieu of evolution.
- And President George W. Bush has launched a faith-based initiative to empower churches and other religious organizations to provide an array of tax-supported services.

Despite the clear national trend, many organizations, including a small but militant group called the Freedom from Religion Foundation (FFRF), are bucking it. FFRF is an IRS 501 (c) 3 non-profit which was founded in 1978 by Anne Nicol Gaylor "to keep church and state separate" and "to promote freethought." It operates out of a headquarters in Madison, Wisconsin, called Freethought Hall, which once served, ironically, as a church rectory. It has a small staff, mostly volunteers, and its national membership is smaller than some mega-churches.

The founder's daughter, Annie Laurie Gaylor, and her husband, Dan Barker, who serve as "co-presidents," are prolific authors, engaging speakers, and skilled debaters. Gaylor's books include *Women Without Superstition: No Gods, No Masters*, and *Betrayal of Trust*. The former highlights courageous women who fought sexism and the subordination of women and the latter chronicles clergy sex abuse of children. Barker is a musician, songwriter, and ex-preacher turned atheist whose autobiography is entitled *Losing Faith in Faith: From Preacher to Atheist*.

The Foundation publishes a newsletter called *Freethought Today* ten times a year as well as a variety of books and brochures in hard copy and on its website. FFRF is very active in litigation over church-state issues in the courts where it has had mixed results. It also holds an annual convention at which it bestows a "Freethinker of the Year Award" and it sponsors high school and college essay contests.

Do groups like FFRF have a future in America? Will they survive to fight for the separation of church and state or will they be marginalized by the powerful and wealthy religious forces in our culture which oppose their mission? Only time will tell.

Funny Moments (September 14, 2006)

ARISTOTLE PROCLAIMED THAT ALL HUMAN beings seek happiness. Unfortunately, the road to happiness has plenty of speed bumps in the form of disappointment, pain, fear, stress, boredom, and tragedy. That is why humor is so important to us. Funny moments in our lives distract us from the dark side of life and they refresh and energize us, much like a cold drink in the hot sun. As we age, we forget much of our past but not the really funny moments. Let me share a few such moments in my life with you.

There I was, a college student and athlete, lying in a hospital bed in Cleveland in November, 1961. I had a 105 degree fever. I was losing weight rapidly. The doctors were frantically trying to diagnose my ailment. Fortunately, they did and I recovered. During my hospital stay, I was given red carpet treatment by dozens of nursing students who came to my room throughout the day to cheer me up. Afterwards, I decided to ask one of them to a Valentine Day mixer. I phoned her at the nurses' dormitory. She was summoned from her room to the telephone at the end of the hall. She was gracious but declined, saying she was already booked that night, but she asked me to phone again. I went to number two on my list. She was less gracious but civil and she, too, declined. I proceeded to number three on my list and she was downright hostile. Only weeks later did I learn that these three women were roommates and that each reported my phone call to the others. Just my luck.

Then there was the case of another young lady whom I asked out during college. When I arrived at her house, her father said that he was happy for me to spend the evening with his daughter but that he would appreciate it if I respected her decision not to use alcohol. That was fine with me since I had a total of six bucks in my wallet. When my date and I arrived at Farragher's Lounge in Cleveland Heights a bit early for a performance by a folk singer, the bartender asked if she'd like a drink. I expected that it would be a pop and I reached for a dollar bill. "Triple Cutty on the rocks," she replied. As a result, one of us abstained that night but it was not the one I expected.

Then there's the sayings of "Cokey Joe," a retired steel worker who frequented a local tavern in Youngstown near YSU daily for years and who was a master of malapropism. One day I walked in after work and Cokey said, "Doc, there was a crash at the Mexico City Airport. The pilot tried to land on the wrong fairway." On another occasion he closed an argument with another fellow over the location of St. Dominic's Church in Youngstown with this comment: "I know where St. Dominic's is. My friend died and I was a poll parrot there."

My all-time favorite funny moment was in Florida about twenty-five years ago the weekend of a NASCAR race at Daytona when the entire weekend was filled with racing. At a local dirt track on Friday night, the announcer asked everyone to stand so that a Baptist minister could lead us in a prayer before the race. We all complied. When the minister started, his prayer was a loud, shrill babble. Alas, the prayer had been recorded and someone pressed 78 instead of 33 on the tape recorder. As the fans squirmed, this observation rang out across the stands from a few rows behind me in a deep Southern drawl: "You'd better get the Reverend off them amphetamines." The whole place exploded in laughter. That made my trip. I don't remember who won the NASCAR race on Sunday but I remember that moment as though it were yesterday.

The next time you're having a bad day, think about some of the funny moments in your life.

Sam Harris – an Update
(September 28, 2006)

IN A PREVIOUS COMMENTARY (FEBRUARY 2, 2006), I reported to you on a new figure on the American literary and philosophical scene, Sam Harris, author of *The End of Faith: Religion, Terror, and the Future of Reason*, which was published in 2004. Harris is a philosophy graduate from Stanford University who studied world religions for some twenty years and who is completing a doctorate in neuroscience. In *The End of Faith* Harris argues that the beliefs of the religions of the world contradict one another, that literalists in the various traditions, especially Islam, seize on passages in the scriptures which command killing infidels and defectors, and that religion in an era of chemical, biological, and nuclear weapons is an impediment to a viable global civilization and a threat to human survival. Today, a Sam Harris update.

Harris is fast becoming the principal anti-religious voice in the country and possibly the world. *The End of Faith*, now available in both hardback and paperback, is a *New York Times* bestseller and winner of the 2005 PEN/Martha Albrand Award for Nonfiction. *Newsweek* magazine featured Harris in an article by Jerry Adler in the September 11, 2006, issue. He has also gotten attention in *The New York Times, The San Francisco Chronicle, The Chicago Tribune, The Economist, The Guardian, The Independent, The Globe and Mail, New Scientist, SEED Magazine*, and many other publications. Harris regularly issues statements on his own website as well as *truthdig* and

The Huffington Post, each of which elicits literally hundreds of replies, mostly supportive. Harris appears regularly on radio and TV and lectures extensively at universities and city clubs or forums. He writes for the humanist magazine, *Free Inquiry,* (1) and publishes op-ed pieces in major newspapers such as *The Los Angeles Times.* He is to be a recipient of an award from the Freedom from Religion Foundation at its annual convention this year.

In a recent op-ed piece in *The Los Angeles Times,* Harris argues that radical Islam is the world's chief threat, saying that:

> ...(W)e are absolutely at war with those who believe that death in defense of faith is the highest possible good, that cartoonists should be killed for caricaturing the prophet, and that any Muslim who loses his faith should be butchered for apostasy. (2)

In the same op-ed, Harris's identifies a new and surprising target, western liberals, who, he says, "foolishly continue to imagine that Muslim terrorism springs from economic despair, lack of education and American militarism." Harris points out that many terrorists are "economically well-off and well-educated." Further, he insists that we are fighting not so much a war on terror as...

> ...(A) pestilential theology and a longing for paradise... (and) I don't know how many more engineers and architects need to blow themselves up, fly planes into buildings or saw off the heads of journalists before liberal naivete will dissipate.

Recently Harris posted a comment on the web on the Pope's recent speech which inflamed many Muslims, and last week he published a second book, *Letter to a Christian Nation,* a reply to critics of his first book, which is now available through online book sellers and will soon appear in local bookstores.

Natalie Angier, science writer for *The New York Times,* says that Harris "writes what a sizable number of us think, but few are willing to say."

Another Harris admirer opines on the web that "there has never been anyone else with (his) guts." While this may be hyperbole, there is no doubt that Sam Harris is drawing more attention and drawing it faster than any other religious skeptic in memory.

---

1. Harris no longer writes for *Free Inquiry*.
2. The remaining quotes from Harris are all from the op-ed piece published *The Los Angeles Times* on September 18, 2006.

Aayan Hirsi Ali – A Voice of Dissent in Islam (October 13, 2006)

FOR MANY WESTERN POLITICAL LEADERS, the problem in today's world is not Islam, which they see as a "religion of peace," but religious extremists who subvert it. But this viewpoint is coming under fire from a growing list of writers, including Aayan Hirsi Ali. Though a young woman at 36, Aayan Hirsi Ali has received no less than a dozen major awards in Europe and the United States for her advocacy of Muslim women and in 2005 she was named one of *Time* magazine's 100 most influential people in the world. Recently she was the subject of one of George F. Will's syndicated columns.

Aayan Hirsi Ali was born in Somalia and raised a Muslim. She lived there and in Saudi Arabia, Ethiopia, and Kenya until, at age 22, she ducked an arranged marriage to her father's cousin and settled in the Netherlands where she learned the language, completed her education, and eventually became a member of Parliament. In 2004 Ali published a book in Dutch which was recently translated and published in the West under the title *The Caged Virgin: An Emancipation Proclamation for Women and Islam*. (1) Ali also wrote the script for a short film – *Submission: Part I* – which highlights passages in the Quran which disparage women. Theo van Gogh, director of the film, was murdered by a Muslim fundamentalist shortly after the film was shown and Ali herself was threatened with death. Ali holds that in the name of religion, Muslim women "are enslaved in their homes" and subjected to genital mutilation and disownment (i.e., abandonment) by their families for any real or imagined offense, and denied education and other opportunities for personal and professional growth.

But Ali's critique of Islam goes beyond this. She says that Islamic culture most needs what it most abhors – skepticism. She calls for an enlightenment in the Islamic world much the same as the one in the Christian world centuries ago. She writes: "We Muslims are already imbued with faith and superstition. What we need are schools of philosophy." "Let us have a Voltaire" is the title of a chapter in her book. "All Muslims," she says, "share the conviction that the fundamental principles of Islam cannot be criticized, revised, or in any way contradicted." This dogmatism explains virtually all the defects in Islamic culture, she says, including the "fanaticism" of terrorists, sectarian strife, lagging the West in "technology, finance, health, and culture," lack of respect for individual autonomy and women's rights, the political authority of mullahs, the failure of Muslims to read important Western thinkers, the lack of "a credible and workable political model," and Muslim hypersensitivity to criticism. On the last point, she writes: "I am outraged that Muslims are not more offended by the invocation of Allah and 'God is great' for murder (by terrorists) than by cartoons." Her own skepticism is evident. "I have come to realize," she writes, "that the existence of Allah, of angels, demons, and a life after death, is at the very least disputable."

Ali recently left Europe for her own safety and accepted an appointment at the American Enterprise Institute in Washington, D.C., where she is now working on a new book in which the Prophet Muhammad has an imaginary dialogue with John Stuart Mill, Friedrich Hayek, and Karl Popper. No doubt we can expect more sparks to fly once she publishes it.

---

1. All the quotations of Aayan Hirsi Ali in this commentary are taken from *The Caged Virgin*.

Liberty or Security – a False Dilemma (October 26, 2006)

MANY HAVE EXPRESSED DISMAY OVER the Patriot Act and other laws and practices adopted by the United States since 9/11 to guard against the threat of terrorism. In essence, the critics charge that the U.S. is sacrificing liberty at the altar of security. Although I, too, have misgivings about many features of the Patriot Act, not to mention poorly justified, planned, and executed military initiatives in Afghanistan and Iraq, I also believe that the line between prudent security measures and overzealous infringement of liberties is not as clear and distinct as one would hope, especially in a climate where suicidal religious zealots perceive every American death as strengthening their claim on heaven. I also recognize that without security there can be no liberty.

Indeed, this is arguably the central insight of two of the greatest political theorists in history – Thomas Hobbes and John Locke – despite the fact that in 17th century England the former espoused the cause of monarchy and absolute government, while the latter espoused the cause of Parliament and limited government.

In his *magnum opus, Leviathan*, published in 1651, Hobbes tells us that liberty, the power to do as one wishes, is dependent upon security (Ch. XIV). Humans, he says, as pleasure-seeking, pain-avoiding animals, will seek their own pleasure and advantage, even at the expense of their neighbors, unless there is a recognized law-maker who possesses sufficient power to make laws and to enforce them. Absent this, Hobbes says, "the life of man" is "solitary, poor, nasty, brutish, and short." (Ch. XIII) Through a social contract, Hobbes says, we collectively agree to establish and recognize a political sovereign, a leviathan, whose power protects our life, liberty, and possessions.

Similarly, in his *Second Treatise of Government*, published some 39 years after Hobbes's *Leviathan*, John Locke, though seeking to limit the powers of government, recognized, as Hobbes did, the necessity of government to provide security, and the line between security and Liberty. Locke argues that in the absence of government, society suffers three serious defects or "wants": 1) lack of a settled, known, established law, 2) lack of a fair and impartial judge; and 3) lack of the power to impose a proper sentence on a wrongdoer. The purpose of government, which people establish through a social contract, Locke says, is to overcome these defects. So essential is a stable and strong government to rights and liberties, Locke observes, that nearly all humans past and present "take sanctuary under the established laws of government and therein seek the preservation of their property." "Property" is Locke's term for our rights under the moral law to life, liberty, and possessions ("estate").

Can government err in the quest to secure us from terrorism and other threats to our welfare? Of course it can. Public discussion and debate are important to help us identify and correct these errors. Nevertheless, we should never forget that security is indispensable to liberty and that no one has a foolproof plan for the perfect blend of security and liberty in the dangerous world in which we live.

Sam Harris, *Letter to a Christian Nation* (November 9, 2006)

IN HIS FIRST BOOK, *THE End of Faith*, published in 2004, Sam Harris, philosopher, religious skeptic, and neuroscientist, wrote *about* religion. In his second book, *Letter to a Christian Nation*, published a few months ago, Harris writes *to* the religious, especially American Christians. Both books are *New York Times* bestsellers. In the *Letter*, which runs for a mere ninety-five pages, Harris outlines the alleged defects of religion and entreats believers to take a fresh look at their worldview so that, in his words, there can follow a "public discourse that encourages critical thinking and intellectual honesty." (p. 87)

His critique of religion includes these points:

1. Religions contradict one another so they cannot all be true. (pp. 5-7)
2. Sizeable segments of the religious community defy the exhaustively confirmed findings of modern science on evolution. (p. x)
3. The Bible is a bad place to look for a moral code. For instance, the Bible condones slavery, beating children and even killing them in certain cases, and stoning people to death for heresy, adultery, homosexuality, working on the Sabbath, and other deeds. A morally praiseworthy part of the Bible, the Golden Rule, was taught

long before Jesus by Zoroaster, Buddha, Confucius, and Epictetus (pp. 8-1) and it amounts to nothing more than intelligent self-interest (pp. 23-24).

4. The stance of many believers on embryonic stem cell research, abortion, contraception, and vaccinations to prevent HPV (human papillomavirus) needlessly perpetuates suffering.
5. Doing good does not require belief in God. For instance, many doctors "are moved simply to alleviate suffering without any thought of God." (p. 33) And surely the members of the National Academy of Science, ninety-three percent of whom reject belief in God, are "at least as well behaved as the general population." (p. 39)
6. Secular societies in the world have a higher level of development and a lower level of crime than religious societies. (pp. 39-44)
7. In the United States, the red states, which are populated by large numbers on the religious right who vote Republican, have higher crime rates than the blue states. (p. 45)
8. "Countries with high levels of atheism are also the most charitable both in terms of the percentage of their wealth (which) they devote to social welfare programs and the percentage (which) they give in aid to the developing world." (p. 46)
9. There is no satisfactory solution to the classic problem of evil. The enormity of human and animal suffering in the world is incompatible with the notion of an all-good, all-powerful God. (pp. 52-57)
10. Beliefs should be based on sufficient evidence, not faith. "…(F)aith is nothing more than the license religious people give one another to keep believing when reasons fail." (pp. 66-67)
11. The traditional arguments for the existence of God are all fatally flawed. (pp. 66-79)
12. Our "competing religious certainties" are killing us, literally. Religious differences exacerbate conflict and impede the creation of stable governments and viable economies in at least thirteen areas of the world. (pp. 79-82)

13. Islam is the greatest single threat to humanity's long-term survival and happiness. "The idea that Islam is 'a peaceful religion hijacked by extremists' is a fantasy…" (p. 85)

Obviously, Harris has given us a highly provocative polemic against religion. It remains to be seen whether believers in great numbers will read it, whether they will carefully evaluate his claims and arguments, and whether they will engage in the public discourse on religion that he recommends.

Garry Wills, *A Country Ruled by Faith* (November 30, 2006)

IT IS NO SURPRISE THAT George W. Bush made campaign promises to his political base – evangelicals. But, as a recent article in *The New York Review of Books* by Pulitzer Prize-winning historian, Garry Wills shows ("A Country Ruled by Faith," Nov. 16, 2006), the ambitious scope of the President's evangelical agenda is surprising.

The President began by ridding government of as many holdover liberals as possible and replacing them with evangelicals. To implement his plan, he appointed Kay Coles James head of the White House Office of Personnel. James had worked for Pat Robertson and James Dobson, two evangelical heavyweights. Also, the President picked key advisors and cabinet members, among them Condoleeza Rice, Karen Hughes, John Ashcroft, Andrew Card, and Michael Gerson, who shared his religious worldview. Even appointees to the Iraqi Provisional Government came largely from a pool of evangelicals, Wills says.

Next, President Bush gave evangelical leaders unprecedented access. Either the President or his key staff consulted them routinely on virtually all issues of interest to them.

Further, the President established the White House Office of Faith-Based and Community Initiatives to funnel money to them. Grants went to Pat Robertson, Chuck Colson, James Dobson, and many others, including selected African-American clergy, such as Bishop Sedgwick Daniels of Milwaukee.

The President also carried the evangelical perspective to scientific and social issues. Saying that the jury is still out on evolution, he proposed teaching intelligent design, a version of creationism, alongside evolution in science classrooms. Also, his administration ignored objections by scientists to the sale of a book at the Grand Canyon "claiming that the Grand Canyon was formed by Noah's Flood," and it scuttled publication of a draft guide for park employees which pointed out that the canyon was not formed in the alleged period of the Flood. Additionally, to pacify the religious right, Wills says, the Bush administration...

- opposed embryonic stem cell research, in defiance of moderates in his own party,
- ignored scientific warnings about global warming,
- spent $170 million on abstinence-only sex education in the public schools while removing from the website of The Centers for Disease Control the findings of a panel that abstinence-only programs don't work,
- refused to make the morning-after pill available to women over-the-counter, despite the recommendations of the board of the Food and Drug Administration,
- sought a Constitutional amendment banning same-sex marriage,
- forbad the expenditure of U.S. foreign aid to any organization which distributed condoms or provided information to women about abortion, despite the fact that birth control and abortion remain legal in the U.S., and
- protected a controversial general who publicly characterized the war on terrorism as a battle of Christians against Satan.

Wills' article shows that he views George W. Bush as a president on a mission to destroy the Establishment Clause of the First Amendment. Yet Wills overlooks an important fact: the President is not universally loved among evangelicals. Some have protested that he politicized the faith-based initiatives by spending mostly in battleground states to help Republicans and there remains a huge gap between the billions which Bush promised to evangelicals and the millions which he actually delivered to them. And surely, if exit polls are accurate, many evangelicals deserted him in the recent election.

David Kuo, *Tempting Faith* (December 14, 2006)

DAVID KUO WORKED IN THE White House Office of Faith-Based and Community Initiatives for three years during the administration of President George W. Bush. Kuo went to Washington as an evangelical Christian to help the President bring compassionate conservatism to America by ending discrimination against religious charities and by providing billions of dollars to them for their work. His recent book, *Tempting Faith*, is a report card on the President's faith-based agenda. Kuo gives the President an F.

But *Tempting Faith* is more than an indictment of President Bush. It is also a tale of his own spiritual journey, a candid report of his experience on the White House staff, a reappraisal of whether faith-based groups are really victims of discrimination by government, and a caveat about the dangers of politics to people of faith.

Some of what Kuo has to say will surprise no one. For instance, he tells us that the White House is one huge spin machine in the service of George W. Bush and that Karl Rove rules the White House roost. But much of the rest of the book is filled with surprises which will shock many evangelicals. Here are three of them.

Firstly, when Kuo and his associates looked for evidence to confirm the evangelical mantra that government discriminates against faith-based groups, they found very little. Dozens of religious charities, it turns out, are recipients of federal grants, among them Catholic Charities and Lutheran

Social Services, which have received $1.5 billion a year for many years running, and Habitat for Humanity, a favorite grantee of the Department of Housing and Urban Development.

Secondly, President Bush's faith-based agenda, Kuo charges, is a charade, a slick and successful political strategy architected by Karl Rove to lure Christian conservatives to the camp of Bush and other Republicans. Although Bush had promised $8 billion a year in new money for compassionate conservatism, only $30 million had been budgeted by the second year of his presidency. The White House staff, Kuo says, showed no support for faith-based programs when federal budgets were drafted. And this was not due to the costs of the war in Iraq or post-9/11 security; there was an active White House non-military domestic agenda all along, Kuo insists. According to Kuo, President Bush talked the compassion talk but he didn't walk the compassion walk. Cynically, the White House invited tens of thousands of ministers and other community leaders to workshops in battleground states and Congressional districts to learn how to apply for federal grants despite the fact that they knew that, at most, only one out of five hundred could realistically expect to receive any of the meager funds. Despite the President's pathetic performance on the faith-based agenda, Kuo says, evangelicals continued to trust and support him. No one asked, "Where's the beef?"

Thirdly, Kuo advises Christians to take a break from politics and go on a two-year political "fast." Christians have been seduced by politicians seeking their votes who "will say anything" to get them. (p. 265) Christians should divert their energy and money from politics to serve God by helping the poor, the homeless, alcoholics and drug addicts, battered women, children of prisoners, and others in need.

David Kuo's *Tempting Faith* is must reading for all people of faith in America. It is an honest and disturbing story of manipulation of millions of Americans by political operatives and a tale of the painful education of the author.

The Costs of College and Perceived Value
(January 5, 2007)

MOST HIGH SCHOOL GRADUATES APPLY for admission to several colleges, as they should, because today the average income of college graduates is twice as much as non-graduates. (1) Once admitted, these young people and their parents face the daunting task of meeting the ever-rising costs of college – room, board, tuition, books, and other fees. The price tag at most private institutions is especially high. The average room, board, and tuition at private, non-profit colleges stands today at $30,367, far more than at public institutions, and costs at private schools rose 81% from 1993 to 2004, more than double the rate of inflation. (2) One private institution, George Washington University, actually charged students over $49,000 last year. Although public institutions cost less as a rule, their fees also predictably go up each year. This is usually attributed to a steady decline across the nation in appropriations by states to public colleges as a percentage of their operating costs. Although scholarships, grants, loans, and student jobs are available to a great many students at both private and public institutions, many graduates and their families find themselves paying off college debts long after commencement.

    A key question about fees is what drives them? How are they set? Although there are no doubt some cases where institutions struggle to keep costs as low as possible, they're few and far between according to a recent series on American higher education published by *The New York*

Times. (3) The *Times* reports, remarkably, that the popularity of a college rises with its cost! (4) For instance, at one private college in Pennsylvania which was losing applicants, the chairman of the Board of Trustees promoted a 17.6% increase in tuition and within four years the size of the first year class rose 35%. "Applicants," the *Times* points out, "had apparently concluded that if the college costs more, it must be better." (5) The *Times* observes that consumer perceived value is a prime factor at countless institutions of higher education which have "sharply increased tuition to match colleges they consider their rivals, while also providing more financial aid..." lest they lose potential revenue or be perceived by prospective students as inferior. (6) For instance, Notre Dame tracks fees at Chicago, Emory, Vanderbilt, and seventeen other schools when it sets fees. (7) Thus colleges exploit the perception of students and their families that there is a direct correlation between cost and quality. As a result, costs go up and up and up. When your customers believe that they get what they pay for, that more means better, charging them less, even if feasible, is institutionally self-defeating.

The research on college costs and types of colleges may surprise many of these families. On the one hand, there is no proven correlation between fees and actual quality. On the other hand, the type of college – public or private, large or small – has no significant effect on a college graduate's occupational achievements or income. (8) Despite this, I do not expect any change soon in consumer perceptions of value in higher education. The situation is somewhat similar to the world of motorcycles. Harley-Davidson cycles cost more than comparable models of other manufacturers despite the fact that there is no proof that they are superior in design and performance. But this doesn't faze Harley owners.

---

1. Rudy Fenwick, "Report to the Ohio Faculty Council on the Effects of College Graduation on Individual Income: A Summary of Research Results in the Sociological Literature," February 2005.
2. *The New York Times*, December 12, 2006.
3. *Ibid.*

Commentaries

4. *Ibid.*
5. *Ibid.*
6. *Ibid.*
7. *Ibid.*
8. Fenwick, *op. cit.*

Nora Ephron, *I Feel Bad About My Neck* (February 1, 2007)

AUTHOR AND DIRECTOR, NORA EPHRON, who gave us *When Harry Met Sally, Silkwood,* and *Sleepless in Seattle,* has published a mini-autobiography entitled *I Feel Bad About My Neck,* in which she reflects with honesty and wit on the highs and lows in her life, the travails of aging, and the certainty of death.

The reader gets a picture of Ephron from her book as an obsessive person. One obsession is with her appearance. She admits that she spends long hours every week at "maintenance." (p. 31) Part of the regimen involves a battery of moisturizers – cream for her face, lotions for her arms and legs, oil for her bath, and Vaseline for her feet. (p. 47) She also dyes her hair and exercises in fits and spurts but with unwanted results. (p. 35)

> Every time I (try to) get into shape, something breaks… (p. 44) So far, in the breakage department, I have managed the following: I pulled my lower back doing sit-ups; I threw out my right hip on the treadmill; I got shin splits from jogging…(and) frozen shoulders (from weight lifting). (pp. 45-46)

And what has all this attention to appearance produced? She estimates that at the age of sixty-six she looks "approximately one year younger" than she is. (p. 139)

Another obsession is with her computer. She concedes that she is a "mouse potato." This is "someone who's as connected to her computer as couch potatoes are to their television sets." (p. 95) Other obsessions are cooking, an apartment in the Apthorp Building on New York's upper west side, cabbage strudel, reading good books, purses, and psychonalysis.

In a chapter entitled "What I Wish I'd Known," Ephron dispenses nuggets of wisdom culled from her own experience. Among them are these:

"Buy, don't rent." (p. 123)

"The last four years of psychoanalysis are a waste of money." (p. 124)

"At the age of fifty-five you will get a saggy roll above your waist even if you are painfully thin." (p. 124)

"The empty nest is underrated." (p. 125)

"When your children are teenagers, it's important to have a dog so that someone in the house is happy to see you (when you come home)." (p. 125)

"There are no secrets." (p. 126)

Ephron also engages the topics of suffering and death. She divulges that her father hastened her dying mother's death with an overdose of sleeping pills to end her suffering (p. 103) but she doesn't tell us if she approved. She worries about her own future: "Is life too short, or is it going to be too long?" (p. 132) She confesses that the death of Judy, her best friend and confidant, from cancer has riveted her attention on death. "Death," she writes, "is a sniper. It strikes people you love, people you like, people you know, it's everywhere. You could be next... Everyone dies." (p. 131) Apparently a secular, Ephron finds none of the consolations in death which traditional religions provide.

Nora Ephron's *I Feel Bad About My Neck* is entertaining but it is too short and too selective. She says next to nothing about her children, her three marriages, or the genesis of her screenplays. Hopefully a larger version is in the works that will fill in the huge gaps in this volume.

Robert Green Ingersoll, *The Shakespeare of Oratory* (February 16, 2007)

Eugene Debs called him "the Shakespeare of Oratory." (1) After hearing him speak, Mark Twain said "What an organ is human speech when it is employed by a master." He was a hero to James Garfield, Walt Whitman, Ulysses Grant, Margaret Sanger, Andrew Carnegie, Thomas Edison, Henry Ward Beecher, and Elizabeth Cady Stanton. Who was this remarkable man? Robert Green Ingersoll.

Born in 1833 in Dresden, New York, Ingersoll moved as a child with his family to Illinois where eventually he became a lawyer and state Attorney General. Originally a Democrat, he bolted to the Republican Party to join in the crusade to end slavery. He was the speaker of choice among prominent Republicans who sought his aid during their campaigns. One of his greatest speeches was the "Plumed Knight" speech in Cincinnati at the Republican convention in 1876 in which he nominated James G. Blaine for president. Although Blaine lost, Ingersoll set the standard for nominating speeches.

Ingersoll's work as a lawyer included representing two clients accused of bribery in the so-called Star Route scandal which involved bidders who were accused of using bribes to get U.S. Post Office contracts. His clients were acquitted. He also worked *pro bono* for Charles B. Reynolds, a prominent freethinker who had been arrested in New Jersey and charged under an archaic blasphemy law. Although Reynolds was convicted and fined $50, which Ingersoll paid, Ingersoll's arguments in court mocking blasphemy laws effectively put an end to blasphemy prosecutions in the nation.

In 1862, during the Civil War, Ingersoll raised the 11th Illinois Calvary Regiment and was given the rank of Colonel. Forever after he would be called Colonel Bob. He and many of his troops were captured by Confederate soldiers in a battle in which they were vastly outnumbered but they were released in exchange for a promise that they would not return to combat.

Ingersoll's career as an orator is unique. During an era in which there was no public address system and no films, TV, or radio, Ingersoll drew spectacular crowds from every walk of life and every class who paid the then hefty sum of $1 to hear him. Although it is hard to believe, a Chicago newspaper reported in 1876 that no fewer than 50,000 people packed into an enormous tent there to hear him. Ingersoll had a photographic memory and committed thirty speeches to memory, some of which lasted as long as three to four hours. He sold out every auditorium, theater, and tent in the north, midwest, and west, where he spoke, and despite his anti-slavery mission, he even drew large crowds in the south. The only states in which he did not speak were Oklahoma, Mississippi, and North Carolina.

What is perhaps most remarkable is that Ingersoll was an abolitionist, an advocate of equal rights and equal pay for women, and an agnostic. Many of his talks openly poked fun at religion and were severely critical of the Bible as a moral guide. Can you imagine tens of thousands of Americans gathering today to hear a religious skeptic?

Ingersoll was a font of wise sayings. One of his most famous is this:

My creed is that happiness is the only good. The place to be happy is here. The way to be happy is to make others so.

You can learn more about this extraordinary man by reading *Robert G. Ingersoll: A Life* by Frank Smith, visiting the Ingersoll Museum in Dresden, New York, or checking out the museum website – rgimuseum.org.

---

1. Some of the information and the quotations here are taken from Frank Smith, *Robert G. Ingersoll: A Life*.

Bernard Rollin, A Dog's Best Friend
(March 1, 2007)

PHILOSOPHERS ARE OFTEN THOUGHT TO be scholarly hermits who distance themselves from the practical world to produce books and papers accessible only by their peers. But there are exceptions, one of whom is Bernard Rollin of Colorado State University.

In 1975 Rollin was asked by his university to design and teach a course in veterinary ethics. This led not only to a new course but a new career path for Rollin. He immersed himself in ethical issues involving animals and eventually he became one of the most influential and respected practitioners of animal ethics in the world. Like other distinguished philosophers, Rollin has an impressive list of publications including fourteen books and over 300 articles and papers. But what sets Rollin apart from mainstream philosophers is a hands on approach in which he works with thousands of people around the world every year to improve the treatment of animals. Rollin moves comfortably and confidently among government officials, corporate executives, scientists, farmers, ranchers, veterinarians, and faculty, staff, and students on campuses. At last count Rollin has given over 1,100 talks on animals and ethics in thirty countries on six continents.

Not surprisingly, Rollin was the principal architect of federal legislation in 1986 dealing with the treatment of laboratory animals. But his focus is not restricted to the laboratory; he also addresses ethical issues involving companion animals, animals used in safety testing, animals used in product development, animals used for food, and animals used for sport.

Rollins's career is built on two foundations. The first is that animals are entitled to fulfill their natures. This means that they have rights to food, mobility, companionship, exercise, treatment of ailments, and freedom from avoidable pain, suffering, and distress. Surveys show that three of four Americans, while still wanting to continue using animals for food and other purposes, agree with him. The second is the belief that patiently working with stakeholders in the world of animals will lead to steady incremental improvement in the treatment of animals. Instead of finger-pointing at a distance, Rollin prefers to meet and talk with stakeholders and explore with them ways to achieve their goals which are compatible with the welfare of animals. After all, he points out, people who deal with animals are pursuing laudable goals such as "trying to cure diseases, protect the public from toxic substances, advance knowledge, or produce cheap and plentiful food." His most recent success is a decision by a huge pork producer to discontinue sow stalls and to shift to traditional grazing.

Rollin hopes that the United States will evolve to match the compassion for animals found in Europe, especially Sweden, but he admits that this will take time and cost Americans more at the super market, perhaps ten-percent to twenty-percent more. He also hopes that ethical sensitivity to animals will continue to grow among scientists, some of whom, he says, have been reluctant to abandon the Cartesian myth that animals are mere machines who experience no felt pain.

It's time to amend the old saying that a dog is a man's best friend. Bernard Rollin is the best friend of dogs, cats, mice, rats, cattle, horses, pigs, chickens, and hundreds of other animals to whom he has dedicated his life.

James Randi (March 16, 2007)

SUPPOSE YOUR NEIGHBOR TELLS YOU that she receives messages regularly from her husband who died five years ago. Whom might you contact to figure out whether your neighbor is psychic or psycho? Your best bet is James Randi.

In the 1970s, Johnny Carson asked Randi to appear on The Tonight Show opposite Uri Geller, a self-proclaimed psychic, who had become an international celebrity. Randi replied that Geller would never agree to such a confrontation but Randi agreed to coach Carson's producer to keep Geller from hoodwinking the audience. Geller bombed, his career promptly took a nose dive, and he would later sue Randi no fewer than six times to no avail.

What Randi did for Geller, he also did for faith-healer Peter Popoff, psychic James Hydrick, and dozens of other charlatans.

Randi was not always a debunker of paranormal claims. For most of his life, he was a celebrated magician and escape artist. As a youngster in Toronto he attended a performance by magician Harry Blackstone, Sr. He was immediately hooked on magic and dropped out of school, eventually becoming a show-stopper around the world. In addition to traditional stage magic, Randi escaped from a straightjacket while suspended from a crane over Niagara Falls, escaped from safes and jail cells, and survived for 104 minutes on The Today Show in a sealed coffin in a hotel swimming pool, breaking Houdini's record of 93 minutes.

As the years passed, Randi saw a growing number of people claiming paranormal powers. He then took on an additional career, unmasking the use of magic or fraud under the guise of occult powers. Today Randi continues to wear two hats, magician and debunker of the paranormal. As a base of operations he established the James Randi Educational Foundation in Fort Lauderdale in the 1960s with the help of two large gifts by an anonymous donor. One enabled Randi to purchase property for his foundation, the other to establish a $1 million prize to anyone who can demonstrate paranormal powers under proper controlled conditions. No one has collected yet. Psychic Sylvia Browne agreed in recent years on Larry King Live to take the Randi Challenge but thus far she has been a no-show.

Randi has published ten books, produced two NOVA specials, and appeared on dozens of TV programs and documentaries. Randi, now 78, remains as busy as ever. One additional task he took on in recent years is organizing an annual conference in Las Vegas for skeptics from around the world. Randi's remarkable career prompted the MacArthur Foundation in 1986 to bestow upon him the so-called "Genius Award" which came with a cash gift of $872,000 payable over five years.

To learn more about Randi, visit his website at randi.org.*

---

* I wish to thank Mr. Randi for participating in a recent telephone interview which helped in the preparation of this commentary.

Would You Vote for an Atheist or Agnostic? (April 5, 2007)

WOULD YOU VOTE FOR AN atheist or agnostic for President of the United States? If you would, you're a member of a distinct minority, particularly if you are religious.

This is the message from a recent study which appeared in the *American Sociological Review*. (1) This study reports the attitudes of religious people in the United States toward non-religious people. Based on a telephone survey of 2,000 households and in-depth interviews with 140 people, the study concludes that believers do not trust non-believers, view them as selfish and uncaring, and oppose their children marrying them. Religious faith, believers say, is central to being a good American and a good person. (2)

These views are worrisome, to put it mildly.

In the first place, they fly in the face of these facts:

1. Article VI of the Constitution says that "no religious Test shall ever be required as a Qualification to any Office or public Trust under the United States."
2. Our political system is built upon the separation of church and state.
3. The word "God" does not appear in the Constitution even once.
4. Many of our founders, including Jefferson, repudiated traditional religion.
5. Some 30,000,000 or more Americans profess no religion. (3)

In the second place, these views denigrate the many atheists and agnostics who are responsible individuals and citizens.

On this point, let me cite a few examples of prominent figures.

Bill Gates and Warren Buffet, the two richest people in the world, are arguably the world's two greatest living philanthropists. Ted Turner, founder of CNN, gave $1 million to the United Nations. Actor Angelina Jolie, a United Nations Goodwill Ambassador, has invested her time and treasure in refugees and children in Africa and Asia. Many other admired entertainers, past and present, are also non-believers. The list includes Diane Keaton, Keanu Reeves, Jodie Foster, Jack Nicholson, Margot Kidder, John Malkovich, Christopher Reeve, Katherine Hepburn, Barry Manilow, Billy Joel, Penn and Teller, Julia Sweeney, George Carlin, Dave Barry, and Andy Rooney, among many others.

Further, non-believers also include Francis Crick and James Watson, co-discoverers of DNA and Nobel laureates; economist Milton Friedman, a Nobel laureate; chemist Linus Pauling, a Nobel laureate; Gene Roddenberry, creator of *Star Trek*; Robert Smith, former Ohio State and Minnesota Vikings running back and now TV football analyst; Annika Sorenstam, world-renowned golfer; George Will, author and syndicated journalist; and Ted Williams, Hall of Fame baseball player.

Hundreds more names could be added to these.

Don't get me wrong. I am **not** saying that all atheists and agnostics are pillars of virtue. I do not put shock-jock Howard Stern, *Hustler* publisher Larry Flynt, or President Bush's master tactician, Karl Rove, on the same moral plane as the other non-believers that I have cited. (4) I **am** saying that whether a person does or does not profess religion tells us nothing about his or her character or whether he or she enhances the lives of others, a key criterion of a moral person. It's high time for people on both sides of the religious divide to recognize this.

---

1. April 2006.
2. mndaily.com, March 24, 2006.

3. American Religion Identification Survey.
4. In an interview on "Fresh Air," National Public Radio, September 5, 2006, Wayne Slater said that Karl Rove is an agnostic. Slater, with James Moore, wrote a biography of Rove entitled *The Architect: Karl Rove and the Master Plan for Absolute Power.*

A Day with Ted Williams (April 19, 2007)

IT WAS THE SUMMER OF 1955. My friend Brian Trainor and I boarded an early morning train at the Erie Terminal in Youngstown for a trip to Cleveland to see the Indians play the Boston Red Sox on a perfect day for baseball. We were twelve years old. Our fathers bought our train tickets, gave us spending money, and instructed us to report to a Mr. Berry at the umpires' entrance at the stadium to pick up our game tickets. After we arrived at Terminal Tower in Cleveland, we walked about a mile to the stadium and tracked down Mr. Berry. Charley Berry, a long-time American League umpire, it turns out, had been a friend of Brian's father, Frank Trainor, since they grew up together in Massachusetts. After handing us complimentary tickets, Mr. Berry told Brian and me that he had a surprise for us. He escorted us through a tunnel to the Red Sox clubhouse where Ted Williams was waiting to greet us. We were awestruck. Brian and I assumed that he would shake our hands, sign an autograph, and send us on our way. How wrong we were.

After making sure that he had our names right, Ted Williams led us to the playing field and stationed us just behind the batting cage so that we could watch him and other players take batting practice. Later, on the field and in the dugout, he introduced us to players on both teams.

Ted Williams spent about two hours with us that day. When game time arrived, he autographed two baseballs for each of us, pointed us in the direction of our seats, shook our hands, and said goodbye.

I don't remember which team won that day or how Ted Williams did at the plate. What I will never forget is the kindness and humility of Ted Williams.

Arguably the greatest batter in history had treated two young strangers as though they were his own kids. When Brian and I met him, Ted Williams was already headed to the Hall of Fame. He didn't need to do a favor for an umpire or anyone else. As I got older, I learned that Ted Williams spent many off-duty hours visiting sick children in hospitals without fanfare. I also learned that Ted Williams was an atheist. (1) Here was a baseball legend that gave up five playing seasons during his prime to serve his nation in two wars. During World War II he was a flight instructor and during the Korean War he was a fighter pilot who flew thirty-eight missions alongside a fellow named John Glenn. (So much for the canard that there are no atheists in foxholes.) Here was the last man to hit .400 for a season. Here was a man with a lifetime batting average of .344. Here was a man who hit 521 home runs, who was a two-time MVP, who was a two-time Triple Crown winner, and who struck out during his career less than one in every ten times at bat. Here was a man who was the oldest batting champ in the Major Leagues at age 40 and who appeared in 17 All-Star games. And here was a man who would be named to the Major League Baseball All-Century Team and All-Time Team. One can only imagine what his career totals would have been had his career not been interrupted by military service.

On that day in 1955 an American icon was simply a good person doing a good deed. And Brian, now a banker in Europe, and I, will never forget him for it.

---

1. Upon learning that Ted Williams' son, John Henry, had his father's body frozen and shipped to a cryonics warehouse in Arizona, Johnny Pesky, Williams' long-time teammate, said "Ted wanted to be cremated. He was an atheist. He didn't believe in religion." See SI.com, July 8, 2002.

Suicide Isn't Always Bad (May 3, 2007)

In *On Liberty* John Stuart Mill proposes that society may interfere by law or custom with the liberty of an adult only when his or her conduct poses a threat of harm to others. He writes:

> (T)he sole end for which mankind are warranted, individually or collectively, in interfering with the liberty of action of any of their number, is self-protection.

> (The) only purpose for which power can be rightfully exercised over any member of a civilized community, against his will, is to prevent harm to others.

> His own good, either physical or moral, is not a sufficient warrant.

When I read this passage in a philosophy class recently, a student posed a question: "Does Mill's harm criterion prohibit suicide?" I paused for a moment, then said that, according to Mill, it depends. If suicide poses a threat of harm to others, it may be prohibited in principle by law or custom, but if it doesn't, it may not. Yet, the more that I thought about it, the more I realized that Mill's harm principle gives us very little guidance on suicide. There are some circumstances where suicide is harmful to others and others where it isn't, and in some specific cases, it isn't easy to figure out which of the two categories we're dealing with.

One case where suicide is clearly harmful to others is 9/11 where terrorists took their lives at the same time that they took the lives of thousands of others. Another case is a man who is wracked with depression after a painful divorce, the loss of his job, and a bankruptcy, but his young daughter loves him and suicide would surely crush her emotionally, perhaps permanently. Sadly, his depression wins out and the daughter suffers. Another case is a brilliant CEO who, while negotiating a merger which will save the jobs and careers of thousands, gets an ALS diagnosis and checks out. In these cases, we regret the suicides, in part, because of the harm that they entail for others.

But in other circumstances, suicide seems beneficial. For instance, if a person is a serial rapist or murderer, such as Ted Bundy, and chooses to take his life, I would argue that his self-induced death is a blessing. Or, if the mentally deranged student at Virginia Tech had chosen to commit suicide before the massacre, I would argue that his suicide is a cause for celebration. And I cannot imagine a finer outcome than suicide for a young Adoph Hitler when he lived in Austria before he came to power, an act that would have spared millions of lives.

I concede that in many cases the only way we can make these judgments is retrospectively. One lesson that I take from this is that we should not instantly shed tears when there is a suicide.

I also concede that there is a gray area. Suppose you are dying from a fatal disease and you want to avoid the mental and physical deterioration which awaits you but you have a family who loves you and wants you with them as long as possible. If you swallow two dozen sleeping pills, should we condemn you as a villain? I'm not ready to do so but I can understand the family's loss and regret. When one's own wishes collide with the wishes of others on a matter as important as living or dying, there is no solution which will satisfy everyone. In such cases I prioritize autonomy and the dying individual's right to choose. Whether we're talking about a good person or a bad person, death is the inescapable last chapter in life, and death, even if self-inflicted, can be helpful to the dying person or to others or both.

A 1981 Warning about Religion and Politics (May 17, 2007)

THROUGH THE 1970S A FAMOUS American political figure observed with deepening concern the increasing political activity of religious groups. He worried that religious groups posed a threat to individual liberty and jeopardized the separation of church and state. Finally, on September 15, 1981, he rose in the Senate chamber to warn the American people about the marriage of religion and politics. (1)

The Senator welcomed President Ronald Reagan's election as a sign that Americans had finally turned to true conservatism, one which prizes the freedoms enshrined in the Constitution over the promise of prosperity by a welfare state. But this rediscovery of the primacy of freedom in America, he predicted, will be short-lived if "single issue religious groups" continue to grow in influence and power. Before Americans inject religion into the affairs of state, he cautioned, they should reflect on the harm caused by religion in Northern Ireland, Iran, and Lebanon. He saw intolerance and factionalism on the horizon. He feared that compromise and the give-and-take essential to American political life were in serious danger. Here are his own words:

> On religious issues there can be little or no compromise. There is no position on which people are so immovable as their religious beliefs. There is no more powerful ally one can claim in a debate than

Jesus Christ, or God, or Allah, or whatever one calls his supreme being.

But, like any powerful weapon, the use of God's name on one's behalf should be used sparingly.

The religious factions that are growing throughout our land are not using their religious clout with wisdom. They are trying to force government leaders into following their positions 100 percent.

In the past couple years, I have seen many news items that referred to the Moral Majority, pro-life, and other religious groups as 'the new conservatism.'

Well, I have spent quite a number of years carrying the flag of the 'old conservatism.' And I can say with conviction that the religious issues of these groups have little or nothing to do with conservatives or liberal politics. The uncompromising position of these groups is a divisive element that could tear apart the very spirit of our representative system, if they gain sufficient strength.

I'm frankly sick and tired of the political preachers across this country telling me as a citizen that if I want to be a moral person, I must believe in 'A,' 'B,' 'C,' and 'D.' Just who do they think they are? And from where do they presume to claim the right to dictate their moral beliefs to me?

And I am even more angry as a legislator who must endure the threats of every religious group who thinks it has some God-granted right to control my vote on every roll call in the Senate.

I am warning them today. I will fight them every step of the way if they try to dictate their moral convictions to all Americans in the name of 'conservatism.'

The great decisions of Government cannot be dictated by the concerns of religious factions. That was true in the days of Madison and it is just as true today.

We have succeeded for 205 years in keeping the affairs of State separate from the uncompromising idealism of religious groups and we must not stop now.

To retreat from that separation would violate the principles of conservatism and the values upon which the framers built this democratic republic.

Now, who said all this? Who issued this warning about religion and politics?
It was, of course, the five-term U.S. Senator from Arizona and the Republican Party's nominee for president in 1964, Barry M. Goldwater.
I leave to your judgment whether Senator Goldwater's warning was justified, and, if it was, whether we Americans have heeded it.

---

1. All quotations are from Senator Barry Goldwater, "To Be Conservative," *Congressional Record – Senate*, September 15, 1981, pages 20589-20590.

Religion and Morality (June 14, 2007)

THE POPULAR VIEW AMONG RELIGIOUS people is that religion is indispensable to morality in that religion affirms the existence of a God who has revealed a law to direct humans how to live. (1) There are problems with this position, however, from the perspective of philosophy. Religion relies on faith while philosophy relies on reason. The three central beliefs of Christianity, Judaism, and Islam which have a bearing on morality and which are embraced on faith are 1) There is a God, 2) God is good and not evil, and 3) God has ordained rules for living which humans can learn. Although some believers past and present have accepted the challenge of philosophy to prove these beliefs by reason, their efforts have fared poorly in the judgment of professional philosophers.

The third belief – that God has issued a moral law which humans can learn – is particularly intriguing.

On the one hand, there are strong differences within and among religious traditions as to where one should look to find this law. Shall we turn to scripture? If so, should we consult the Bible, the Talmud, the Quran, or another holy writing? Shall we turn to a prophet? If so, should we consult the teachings of Moses, Abraham, Jesus, Mohammed, Bahaullah, or another holy person? Or shall we turn to our local pastor or a famous televangelist or to our central church administration or to ourselves?

On the other hand, within the same religion, it is difficult to find a moral consensus. There are often strong differences over issues such as divorce, plurality of spouses, the status of women, abortion, homosexuality, same sex marriage, birth control, stem cell research, and how to deal with followers of other religions, sects, and the non-religious. On this point consider the gulf between Episcopalians and Baptists in America, and Sunni and Shia in Iraq.

The fact is that religion is not nearly as important to morality as widely believed. Consider these points:

Firstly, some of the most perceptive and inspiring discussions of ethics in the past generation have come from seculars such as Paul Kurtz, Kai Nielsen, Peter Singer, and Arthur Kaplan.

Secondly, largely secular groups, such as scientists, and largely secular societies, such as the Netherlands, are at least as well-behaved as predominately religious groups and societies.

Thirdly, Utilitarianism (Always seek the greatest happiness of the greatest number of people) and Ethical Egoism (Always seek your own long-term happiness), the major classical teleological or consequence-based moral theories, and Kantianism (Always act on a maxim that you can wish to universalize), the major deontological or duty-based moral theory, are all products of reason.

Fourthly, the Constitution of the United States and the United Nations Declaration of Human Rights, documents which set out moral frameworks for modern living, make no reference to God or religion except to guarantee freedom to practice religion.

Fifthly, research by Harvard anthropologist Marc Hauser shows that religious and non-religious people have the same moral intuitions when faced with the same ethical dilemmas. (2)

Finally, the Golden Rule, the only moral rule which all the world's religions affirm, has been established on entirely rational grounds by Immanuel Kant, arguably the most important writer on ethics in modern history, as what he calls the categorical imperative.

---

1. One prominent scientist, Stephen Jay Gould, also seems to support the view that we should turn to religion to learn how to live. See "Nonoverlapping Magisteria," *Natural History* 106 (March 1997): 16-22. Here Gould argues that science and religion are not in conflict for their

teachings occupy different domains or magisteria. Science tells us how the universe works and religion tells us how to live. Science tells us how the heavens go and religion tells us how to get to heaven.

2. Marc Hauser, *Moral Minds: How Nature Designed Our Universal Sense of Right and Wrong*. Also, see M. Hauser and P. Singer, "Morality without religion," *Free Inquiry* 26: 1, 2006, 18-19.

Hein v. Freedom from Religion Foundation, Inc. (July 19, 2007)

SUPPOSE YOU PICK UP THE daily newspaper and read that President George W. Bush has authorized the expenditure of $5 million of public funds under his faith-based programs for construction of a new Baptist church in Texas by young Christian building trades apprentices. You are incensed at what you see as a flagrant violation of the Establishment Clause in the First Amendment. But what can you do, legally, to stop the President and preserve the Constitution? You can write a letter to the editor, you can picket the White House, you can erupt on social media, and you can unload on a blog. What you cannot do, however, as of June 25, 2007, the date of the U.S. Supreme Court ruling in *Hein v. Freedom from Religion Foundation, Inc.* (Case No. 06-157), is to file a lawsuit.

The Freedom from Religion Foundation, Inc., which is dedicated to preserving the separation of church and state, had challenged the Bush administration's faith-based programs by filing suit against the director of the White House Office of Faith-Based and Community Initiatives and the heads of eight additional faith-based programs in the executive branch. President Bush had created these by executive orders soon after he took office after attempts by the White House to get Congressional approval of them failed. In the 5-4 *Hein* ruling, the Court's right wing caucus – Justices Roberts, Alito, Thomas, and Scalia, joined by swing-vote Kennedy, held that there is an important distinction between expenditures authorized by Congress and those authorized by the President. Taxpayers, the majority said, have standing to challenge the former but not the latter. Since "the White House Office of Faith-Based and Community Initiatives was set up by executive order rather than by Congressional line item, the case was dismissed for lack of standing." (1)

Remarkably, Justice Alito, writing for the majority, didn't even try to defend this distinction. Justice Souter, in his dissent, said: "I see no basis for this distinction in either law or precedent." Further, commentators by the dozens have attacked it. For instance, Vikram David Amar, professor of law at the University of California, Hastings College of Law, says that "The line the Hein Court draws – between Congress and Executive programs to promote religion – makes absolutely no sense." The reason, Professor Amar points out, is that the Constitution says that "no Money shall be drawn from the Treasury, but in Consequence of Appropriations made by Law." In other words, "...all expenditures owe their legitimacy to Congressional authorization." Give this, "it makes little sense," he observes, "to distinguish between expenditures" explicitly directed by Congress and "those which arise from Executive discretion" because "Congress can be assumed to agree with (such Executive spending) or else it would cut off or limit the appropriations." (2)

As misguided as the *Hein* decision was, it could have been worse. Justices Scalia and Thomas sought, unsuccessfully, to persuade their peers to deny standing to taxpayers to challenge appropriations for religion **by the Congress** by overturning the *Flask v. Cohen* ruling of 1968. But stay tuned. The five justices who closed the court house doors to those seeking to block spending by a President to promote religion are relatively young and have many, many years to recast the law.

---

1. Garrett Epps, "Free Speech for the Rich and Powerful," *Salon*, June 29, 2007.
2. http://writ.news.findlaw.com/aram/20070706.html

The Religious Right in the Post-Falwell Era (August 2, 2007)

IF YOU'RE ONE WHO BELIEVES that the Religious Right suffered a serious blow on May 15 when the Reverend Jerry Falwell died, you're badly mistaken, according to Rob Boston, a long-time student of the movement. In a recent issue of *Church & State* magazine, Boston reports that the Religious Right today is flourishing. (1)

After pointing out that Falwell's eminence in the Religious Right "waned" when he focused his efforts on Liberty University, Boston says that leaders of the Religious Right have learned important lessons from Falwell's mistakes. One the one hand, they have toned down their public rhetoric and abandoned Falwell's relish for notoriety, preferring instead to communicate with the faithful through their own media outlets instead of mainstream media. Indeed, some of the most influential organizations in the Religious Right, such as the Reverend Donald Wildmon's American Family Association, which owns 170 radio stations and generates $17 million in revenues annually, operate largely "beneath the mainstream media radar." (p. 5) On the other hand, they have prioritized grassroots organizing. By the time Falwell's Moral Majority collapsed in 1989, Boston observes, it was "essentially a large mailing list with little local presence." (p. 4) The new Religious Right, by contrast, immerses itself in races from the local to the national level by linking itself to the Republican Party and requiring candidates seeking its support to endorse its agenda. This works,

Boston says, because evangelicals are a huge percentage of Republican voters, especially in primaries. (p. 5) This also explains why so many candidates seek the endorsement of leaders of the Religious Right and why so many members of Congress meet weekly with them to collaborate as a "Values Action Team." (p. 5)

Also, Boston observes, the Religious Right today continues to exploit large and small tax-exempt organizations effectively to promote its goals. Among the larger ones is Dr. James Dobson's Focus on the Family, a radio and publishing empire which took in $137 million in 2005, and the Reverend Pat Robertson's Christian Broadcasting Network, which has nearly a million daily viewers and which took in $236 million in the same year. Among the smaller ones is Louis Sheldon's Traditional Values Coalition, which has a budget of $56 million a year to lobby in Washington and California, its home base; Tony Perkins' Family Research Council, which draws on an annual budget of $10.8 million to lobby and to organize evangelical voters; The Alliance Defense Fund, an Arizona-based legal group, which uses its $27 million annual budget to promote the interests of the Religious Right in the courts (p. 5); and the American Center for Law and Justice, a $14.5 million a year operation, which, among other things, works to influence the White House's choice of nominees to the Supreme Court.

Thus, Jerry Falwell's quest for theocracy in America proceeds apace despite his absence. Indeed, the Religious Right has more resources than ever to ban abortions, block legal rights for gays, install creationism, Bible courses, and prayer in the schools, promote abstinence-only sex education, spend tax dollars on religious schools and ministries, pack the Supreme Court, and impede stem cell research. Only time will tell if these resources are up to the challenge from moderates and liberals which the Religious Right faces.

---

1. *Church & State*, Vol. 60, No. 7, July/August 2007, pages 4-6.

The Christian Reconstructionists
(August 16, 2007)

ON JULY 12 OF THIS year, Hindu Chaplain Rajan Zed of Nevada gave the opening prayer in the U.S. Senate. The prayer was disrupted by Christian activists who called prayer in the Senate by a non-Christian an "abomination." The live protest had been preceded by virulent opposition to a non-Christian by the Reverend Donald Wildmon, leader of the American Family Association, and David Barton, a "Christian nation" activist. (1)

This type of intolerance is not new to the Religious Right in the United States. Indeed, a sizeable segment of the Religious Right, Christian Reconstructionists, also called Dominionists, hopes to supplant democracy based on the separation of Church and State with theocracy. The laws, policies, and customs in this theocracy will be grounded in the Bible, including parts of the Old Testament that moderate Christians long ago repudiated, which require "the death penalty for homosexuals, adulterers, fornicators, witches, incorrigible juvenile delinquents and those who spread false religions." (2)

In May of this year Christian Reconstructionists gathered for a four-day conference in Asheville, North Carolina, hosted by a large, wealthy group called America Vision which is based in Powder Springs, Georgia. It is a mistake to view American Vision as an isolated, fringe voice in the Religious Right because it has close ties with the Alliance Defense Fund, which promotes the agenda of the Religious Right in the courts, the Home School Legal Defense Association, the Liberty University School of Law, *World* magazine, the Traditional Values Coalition, the Southern Baptist Convention, and other influential groups. (3)

Speakers at the May conference were bold and clear about their hopes and wishes:

- American Vision President Gary DeMar told the audience that it was time to restore "the sovereignty of God" at home and abroad.
- Gary Cass called for Americans to proclaim that America "was and is a Christian nation" with a mandate from God to Christianize the world.
- The Reverend Voddie Baucham, Jr., and Doug Phillips called on all Christians to withdraw their children from public schools and to immerse them in a Bible-based worldview at home.
- Jeff Ventrella and Ken Fletcher of the American Defense Fund assured the assembly that efforts to restore America's Christian heritage are being redoubled in the courts and that authentic Christians have a directive from God to "win the world for Christ."
- Finally, Janet Folger, a lobbyist for fundamentalists, urged stronger efforts by Christian fundamentalists *against* gays and *for* a "values" candidate for President whose Supreme Court appointees will overturn *Roe v. Wade*. (4)

Christian Reconstructionists see America and the world at a critical point where the forces of good – the followers of Jesus, are arrayed against the forces of evil – seculars, lukewarm Christians, and non-Christians, and they promise salvation to all Christians who join the fray in the name of Jesus. All this sounds painfully familiar, doesn't it? It is time that all of us who are committed to Constitutional democracy, mutual respect and toleration, and the value of public schools learn that religious zealots in distant corners of the planet are not our only threat.

1. Press Release, Americans United for Separation of Church and State, July 12, 2007.
2. Jeremy Leaming, "Fringe Festival," *Church & State*, July/August 2007, Vol. 60, No. 7, p. 10.
3. Leaming, p. 10.
4. Leaming, pp. 11-113.

Paul Kurtz (August 30, 2007)

IN THE CURRENT ISSUE OF *Scientific American* (September 2007), Michael Shermer, publisher of *Skeptic* magazine, sends an "open letter" to four religious skeptics – Richard Dawkins, Daniel Dennett, Sam Harris, and Christopher Hitchens. (1) Books by all four of these authors are currently on the *New York Times* best-seller list. In his letter Shermer warns the authors that the militant, in-your-face tone of their narratives is likely to be counterproductive. He writes: "It is irrational to take a hostile or condescending attitude toward religion because by doing so we virtually guarantee that religious people will respond in kind." (2) He counsels the authors against "passionate diatribes," urges them to be respectful and tolerant of religious moderates, and calls on them to supplement the case *against* religion with the case *for* humanism. (3)

Is it possible to do what Shermer recommends? Is it possible for one to criticize religion without bashing people of faith? And is it possible to make a strong case that humanism is the path to morality, happiness, and social progress? If you reflect on the remarkable life and work of Paul Kurtz, the answer to these questions is a resounding "Yes!"

Paul Kurtz was born in Newark, New Jersey, in 1925. (4) After high school he enlisted in the U.S. Army and served in General Patton's army in Europe. He saw the horrors of Dachau and Buchenwald with his own eyes and spent eighteen months in Germany in the army of occupation. After the war, Kurtz enrolled at New York University where he majored in philosophy, political science, and economics and took Sidney Hook's course entitled "Philosophy of Democracy," which had a powerful impact on him. Later he took his doctorate in philosophy at Columbia University where former students of John Dewey imbued him with Pragmatism, a philosophy that emphasizes the practical application of ideas.

Kurtz then taught philosophy at a string of institutions and spent the last twenty-six years of his teaching career at the State University of New York at Buffalo. Along the way he published forty books and over six hundred articles and reviews. As a "public philosopher who refused to hibernate in his office," (5) Kurtz also edited the *Humanist*, a magazine for a general educated audience, appeared dozens of times on radio and television as a spokesperson for science and reason, established the Committee for the Scientific Investigation of Claims of the Paranormal (1976) and the Council for Democratic and Secular Humanism (1980), and launched two successful magazines – *Free Inquiry* and the *Skeptical Inquirer*. What really sets Kurtz apart, though, is that while he delivered a brilliant critique of religion in his 1986 book *The Transcendental Temptation*, he simultaneously promoted dialogue between humanists and many religious groups, including Catholics, Baptists, Mormons, and others, and he published dozens of books outlining the moral and intellectual foundations of secular humanism. My favorite is *Embracing the Power of Humanism*. (6)

In his open letter Michael Shermer closes with this comment: "Rational atheism values the truths of science and the power of reason, but the principle of freedom stands above both science and religion." (7) Paul Kurtz' s life and work embody the principle of freedom with unmatched success. Reflecting on his eighty plus years, Kurtz says that "I have tried to get along with everyone on the basis of our common humanity." (8) In this he is a model to all of us, religious and secular.

---

1. "Rational Atheism," p. 44, p. 46.
2. *Ibid.*, p. 46.
3. *Ibid.*, p. 46.

4. This and other biographical material on Kurtz are from Brandon M. Stickney, in Paul Kurtz, *Embracing the Power of Humanism*, Rowman & Littlefield Publishers, Inc., 2000, pp. ix-xvii.
5. Stickney, p. xiv.
6. Rowman & Littlefield Publishers, Inc., 2000.
7. Shermer, *op. cit.*p. 46.
8. Personal interview by Tom Shipka, August 17, 2007.

The Power of Belief (September 13, 2007)

WE'RE NOT FAR AWAY FROM the holiday shopping season when all of us will be searching for gifts for special people in our lives. I have a suggestion of a gift that is inexpensive, educational, and entertaining and that is suitable for either adults or children aged twelve or older. It will also make a superb addition to the media collection of a school or library. I'm referring to a forty-five minute film entitled *The Power of Belief* which first aired as an ABC News Special hosted by John Stossel on October 6, 1998. It can be purchased online in several formats at abcnewsstore.com.

The Power of Belief is four things: a critique of paranormal claims and practitioners, an illustration of self-delusion, a demonstration of how stubbornly we cling to cherished beliefs which lack evidence, and an invitation to critical thinking. It proposes that we use a double standard in evaluating claims. In some cases we demand proof. For instance, if I am buying a used car, I'll likely examine it carefully to make sure that runs well and doesn't need expensive repairs. But in other cases, we don't demand proof. For instance, if I get a fatal cancer diagnosis and I'm told by a friend that an experimental drug available only in Mexico can save me, I'll quickly book a flight to Mexico. Here we suspend our critical faculties because we want to believe.

Each segment of the film illustrates one or more of these themes:

- A stock broker convinces himself that he is levitating when he is actually only bouncing on a mattress.

- Fire-walkers who believe that they have special powers discover to their amazement that anyone can fire-walk on wood embers simply because wood is a poor conductor of heat.
- Psychics who claim to possess the power to move or change objects without touching them – psychokinesis – are unmasked by James Randi as conjurers.
- A voodoo priest who puts a curse on John Stossel fails.
- Therapeutic touch practitioners consistently fail to demonstrate their powers in a simple test designed by a nine-year old school girl.
- The members of a group of students who are given a sugar pill but told that it is a stimulant report greater energy while the members of the group who are told that it is a sleeping pill report improved sleep.
- A victim of Hodgkin's Disease dies after she abandons traditional treatment in favor of alternative medicine.
- James Randi fools the media and hundreds of thousands of people in Australia into believing that a man that he has trained to pose as a channeler actually has the power to contact the dead.
- A Texas police chief shows that a psychic detective is either self-deluded or a fraud.
- A group of people who are given a horoscope of a mass murderer are convinced that it accurately describes them.
- A U.S. Navy aerospace scientist offers a natural explanation of so-called near-death experiences based on his experience with pilots in a centrifuge.

Other segments deal with children who perceive a non-existent fox in a box, the use of cold and warm reading techniques by psychics, a faith healer, and the James Randi $1 Million Challenge.

Despite the passage of time since *The Power of Belief* first aired, it remains an outstanding educational film which is worth your time and money.

Mark Lilla on the Great Separation (September 27, 2007)

IN A RECENT ARTICLE AND book, Mark Lilla, professor of humanities at Columbia University, gives us a refresher course in how the United States of America and European nations came to separate theology and politics while most other nations did not. (1) Lilla points out that the Reformation destroyed the unity of Christendom and left 16th century Europe a hodge-podge of churches and sects where doctrinal differences and political ambitions fueled one another. This led to the "madness" of a century and a half of religious wars in Europe in which, Lilla says, Christians killed one another with "maniacal fury." (2)

Facing a certain early death, the disparate and desperate Christians frantically sought a way to establish peace and preserve their lives. Aid came from an unlikely source, Thomas Hobbes, a materialist with repugnance for traditional religion, who seized on their fear to propose a path to mutual survival, namely, erecting through common consent an all-powerful political sovereign, a Leviathan, whose unbounded power would intimidate them into mutual tolerance. John Locke would amend this proposal significantly soon after with the introduction of limited government, the division of powers, majority rule, and human rights, but even for Locke, secular power over a religiously diverse community would ensure peace and mutual toleration. Professor Lilla calls this separation of theology from politics by Hobbes and Locke "the Great Separation." "In order to escape the destructive passions of messianic faith," he notes, "political theology centered on God was replaced by political philosophy centered on man." (p. 33)

Professor Lilla cautions us that the Great Separation is a work in progress, "an experiment," not a *fait accompli*. Why? Because the temptation to inject religion into politics "can be reacquired by anyone who begins looking to the divine nexus of God, man and world to reveal the legitimate political order." (3)

Finally, Professor Lilla reflects on the prospects for a Great Separation among Muslims in today's world. He says that it is unlikely that Islam will take a path similar to Christianity in Europe because Muslims "believe God has revealed a law governing the whole of human affairs" and "not some arbitrarily demarcated private sphere." (p. 50, p. 54) Instead, Muslims "have to find the theological resources within their own traditions" to institute change. (p. 54) Lilla is skeptical about the prospect of "liberal Muslims" to spark this because they don't fully grasp the theological currents at work in Islam and they are viewed by mainstream Muslims as deviants. Lilla does see a ray of hope in what he calls "renovators." Unlike liberals, "renovators," such as Khaled El Fadl, and Tariq Ramadan, "stand firmly within their faith and reinterpret political theology so believers can adapt without feeling themselves to be apostates." (p. 54)

No doubt Mark Lilla can be faulted on one point or another. Nevertheless, in retelling how and why the Great Separation arose, and in reminding us that we need to find ways to manage the interplay of theology and politics if there is to be a future worth living, his work deserves our attention and our gratitude.

---

1. See "The Politics of God," *The New York Times Magazine*, August 19, 2007, and *The Stillborn God: Religion, Politics, and the Modern West*, 2007. Quotes here are from "The Politics of God."

2. Each sect – Roman Catholics, Anglicans, Lutherans, Calvinists, Anabaptists, Quakers, Ranters, Muggletonians, Fifth Monarchy men, and others – had its own "path to salvation and blueprint for Christian society" which it struggled to impose at any cost. (p. 33)

3. Page 50. Americans need to remember this, Lilla writes, as they face "potentially explosive religious differences over abortion, prayer in schools, censorship, euthanasia, biological research and countless other issues…" (p. 50)

World Religions in Modesto
(October 25, 2007)

THE UNITED STATES IS NOW the most religiously diverse nation in the world. Despite the fact that during their lives young Americans will deal with followers of religions other than their own, few of them know much about any religion except their own. Seven years ago Modesto, California, a city of 200,000 residents ninety miles east of San Francisco, decided to do something about this. It was then that the Modesto public schools established a mandatory, semester-long course in world religions for ninth grade students. (1) Teacher-led committees, which designed the course with the help of the Arlington, Virginia-based First Amendment Center, consulted extensively with parents and clergy in the community served by the schools during each stage of development. (2) This strategy not only secured important input but also defused potential resistance.

The Modesto world religions course begins with an overview of First Amendment rights and responsibilities, then focuses on six religions – Buddhism, Christianity, Hinduism, Islam, Judaism, and Sikhism. Each tradition gets the same amount of attention. Students study the history of each faith, its basic teachings, and its social impact. Teachers are forbidden from proselytizing or revealing their own faith stance, if any. Their job is to teach *about* religion in a fair and neutral way, not to promote it. "Every class in the district reads the same textbook, watches the same videos and follows the same scripted lesson plans." (p. 42) In every section students are encouraged "to share their own beliefs and (to) ask questions." (p. 42) Remarkably, over the seven years of the program's existence, only ten families have exercised an opt-out provision which excuses their children from the course.

Recently, the First Amendment Center evaluated the course. In the evaluation researchers interviewed students four times: prior to the course, during the course, immediately after the course, and six months after the course. Among other things, they found the following:

- Students became "more tolerant of other religions and more willing to protect the rights of other faiths." (p. 44)
- Students learned a lot about all six faith traditions studied.
- A significant number of students learned about aspects of their own religion that they had not known previously.
- Students who embraced a faith tradition at the start of the course also embraced it at the end of the course. Learning about other religions did not prompt students to abandon their own; and
- The greatest barrier to teaching about religion in the public schools is not the law, parents, or the community; rather, it is a scarcity of teachers qualified to teach the subject.

Accordingly, researchers from The First Amendment Center recommended a world religions requirement in college teacher preparation programs for all social studies majors, and ongoing in-service training for teachers who are involved in a Modesto-like program. (p. 46)

Despite its benefits, the Modesto world religions course has two defects. Firstly, it ignores many religions with a significant following. Secondly, coverage of the non-religious perspective, atheism, is optional with the teacher. Nevertheless, the Modesto schools are to be congratulated for taking the lead in America in preparing their students to live and work in a religiously diverse world.

---

1. See Carrie Kilman, "One Nation, Many Gods," *Teaching Tolerance*, Fall 2007, pp. 38-46. References to this article here are by page number.
2. See www.firstamendmentcenter.org.

Kitzmiller v. Dover Area School District (November 8, 2007)

NEXT MONTH MARKS THE SECOND anniversary of the landmark ruling by Judge John E. Jones III in the U. S. District Court in Harrisburg in the case of *Kitzmiller v. Dover Area School District.* (1) Tammy Kitzmiller was one of eleven parents of students in the public schools of Dover, Pennsylvania, a township about twenty miles south of Harrisburg, who sued the school district after the Board of Education adopted a policy requiring the reading of a statement in ninth-grade biology classes which cast doubt on the scientific adequacy of evolution, said that "Intelligent Design" is a plausible alternative explanation, and referred students to an Intelligent Design textbook entitled *Of Pandas and People.* (2) Intelligent Design, or ID, holds that "living organisms are so complex that they must have been created by some kind of a higher force." (3) In their lawsuit, the first challenge to ID in the courts, the plaintiffs asked the Court to stop the reading of the pro-ID statement because ID is a religious doctrine, not a scientific theory.

In his 139-page ruling on December 20, 2005, Judge Jones found for the plaintiffs. He said that ID is not science but a thinly veiled form of creationism and that it is unconstitutional to teach it in a public school. (4)

Judge Jones learned a lot during the trial about science and the relation of science to religion, thanks to the testimony of expert witnesses for the plaintiffs, including Kenneth R. Miller, a cell biologist from Brown University, and John F. Haught, a theologian from Georgetown University, both of whom are practicing Roman Catholics. They pointed out that scientists seek *natural* causes of *natural* events, a strategy called methodological naturalism, and that ID violates this because it posits non-natural or supernatural causes. For this reason, Dr. Miller said, ID is a "science stopper."

We can illustrate this point with an example. Suppose you visit your doctor to seek relief of pain in your right arm, your doctor examines you and reviews the results of an MRI, and then reports that a herniated disk is the cause, a problem correctible with surgery. Here your doctor followed methodological naturalism. But suppose that instead of doing this, your doctor tells you that your pain has no cause within your body but is due to an evil spirit. By hypothesizing a non-natural or supernatural explanation of a natural condition, your doctor, like the advocates of ID, abandons science.

Judge Jones took no stance on whether the cosmos has an intelligent cause, declaring, properly, that such matters are outside the province of science. His ruling was informed and brave. And who appointed this Republican church-goer to the federal bench? None other than ID enthusiast President George W. Bush in 2002!

You can learn more about this famous case on NOVA on your local PBS station at 8:00 p.m. on Tuesday, November 13, when a two-hour film entitled "Judgment Day: Intelligent Design on Trial" will be aired.

---

1. Case No. 04cv2688.
2. The vote was 6-3. The three Board members who opposed the ID policy resigned in protest. At the next election, all of the Board members who voted for the ID policy and sought reelection were defeated by candidates opposed to the policy.
3. MSNBC.com, December 20, 2005.
4. Judge Jones also lambasted the members of the pro-ID faction of the Dover Board of Education who, he charged, lied under oath "time and again" to camouflage the religious motives behind the ID policy. See page 132 of the ruling. Judge Jones awarded attorneys' fees to the plaintiffs, costing the school district over $1 million. The newly constituted Board declined to appeal Judge Jones's ruling.

Thanksgiving Day – a Modest Proposal (November 29, 2007)

ON THE FOURTH THURSDAY OF November every year, we celebrate Thanksgiving in the United States to give thanks to the Almighty. This purpose has been affirmed and reaffirmed since colonial days. (1) On Thanksgiving millions of Americans enjoy a feast with their families, one usually featuring turkey, dressing, mashed potatoes, gravy, and rolls. Just before the meal, most families bow their heads in grateful prayer to God.

I know that it is impolitic to say so but I have a problem with Thanksgiving. My problem is not so much that Thanksgiving is a pretext for gluttony from New York to San Francisco. I see no problem with gluttony as long as it is infrequent. Nor is my problem that Thanksgiving ushers in a frenzy of shopping that increases family debt. Although all of us would like to be debt-free, debt is a fact of life for the typical family and debt acquired by shopping for self or loved ones is preferable to debt acquired by gambling, drugs, and alcohol. One problem I do have with Thanksgiving is that it glosses over the problem of evil, namely, "Is the God responsible for our blessings also responsible for our curses – epilepsy, cancer, deformed babies, Alzheimer's, ALS, and weather disasters?" If the answer is yes, one wonders why we have Thanksgiving. (2) But, I digress. The problem of evil is not my main concern about Thanksgiving. So what exactly is my gripe? It is this. On Thanksgiving we applaud God but we are silent about the many people who have helped us and enriched our lives over the past year.

On a day called Thanksgiving, we should acknowledge all our benefactors, not just one.

Some months ago a man in a late-model car, accompanied by two children, approached me in a parking lot near a local interstate to ask for help. He said that one of the cars driven by choir members from his church had broken down on I-80 and had to be towed to Akron, but that the group needed $20 more to pay for the tow. After I handed him $20, he instantly proclaimed, "Hallelujah? Thanks be to God! Thank you, sir, and remember, when you are in trouble, trust in God, and He will rescue you just as He has rescued us!" And then he drove away.

I got the distinct impression that this gentleman was far more grateful to God than to me, and that he viewed my role as minor and insignificant. In his eyes I was only a tool that God had used, not an autonomous, generous person who freely chose to help.

I therefore propose that, on Thanksgiving, we spread out our gratitude. If we acknowledge God before the meal, perhaps we can acknowledge other benefactors during dessert. Perhaps each person around the table could identify one or two special benefactors and explain briefly how they helped. Thanks might go to an infectious disease specialist who saved a family member's life, or a computer technician who recovered weeks of work from a diskette that had been invaded by a computer virus, or a scientist who discovered a medication that enables us to manage our arthritis, or a songwriter whose lyric gives up inspiration, or an author whose novels entertain us, or a friend whose sense of humor gives us a smile regularly.

On Thanksgiving I leave for you to decide if there's a deity in the heavens who deserves your gratitude. I ask only that you also remember the caring and competent people on earth, near or far, who have made an important difference in your life over the past year. (3)

---

1. The explicit purpose of celebrating Thanksgiving to acknowledge the blessings bestowed by the Almighty was declared by colonists in Virginia and Massachusetts, and by the Continental Congress in 1777, George Washington in 1789, Abraham Lincoln in 1863, and Franklin D. Roosevelt in 1939. During the Depression Roosevelt moved up the celebration of Thanksgiving

by one week to "give merchants a longer period to sell goods before Christmas." See *Wikipedia*, "Thanksgiving."

2. In practice it seems that God gets all the credit for the good things but none of the blame for bad ones.

3. In an early celebration of the fall harvest, the precursor of Thanksgiving, Pilgrims in Plymouth, Massachusetts, "were particularly thankful to Squanto, the Native American who taught them how to catch eel and grow corn and who served as an interpreter for them… Without Squanto's help the Pilgrims might not have survived in the New World." *Wikipedia*, "Thanksgiving." In a sense, then, my modest proposal is a plea to return to our roots in America.

Judge John E. Jones III
(December 13, 2007)

JOHN LOCKE, AMERICA'S PHILOSOPHICAL FATHER, cited as a key objective of government to provide "known and indifferent judge(s) with authority to determine all differences according to the established law..." (1) Locke's ideal of an independent judiciary guided only by the law has not always been realized in practice in the United States. One clear case in which it was involves federal Judge John E. Jones III who sits on the U.S. District Court for the Middle District of Pennsylvania. On December 20, 2005, Judge Jones issued a 139-page ruling in *Kitzmiller v. Dover Area School District*. The case involved a challenge by eleven parents to a decision by the Dover, Pennsylvania, school board to introduce the doctrine of Intelligent Design (ID) in ninth grade science classes as a plausible scientific alternative to evolution. The parents alleged that this constituted a violation of the First Amendment prohibition against government endorsement of religion because ID is a religious doctrine and not a scientific one.

To rule on this case competently, Judge Jones was required to know and apply not only the relevant law, including the Constitution of the U.S., the Constitution of Pennsylvania, and dozens of complicated prior rulings, but also to understand the methodology of science, the theory of evolution, and the doctrine called ID. To rule on this case fairly, Judge Jones was required to distance himself from the culture wars in America and from the intense passions which surrounded the case in Dover.

In his ruling Judge Jones found that ID is not a testable scientific hypothesis but "a mere relabeling of creationism" that has no place in a public school science curriculum. His clear and cogent ruling followed weeks of testimony by expert witnesses to whom he obviously listened intently.

As *Time* magazine observed, "Had (Judge) Jones been a Democrat or an atheist, his judgment might have had less impact." (2) The fact that he was a Republican, a Bush appointee, and a Lutheran, took a lot of the steam out of the ID movement nationally. (3)

In the conclusion of his ruling, Judge Jones hit upon a key point. He wrote that the proponents of ID have made a "bedrock assumption which is utterly false," namely, that they must choose between God or science. (4) Drawing on the testimony of expert witnesses in the case, he insisted that evolution and other well-established scientific theories are compatible with "belief in the existence of a supreme being and religion in general." (5)

After Judge Jones issued his ruling, he and his family were put under the protection of federal marshals because of death threats and he was also rebuked by critics, such as Phyllis Schlafly, who said he had "stuck the knife in the backs" of evangelical Christians in Pennsylvania. (6) Judge Jones replied to Schlafly in a speech on February 10, 2006, in which he reminded all of us that "judges must be impartial and that the independence of the judiciary is premised on a judge's pledge of freedom from partisan influences." (7)

Judge Jones's speech probably did not win over those disappointed by his ruling. Nevertheless, by his knowledge, courage, and devotion to judicial impartiality, he is a model to his peers and a judge who deserves consideration for appointment to the U.S. Supreme Court when there is a vacancy.

---

1. *The Second Treatise of Government*, Chapter IX, "Of the Ends of Political Society and Government," 1690.
2. Matt Ridley, *Time*, April 30, 2006.
3. *Ibid.*
4. Case No. 04cv2688, p. 136.
5. *Ibid.* Two of the expert witnesses in the trial have written books aimed at showing the compatibility of evolution and belief in God. See Kenneth R. Miller, *Finding Darwin's God*, and

John F. Haught, *God after Darwin*. Miller is a cell biologist at Brown University and Haught is a theologian at Georgetown University. Both are Roman Catholics.

6. Phyllis Schlafly, *Townhall.com*, January 2, 2006.

7. Speech by U.S. District Judge John E. Jones III to the Anti-Defamation League, National Executive Committee Meeting, Palm Beach, Florida, February 10, 2006. See www.adl.org/Civil_Rights/speech_judge_jones.asp

Government-Sponsored Nativity Scenes – a Prediction (January 24, 2008)

THUS FAR THE SUPREME COURT of the United States has interpreted the Establishment Clause of the First Amendment (1) to mean that government may sponsor a Christmas nativity scene only if it is part of a broader display which features secular elements such as Santa, the reindeer, and a Christmas tree. The idea that government may display a crèche, a cross, or some other Christian symbol in a standalone display during the holiday season has thus far gotten no support from the Supreme Court. For a variety of reasons – the rationale of the majority in previous Supreme Court decisions, the composition of the Roberts' Court, the persistent pressure of Christian Dominionists to Christianize America, the overwhelming support by Americans of displays of Christian symbols on public property, (2) and the pandering to the Religious Right by the current crop of presidential candidates – I expect this to change. In the next decade, the Supreme Court, I predict, will approve the use of Christian symbols by government in a standalone display during the Christmas season and perhaps year round.

Consider the Court's 1984 decision in *Lynch v. Donnelly*.

During the Christmas season every year the city of Pawtucket, Rhode Island, erected a display that included a crèche as well as Santa Claus, reindeer, and other secular elements. In the early 1980s a lawsuit challenging the constitutionality of this display was filed in federal court. Eventually the U.S. Supreme Court reversed rulings by the district and appellate courts and ruled that the Pawtucket display is constitutional.

The 5-4 decision in *Lynch v. Donnelly* held that the Pawtucket display is constitutional because, in the Court's view, the display had a secular purpose, the celebration of a national holiday; it acknowledges the historic importance of Christianity in our culture but does not endorse this religion; and it creates no excessive entanglement of government and religion since the Pawtucket display did not involve church authorities. (3)

What leads me to expect a dramatic new direction from the Roberts' court is that *Lynch v. Donnelly* affirms that the Constitution not only does not require a strict separation of church and state but permits government to "acknowledge" religion's traditional role in America and obligates it to "accommodate" religion. It cites a litany of examples of accommodation, including chaplains in the Congress and the military, chapels in the Congress, prayers before legislative sessions, Presidential Thanksgiving Proclamations, "In God We Trust" on currency, "One nation under God" in the pledge of allegiance, and many others. (4)

The Court Observed: "If the presence of the crèche in (the Pawtucket) display violates the Establishment Clause, a host of other forms of taking official note of Christmas, and of our religious heritage, are equally offensive to the Constitution." The Court was apparently unprepared to entertain the possibility that some or all of the "accommodations" are constitutionally suspect.

Once the Roberts' court faces a case involving a standalone nativity scene, my money says that it will give the crèche a green light. And guess what. The case may come out of Ohio where standalone nativity scenes graced two state parks during the Christmas season. (5)

---

1. The First Amendment of the Constitution provides that "Congress shall make no law respecting an establishment of religion, or prohibiting the free exercise thereof..."
2. *The Pew Forum on Religion & Public Life,* June 2007, reports that in 2007 83% of Americans supported the display of Christian symbols on public property during the Christmas season, and that in 2005 74% supported the display of the Ten Commandments in government buildings year round.

3. These criteria were established in the case of *Lemon v. Kurtzman*, 1971.

4. Others mentioned are paid vacation days for federal employees on Thanksgiving and Christmas, religious art work in the Supreme Court chambers and thousands of other public buildings, national days of prayer, tax-exempt status for churches, busing of and texts for students in church-related schools, and grants to students in religiously-affiliated colleges. Approval by the Roberts' Court in 2007 in *Hein v. Freedom from Religion Foundation, Inc.* of the White House faith-based initiatives can be added today.

5. The Freedom from Religion Foundation has protested a decision by Ohio's Governor to reinstitute nativity scenes in 2007 at Shawnee State Park and Malabar Farm after a complaint by a citizen led to their removal.

Justice Brennan's Dissent (February 7, 2008)

THERE ARE POWERFUL FORCES IN America today promoting the entanglement of church and state. Dozens of religious organizations intrude into politics in defiance of the laws granting them tax-exempt status. (1) The courts are ever more receptive to entanglement as was shown last year when the Supreme Court approved President Bush's faith-based initiatives which distribute huge grants to religious organizations. (2) The Congress is ever more receptive to entanglement as was shown in December when the U.S. House of Representatives, anxious to pander to the religiosity of their constituents and to placate the religious right, approved a resolution "Recognizing the Importance of Christianity and the Christian Faith." (3) And mainstream America is also receptive to entanglement. Surveys show that 74 percent of Americans believe it is proper to display the Ten Commandments in government buildings year round and 83 percent believe that displays of Christian symbols should be allowed on government property during the Christmas season. (4)

So, what's wrong with church and state cozying up to one another? In 1984 Supreme Court Justice, William Brennan, an Irish Catholic, gave four major objections to church-state entanglement in his dissent in a 1984 decision which approved a nativity scene in Pawtucket, Rhode Island. (5)

Firstly, he wrote, it violates the Constitution. The Establishment Clause requires government to be neutral to religion, neither helping nor hindering it, and to treat all sects equally. A government display of Christian symbols goes beyond mere acknowledgement or accommodation of religion to an endorsement of it. Proof of this is found in the fact that governments which erect a display with religious symbols seldom if ever post a disclaimer alongside the display saying that the display does not imply endorsement of religion.

Secondly, a government display of Christian symbols threatens religious diversity and marginalizes citizens of other faiths or no faith. Such displays send the message that they are outsiders whose views "are not similarly worthy of public recognition or entitled to public support."

Thirdly, the sectarian significance of a government-sponsored nativity scene is not diminished if secular components such as a Santa are added because a nativity scene "is the chief symbol" of the uniquely Christian belief that Jesus is "the divine Savior" who was brought into the world miraculously "to illuminate a path toward salvation and redemption."

Fourthly, just because Christmas is a national holiday does not imply that it is constitutionally proper for government to celebrate the holiday in a sectarian fashion. Government may "recognize the holiday's traditional secular elements of gift-giving, public festivities, and community spirit..." but it may not "embrace the distinctively sectarian aspects of the holiday" such as a nativity scene, a cross, or a Bible.

Jurists such as former Justice Brennan are swimming upstream in American culture today and that is all the more reason to summon his counsel. In America all of us have a constitutional right to display religious symbols in our homes, in our churches, and in our businesses. That should satisfy any reasonable believer. Those who work to entangle church and state are undermining the First Amendment, threatening religious diversity, and promoting the tyranny of the majority.

---

1. Americans United for the Separation of Church and State monitors and publicizes this problem. See www.au.org.
2. *Hein v. Freedom from Religion Foundation, Inc.*, 2007.
3. *H.* Res. 874, introduced by Rep. Steve King, Republican of Iowa, had 51 co-sponsors and passed with 372 votes. 9 members voted "nay," 10 voted "present," and 40 didn't vote. See News Release of the Freedom from Religion Foundation 12-14-07 at www.ffrf.org.

4. *The Pew Forum of Religion & Public Life*, June 2007, p. 1. In this vein, a newly constructed 9/11 memorial in Austintown, Ohio, includes a mini-church adorned with a cross. It is apparently on public property adjacent to a township ball field, a township parking lot, and a township drop-off for recyclables.

5. *Lynch v. Donnelly*, 1984.

The Gospel of Prosperity Under Fire (February 21, 2008)

HE WEARS ELEGANT SILK SUITS, he drives a $350,000 Bentley, he lives in a $10 million oceanfront mansion, and he flies around the world in a private jet. Is he a billionaire investor, a corporate CEO, or a Hollywood celebrity? None of the above, it turns out. He's a pastor of one of the six mega-churches which are a target of an investigation by Senator Charles Grassley of Iowa, ranking Republican on the Senate Finance Committee, who has requested a mountain of financial information from them. All six ministries preach the Gospel of Prosperity, the message that God bestows earthly riches on the faithful. (1) They are Benny Hinn's World Healing Center; the Reverend Creflo Dollar's World Changers Church; Paul and Randy White's Without Walls International Church; Joyce Meyer Ministries; Kenneth Copeland Ministries; and Bishop Eddie Long's Ministry.

Senator Grassley got leads about possible abuses of the tax-exempt status of these Gospel of Prosperity churches from reporters and whistleblowers. He assures us that his investigation is not "an attack on ministries in particular or tax-exempt groups in general. The strong majority of non-profit groups, including churches," the Senator says, "operate above-board and perform good works that make their tax exemption a bargain for the American people." (2) "But," he continues, "when I hear about leaders of charities being provided a $300,000 Bentley to drive around in, my fear is that it's the taxpayers who subsidize this charity who are really being taken for a ride." (3)

It will be difficult for the targeted ministries to impugn Senator Grassley's motives for three reasons: firstly, he is a darling of the religious right who got an 87% approval rating by the conservative Family Research Council in 2006; secondly, after 9/11 he spearheaded investigations into secular charities such as the Red Cross and the Smithsonian Institution; and thirdly, many members of the evangelical community are as suspicious of the targeted ministries as Senator Grassley is.

For instance, Ole Anthony, head of the Texas-based Trinity Foundation, an evangelical group which has spoken out for years against the lack of financial transparency by television ministries, welcomes Senator Grassley's initiative and says that it wouldn't be necessary if the established churches had stood up to the televangelists over the years. (4) Interestingly, none of the targeted ministries belongs to the Evangelical Council for Financial Accountability, a voluntary oversight group of Christian ministries to ensure transparency and compliance with the law.

It remains to be seen whether the information sought by Senator Grassley will be provided by the mega-churches. A December 2007 deadline came and went with only two of the ministries submitting any of the requested documents. Reverend Dollar openly defied the request for information. Reverend Long said that he considers the Senator's request "an attack on… religious freedom and privacy rights." (5) Senator Grassley is unlikely to relent, however. He says that his goal is to ensure that money that is donated under tax exemption is used according to the law for legitimate non-profit purposes and not to enrich church officials. (6) My suspicion is that we've seen only the first skirmish in a protracted war. In reminding evangelists that they are not above the law, Senator Grassley has taken an important step which deserves our support and encouragement.

---

1. Rob Boston, "Prophets, Profits, and Federal Tax Law," *Church & State*, January 2008, p. 7.
2. Ibid., p. 5.
3. *Ibid.*, p. 4.

4. *Ibid.*, p. 6.
5. *Ibid.*, p. 5.
6. *Ibid.*, p. 5.

Senator Obama on Religion (March 6, 2008)

PRESIDENTIAL ASPIRANT BARACK OBAMA TELLS us he wants to overcome divisions in America and refocus Americans on the pressing problems that face the nation and the world. One such division is between evangelicals, on the one hand, and liberals and seculars, on the other. How exactly does the Senator hope to bridge this gulf? He answers this question in a chapter on religion in his book *The Audacity of Hope*. (1)

Senator Obama first tells us that he was not raised in a religious household. His father, originally a Muslim, was an atheist at the time of his marriage to Obama's mother, and his mother, the primary influence in his early life after his parents divorced when Obama was only two, gave him an anthropologist's perspective on religion, schooling him in the great religions and their scriptures, and teaching him to treat religion "with suitable respect" but also "with suitable detachment." But as he aged and got a job working "for a group of churches in Chicago that were trying to cope with joblessness, drugs, and hopelessness," he discovered the value of religion as a source of hope, stability, and personal responsibility, eventually submitting to baptism at Trinity United Church of Christ in south Chicago. (2)

As to his proposals to bridge the evangelical-liberal gulf, Senator Obama sees a need for self-evaluation in both camps. Liberals need to appreciate how broadly and deeply religion pervades American society, that religious people share their commitment to the next generation and the focus on "thou" and not just "I," and that liberals should stop squandering time, energy, and money trying to remove "In God We Trust" from our currency and "One Nation Under God" from the Pledge of Allegiance. As for evangelicals, he says that they fail to understand the rationale against entanglement of church and state of our founders and clergy, (3) and fail to appreciate the dangers of sectarianism in America's religiously diverse society today. "Whatever we once were," he writes, "we are no longer a Christian nation; we are also a Jewish nation, a Muslim nation, a Buddhist nation, a Hindu nation, and a nation of nonbelievers." Moreover, the Senator observes, even if nearly all Americans were Christians, religious conflict would remain. "Whose Christianity would we teach in the schools," he asks, "James Dobson's or Al Sharpton's?" And which passages of scripture would we emphasize? Would it be Leviticus which approves slavery and condemns eating shellfish? Or Deuteronomy "which suggests stoning your child if he strays from the faith?" Or the Sermon on the Mount, "a passage so radical," he says, "that it's doubtful that our Defense Department would survive its application?"

Finally, Senator Obama admonishes evangelicals that it is not enough to "simply point to the teaching" of their church or "to invoke God's Will" on an issue. Their proposals, the Senator insists, "must be subject to argument and amenable to reason." For instance, on abortion, he writes, "If I want others to listen to me, then I have to explain why abortion violates some principle that is accessible to people of all faiths" and "those with no faith at all."

Only time will tell whether Senator Obama succeeds in his quest to be President, and if he does, whether evangelicals and liberals will respond to his call to dialogue and collaboration.

---

1. Crown Publishers, 2006, pp. 195-226. Quotations here are taken from this chapter.
2. His utilitarian view of religion also appears in other comments. For instance, he notes that "...faith can fortify a young woman's sense of self, a young man's sense of responsibility, and the sense of reverence all young people should have for the act of sexual intimacy." (p. 215)

3. He notes that "the religious right who rail against liberal judges don't understand that their fight is with the drafters of the Bill of Rights and the forebears of today's evangelical church." (p. 217) He gives special recognition to Baptist minister John Leland who campaigned for separation of church and state.

Alan B. Krueger, *What Makes a Terrorist?* (March 20, 2008)

ALAN B. KRUEGER IS AN authority on terrorism and a professor of economics at Princeton University. In 2006 he gave a series of lectures on terrorism at the London School of Economics which he published recently under the title *What Makes a Terrorist?* (1)

Throughout Professor Krueger's book he attempts to debunk a myth about terrorists which, he says, is perpetuated by leaders of government including President George W. Bush and former Prime Minister Tony Blair. The myth is that terrorists are products of poverty and lack of education who have nothing to live for. With a mountain of evidence drawn from his study of terrorist organizations across the globe, Professor Krueger demonstrates that most terrorists come from "well-educated middle-class or high-income families. (p. 2, p. 5, p. 76, p. 80) (2) For instance, 60% of Palestinan terrorists are educated through high school and beyond compared to only 15% of the general Palestinian population. (p. 35) Understandably, Krueger points out, Hamas and the Palestinian Islamic Jihad recruit mainly on college campuses. (3)

What turns people into terrorists, Krueger insists, is not poverty, illiteracy, or lack of opportunity, but a passionate commitment to political goals which they seek to accomplish through violence and, if necessary, the sacrifice of their own lives. (4)

Krueger's other findings include the following:

1. Most terrorism is local. 88% of terrorist attacks occur in the perpetrators' country of origin. 9/11 is the exception. (p. 71)
2. Religion figures prominently in suicide attacks. In 90% of suicide attacks, the perpetrators and the victims are of a different religion or sect. (p. 72) (4)
3. Nations which suppress political and civil rights, such as Saudi Arabia, produce a lot of terrorists while nations which promote and safeguard political and civil rights produce few of them. (p. 73, p. 79)
4. Wealthy nations are more likely to be targets of terrorism than poor ones. (p. 76)
5. The insurgents in Iraq are mostly Iraqis. Of the approximately 20,000 insurgents there, only 4% are non-Iraqis. (p. 85)
6. Terrorist attacks have an economic impact. Isolated or infrequent attacks usually have little economic impact but there are exceptions. For instance, the 9/11 attack crippled the travel and convention industry in the United States. (p. 119) Sustained attacks, however, such as those by Basque separatists in Spain, usually cause significant economic harm such as a drop in the Gross Domestic Product or stock market volatility. (pp. 111-113)
7. Terrorist attacks have a psychological impact. After 9/11, for instance, in New York City alcohol consumption increased 25% and visits to doctors went up appreciably and across America stress levels rose by double digits for many months. (pp. 119-121)
8. Terrorist attacks have a political impact. In Israel, for instance, terrorist attacks increase support for right-wing political parties and in the United States terrorist attacks result in higher approval ratings for Republicans. (pp. 130-131)
9. The invasion of Iraq by the United States was a costly mistake. (p. 160) (5)

Krueger's book deserves a large audience because his observations and recommendations are data-driven. It is one of the most valuable studies on the topic of terrorism that has ever been published.

---

1. Princeton University Press, 2007.

2. Krueger finds one exception to the rule – Northern Ireland – where terrorists come mainly from the working class. (p. 45)

3. One Hamas leader told Krueger that "Our biggest problem is the hordes of young men who beat on our doors, clamoring to be sent to suicide missions. It is difficult to select only a few." (p. 33)

4. On this topic, while Krueger concedes that in Iraq insurgents are mainly Muslims (p. 87), he does not demonize Islam. He writes: "Although the world's attention is currently focused on Islamic terrorist organizations, they are by no means the only source of terrorism. No religion has a monopoly on terrorism." (p. 81)

5. On March 11, 2008, McClatchy Newspapers reported that a Pentagon-sponsored study of more than 600,000 Iraqi documents captured after the 2003 U.S. invasion has concluded that Saddam Hussein's regime had no link with al-Qaeda. *The Vindicator*, March 11, 2008, p. A3.

U.S. Religious Landscape Survey
(April 24, 2008)

IN FEBRUARY OF THIS YEAR, the Pew Forum on Religion & Public Life released the results on one of the most extensive surveys in history of the views of Americans toward religion. The survey, titled the *U.S. Religious Landscape Survey*, was conducted in 2007 among a sample of 35,000 adults. (1) Thousands of facts about believers and non-believers in America can be found in the narrative or tables in this 250 page document, including these:

- Members of historically black churches are least likely to be married (p. 67); (2)
- More men than women are likely to claim no religious affiliation (p. 62);
- Hindus, Jews, and Buddhists have much larger percentages of members with high incomes and advanced education than members of other religious groups (p. 9); and
- Approximately one in twenty-five Americans are atheists or agnostics. (p. 24)

But these interesting revelations are peripheral to the principal findings of the survey. Let's focus on three such findings.

Firstly, "...religious affiliation in the U.S. is both very diverse and extremely fluid." (p. 5)

More than one-quarter of us - 28% - have left the faith in which we were raised in favor of another religion or no religion. (p. 5) The fastest growing segment of the population is the unaffiliated which comprises two groups – those who say they are religious but connect with no particular church and those who say they are atheist or agnostic. 16.1% of Americans fall into this unaffiliated category today. (p. 5, p. 7) In the 18 to 29 age group, one in four are unaffiliated. (p. 5)

Secondly, the fluidity of the American religious landscape is particularly evident in the declines in Catholicism and Protestantism.

The survey notes that "Catholicism has lost more people to other religions or to no religion at all than any other single group." (p. 19) While 31.4% of U.S. adults were raised Catholic, only 23.9% identify with the Catholic Church today. (p. 23) More than one in ten Americans today who were raised Catholic no longer are. (p. 25) Despite the huge loss of Catholics raised in the faith in the U.S., the Catholic Church, paradoxically, has retained its traditionally large share - 25% - of the American adult population. (p. 19) This is due to immigration:

- Nearly half of all immigrants to our shores are Catholic. (p. 36)
- Half of all adult Catholics in the U.S. under age forty are Hispanic. (p. 45)
- One in five Catholics in the U.S. was born outside the U.S., and of these, four of five are from Latin America and the Caribbean. (p. 53)

Protestantism has also declined in America. Through the 1970s, 60% to 65% of Americans identified themselves as Protestant. (p. 18) Today that figure has dropped to 51%, a bare majority. (p. 18) Further, the survey divides Protestantism into three groups – mainline, evangelical, and historically black – and notes that "the proportion of the population identifying with the large mainline Protestant denominations has declined significantly in recent decades, while the proportion of Protestants identifying with the large evangelical denominations has increased." (p. 18) Today only 18.1%

of the U.S. adult population are members of mainline Protestant churches compared to 26.3% who are evangelicals. (p. 10)

The Pew Forum on Religion & Public Life is to be applauded for producing the *U.S. Religious Landscape Survey*. It will be an important resource for a long time for all of us with an interest in religion in America.

---

1. The Pew Forum on Religion & Public Life, *U.S. Religious Landscape Survey*, 2008. See religions.pewforum.org for the online presentation of the findings of the survey. Quotes of the survey and references to it here are by page number.

2. Hindus and Mormons are most likely to be married – 78% and 71% respectively – and Hindus have the lowest divorce rate – 5%. Only 33% of members of historically black churches are married and 34% were never married. (p. 67)

Confronting the Debt Culture
(May 8, 2008)

NEXT WEEK AT THE WASHINGTON, D.C., Marriott, a national conference will be held with the theme "Confronting the Debt Culture." It is co-sponsored by five organizations, including the Institute for American Values and the New America Foundation. (1) The conference will attract consumers and consumer advocates, scholars, elected and appointed government officials, philanthropists, and representatives from foundations, banks and credit unions, among others.

The highlight of the conference will be the release of a report entitled *For a New Thrift: Confronting the Debt Culture* which the co-sponsors have been researching and writing for many months.

What prompts this conference? The conference co-sponsors are convinced that we Americans are living beyond our means and accumulating debt at a staggering, unprecedented rate, and that the time is ripe to transform a debt culture into a thrift culture. Consider these "debt facts" which they cite:

- The subprime mortgage crisis, which is due to "over(ly) lenient lending and over(ly) exuberant borrowing," has resulted in millions of foreclosures and sharp declines in local property tax revenues. (2) In 2008 two million Americans will lose their homes. (3)

- In 2005 and 2006, for the first time since the Depression, Americans spent more than they saved. (4)
- "More than 20% of lower-income families spend at least 40 percent of their income in debt payments." (5)
- "One in seven families is dealing with a debt collector." (6)
- "Nearly half of all credit card holders have missed payments in the last year." (7)
- One-of-four undergraduate students "carry credit card balances in excess of $3,000." (8)
- A typical college graduate completes his or her degree with $20,000 in debt, up from $9,000 a decade ago. (9)
- "More than 40 percent of college graduates who don't pursue graduate school blame student loan debt." (10)
- Two-thirds of Americans acknowledge that they don't save enough. (11)
- On average Americans save less than citizens of nearly every other developed nation. (12)
- Payday loans doubled every year from 2001 to 2006 and topped $28 billion in 2006. (13)
- 36% of Americans say that they lost control over their finances at one point or another. 45% in the 30-49 age group admit this, as do 40% of parents with children under 18 and 46% of African-Americans. (14)

Although we have yet to see the blueprint to increase savings and decrease debt which will be released at the Washington conference, and we cannot judge whether the proposed strategies will work, we can anticipate strong opposition to the plan from predatory lenders and others who "feed upon and aggravate the debt culture," (15) and we can applaud the ambitious efforts of the Institute for American Values and the other four organizations for taking this initiative. Although debt is virtually unavoidable, even for the most frugal among us, America is on a protracted debt binge. Debt for an individual or a family can be reasonable and manageable or it can be crushing and out-of-control. When debt is overpowering, people are robbed of autonomy, pride, and the fruits of their labor. Hopefully the Washington conference and the report which it issues will be important first steps in resuscitating American thrift.

---

1. The conference is May 12-13 at the Washington Marriott, 1221 22nd Street, N.W. See www.NewThrift.org. The Institute for American Values is a nonprofit, nonpartisan organization which seeks to strengthen the American family and the virtues of competence, character, and citizenship. See www.americanvalues.org. The New American Foundation is a nonprofit public policy institute which seeks to bring new voices and new ideas to public discourse on domestic and global issues. See www.newamerica.net. Other co-sponsors of the conference are the Institute for Advanced Studies in Culture, University of Virginia; Demos; and Public Agenda.
2. *For a New Thrift: An Appeal to Prospective Colleagues*, p. 4.
3. *Ibid.*, p. 3.
4. *Ibid.*
5. *Ibid.*
6. *Ibid.*
7. *Ibid.*
8. *Ibid.*
9. *Ibid.*
10. *Ibid.*
11. *Ibid.*
12. *Ibid.*
13. Sheila Bair, Chairman, Federal Deposit Insurance Corporation, April 19, 2007. Quoted in *Confronting the Debt Culture: A National Conference*, p. 4.
14. *For a New Thrift…*, p. 4.
15. *Ibid.*, p. 14.

So You Want to Be a Professor?
(May 22, 2008)

EVERY YEAR IN THE SPRING the American Association of University Professors (AAUP), an old and respected national organization of higher education faculty, publishes a report on the economic status of the profession. This year's report deals with two issues, faculty salaries and shifts in staffing. (1) The report was authored for the AAUP by economist Saranna Thornton of Hampden-Sydney College who chairs the AAUP Committee on the Economic Status of the Profession.

On faculty salaries, the AAUP report has plenty of bad news for current and prospective faculty:

- Faculty salary increases have lagged behind inflation in three of the past four years. (p. 9)
- The pay gap between faculty at private and public institutions continues to widen.
- In 1971 full professors at public institutions earned 91% of the salary of full professors at private institutions. Today that percentage has dropped by 15% to 76%. (p. 11)
- At universities with I-A football programs (2), head football coaches now earn ten times more than the average full professor at those institutions. (p. 11)

* And, over the past ten years, the average salary increase of college presidents was more than six times the average salary increase of faculty. (p. 13)

What is more worrisome to would-be professors than data on salary, however, is the staffing trends cited in the AAUP report. Over the thirty-year period starting in 1976, as enrollment in America higher education grew by 60%, the number of employees grew by 84%. But the lowest growth - 17% - was in tenure-track faculty positions. The segments of the work force which grew the most were full-time non-faculty staff, which grew by 281%, and full-time administrators, which grew by 101%. (p. 16) There were significant increases in faculty but only in part-time and non-tenure track positions which are characterized by low pay and a lack of job security. (3) Over the same period, the number of non-tenure track faculty grew by 223% and the number of part-time faculty grew by 214%. (pp. 15-16)

Simultaneously, American colleges were containing labor costs by outsourcing. Many full-time jobs in food services, maintenance, grounds, janitorial services, and other areas – jobs which typically carried good wages and benefits – disappeared as private vendors came on campuses with employees at or near the minimum wage. (p. 17) Institutions which employed personnel in the skilled trades such as carpenters, electricians, and plumbers, reduced their numbers significantly and in some cases to zero. This trend prompted a comment many years ago by a YSU skilled trades worker who said: "When I came to YSU we had one provost and three plumbers. Now we have three provosts and one plumber." (4)

What can we gather from all this? One clear implication is that newly-minted Ph.D.'s will face heavy competition for tenure-track positions. After long years of schooling, they will likely find the academic marketplace cruel and hostile. If they insist on college teaching, many will have to settle for non-tenure track positions. (5) If they opt for part-time, they may find themselves working at three or four campuses and spending twelve to fifteen hours a week, or more, behind the wheel as academic nomads. What a far cry this is from the romanticized lives of professors furnished by Hollywood.

---

1. *Where Are the Priorities? The Annual Report on the Economic Status of the Profession, 2007-2008.* See www.aaup.org. References here are by page number.

2. The designation I-A was changed several years ago to "Football Bowl Subdivision."

3. The AAUP estimates that many institutions can employ as many as eight part-time faculty, each teaching three courses a year, for approximately the same cost as one full-time tenure-track faculty member. (p. 17) Usually part-time faculty members have no insurance benefits.

4. This was said at a campus meeting called by a professional search firm who had been hired by YSU to identify suitable candidates to fill a vacancy in the post of provost.

5. Full-time non-tenure track and part-time faculty are now called "contingent" faculty.

The Costs of Family Fragmentation to Taxpayers (June 5, 2008)

THE INSTITUTE FOR AMERICAN VALUES and three other groups dedicated to strengthening the family commissioned a study which was published recently. It is entitled *The Taxpayer Costs of Divorce and Unwed Childbearing: A Report to the Nation*. (1) The principal investigator is Benjamin Scafidi. The report confirms that due to divorce and unwed childbearing, the institution of the family is in trouble, and the fragmented family comes with a staggering price tag which the report estimates, conservatively, at $112 billion a year. (2)

Although the rate of divorce in the United States has moderated in recent years, it is still very high. Moreover, one of three children born in America today is born outside of wedlock. 25% of non-Hispanic white babies are born to single mothers, 46% of Hispanic babies are born to single mothers, and 69% of African-American babies are born to single mothers. (p. 7) Over the past forty years, the proportion of children in America living with two married parents dropped by 17% from 85% to 68%. (p. 7)

One reason for the huge costs to taxpayers cited in the report is the link between single mothers and poverty. A huge percentage of single mothers and their children qualify for a variety of federal, state, and local programs that serve the poor. Among these programs is Temporary Assistance for Needy Families (TANF), Food Stamps, Housing Assistance, Medicaid, the State Children's Health Insurance Program (SCHIP), Women, Infants, and Children Assistance (WIC), the Low Income Home Energy Assistance Program (LIHEAP), Head Start, and school breakfast and lunch programs. (pp. 12-13)

According to the report, only 1% of women with an intact first marriage live in poverty while more than 24% of divorced mothers live in poverty. (p. 10) Further, if 60% of the single mothers were married, the number of people in poverty would decline by 31.7% and the number of children in poverty would decline by 36.1%. (p. 14) Surprisingly, lower-income married couples are far less likely to choose to use government benefits for which they are eligible than single-mother households. (p. 19)

Moreover, there is a link between single-mother households and crime, triggering huge costs in the criminal justice system. Boys raised in single-parent households are more than twice as likely to commit crimes than boys raised in married households. (p. 16, p. 28) Further, children from single-parent households, once adults, are more likely to be criminals than children raised in married households. (p. 16) Also, girls born in poverty are more likely to drop out of school, become pregnant as teenagers, and live unmarried than girls from intact marriage households. (p. 16)

This report teaches us two lessons. Firstly, we Americans have to redouble our efforts to strengthen the family by reducing unnecessary divorce and childbearing and secondly, we should stop demonizing gay couples as a threat to the institution of marriage. Marriage has suffered in America not because gay couples, a tiny fraction of the population, seek civil unions or legal marriages but because millions of heterosexuals have failed to practice safe sex or have failed to build and maintain stable marriages. (3)

---

1. *The Taxpayer Costs of Divorce and Unwed Childbearing: A Report to the Nation*, Benjamin Scafidi, Principal Investigator, © 2008 by Georgia Family Council and the Institute for American Values. Other sponsors are the Institute for Marriage and Public Policy and Families Northwest. See www.americanvalues.org. References to this report are by page number.

2. Of this amount, the federal government spends $70.1 billion, the states spend $33.3 billion, and local governments spend $8.5 billion. Ohio ranks fourth among the states, spending $2.7 billion a year, while Pennsylvania ranks fifth, spending $2.3 billion a year. (p. 7)

3. The report does not say that all marriages must be saved. It acknowledges that about one-third of marriages ending in divorce are "high-conflict" marriages and that children in such families are usually "better off when those marriages end." (p. 12)

Edward Filene, Father of the Credit Union (June 19, 2008)

FILENE'S WAS A BOSTON-BASED DEPARTMENT store chain founded by William Filene, a German Jewish immigrant, in 1881. When William became ill, his son Edward left Harvard in 1890 to run the business. Edward oversaw the expansion of the chain and the introduction of marketing innovations such as the bargain basement, money back guarantees, and automatic markdowns. With these markdowns, the cost of an item dropped the longer it remained on the selling floors. (1)

Although Edward Filene was a hugely successful entrepreneur, he was also deeply committed to his employees and their families. To promote the quality of their work and their lives, Filene…

- Established "a profit sharing program…, a 40 hour work week, health clinics and paid vacations…," (2)
- Lobbied for the first Workmen's Compensation Law in 1911,
- Organized a community council to deal with urban problems such as crime and run-down housing, and
- Submitted to collective bargaining and arbitration long before passage of federal law conferring the right to unionize on private sector workers. (3)

But Edward Filene's most important and lasting contribution to American workers is the credit union. Early in the twentieth century, few banks offered small loans to workers. Those who needed a loan usually turned to street lenders or loan sharks who charged excessive interest rates. To provide people of modest means with access to low-cost credit, and to help them cultivate a habit of saving, Filene launched the credit union movement in the United States, first in Massachusetts, with the passage of the Massachusetts Credit Union Act of 1909, and then state by state across the nation. (4)

One of Filene's smartest decisions was to hire Roy Bergengren, a Harvard-educated lawyer, to lead his nationwide campaign for credit unions. Bergengren joined the project in 1921. Within fourteen years his accomplishments were staggering. Thirty-eight states had credit union laws. A national credit union law had been signed by President Franklin D. Roosevelt. There were 3,600 credit unions in the nation with 750,000 members. Credit unions were growing at a pace of 100 per month. Each month brought 6,000 new credit union members. And a national credit union organization had been formed. It continues today as CUNA, the Credit Union National Association. (5) Filene spent more than $1 million of his own funds to bankroll this cultural revolution.

Today there are more than 8,100 credit unions which serve more than 86 million members. (6) Nevertheless, despite all the good that credit unions have done, Filene's goal for workers – low-cost credit and regular savings – are once again in jeopardy in America. As a people we are spending more than we save. Payday lenders, today's version of loan sharks, give $28 billion in loans a year at triple digit interest rates. Credit card debt is off the chart. And there is a national epidemic of foreclosures and bankruptcies. (7) One wonders if the heroic efforts of Edward Filene and Roy Bergengren were in vain. Next time we'll take a look at a group that believes it has a workable plan to revive Filene's hopes for American workers.

---

1. http://www.filenesbasement.com. Click on "Our Story."
2. http://en.wikipedia.org/wiki/Edward_Filene
3. *Ibid.* Filene also established the Boston, U.S., and international chambers of commerce and a major philanthropic foundation which still exists.
4. *For a New Thrift - Confronting the Debt Culture: A Report to the Nation*, Institute for American Values, 2008, p. 44.

5. *Ibid.*, p. 44.
6. *Ibid.*, p. 46.
7. See *For a New Thrift: An Appeal to Prospective Colleagues* at www.NewThriftt.org.

For a New Thrift: Confronting the Debt Culture – Part 1 (July 3, 2008)

A REPORT ENTITLED *For a New Thrift: Confronting the Debt Culture* was released recently in Washington, D.C. (1) Its sixty-two signatories, called the "Commission on Thrift," aim to reduce debt and to cultivate a habit of saving among Americans of modest means. Today I'll deal with the first part of the report which tells us what went wrong in our culture and next time I'll deal with the second part which outlines a cure.

For a New Thrift points out that America's pro-thrift culture (2) of the post-Depression era has been transformed over the past generation by anti-thrift organizations. These include credit card companies, payday lenders, check cashing outlets, rent-to-own stores, auto title lenders, private student loan companies, franchise tax preparers, subprime mortgage brokers and lenders, and state lotteries. (p. 7) The sad outcome of all this for Americans in the lower economic tier of society, who are the prime target of these groups, is that they forego saving and amass huge debt. Let's focus on credit cards, payday lenders, and the lottery.

The report explains that credit cards were initially sent to financially solvent customers who paid off their balances in full when they received their monthly bills. Since this generated little profit for the industry, it chose a new target in the 1990s – "lower-income users" who wanted or needed credit "but would be likely to carry a monthly balance." (p. 16) This move resulted in a staggering increase in credit card usage and higher revenues in interest and fees. Last year credit card debt reached $937.5 billion – nearly $1 trillion – and nearly half of all credit card holders missed at least one payment. (p. 18) Today there are more than a billion credit cards in use in America. (p. 15)

Next, payday lenders target customers with annual incomes between $18,000 and $25,000. Over 20,000 payday loan outlets dispense so-called "fast cash" to 15 million people every month typically at three digit annual interest rates. (p. 23) Why are such exorbitant interest rates legal, you ask? Because in the 1980s most states eliminated usury caps. (p. 16) Further, "(S)ix out of ten (borrowers) take out at least twelve loans per year, each time paying a fee for their 'cash advance'." (p. 24)

As to lotteries, the report tells us that:

- 42 states and the District of Columbia run lotteries which generate $57 billion a year in revenues, (p. 25)
- Twenty percent of all Americans are frequent lottery players, (p. 25)
- "Three-quarters of state advertising dollars go to the lottery," (p. 26)
- Public approval of lotteries is high – around 75%, (p. 26) and
- Household income varies inversely with lottery spending. For instance, households with incomes under $12,400 a year spend an average of $645 a year on the lottery while households with incomes ten times that amount spend an average of only $419 a year or $226 less. (p. 28) (3)

How, then, does the Commission on Thrift propose to bring consumer debt under control and to restore a habit of regular saving among people of low income? I'll outline their plan next time.

---

1. ©2008 Institute for American Values. See www.NewThrift.org. References to this report here are by page number.
2. Pro-thrift institutions which the report lists include credit unions, mutual savings banks, savers' clubs, savings and loan associations, savings bond programs, labor-union sponsored savings plans, and low caps on loan interest rates mandated by law. (p. 6)

3. In Texas the lottery is targeting the 18 to 25 year old age group as the group most likely to produce greater revenues. In 2006 the median spending in this group was $50 a month, the highest level of lottery spending among all age groups. (p. 33)

For a New Thrift: Confronting the Debt Culture – Part 2 (July 17, 2008)

WITH AMERICANS MIRED IN UNPRECEDENTED debt, a group called the "Commission on Thrift" has issued a report with a plan to shrink debt and encourage saving among Americans of modest means. (1) Here are the highlights of the plan.

The Commission on Thrift proposes a National Thrift Initiative. This is mainly a public education campaign for thrift similar to campaigns to reduce drinking, reduce smoking, and encourage seatbelt wearing. (p. 49) (2) As part of this, the Commission calls for revival of National Thrift Week which was celebrated in America from 1917 to 1966.

Another component of the thrift plan is the creation of a savings plan available to all Americans modeled on the U.S. Thrift Savings Plan. The U.S. Thrift Savings Plan was created by the federal government in 1986 for all federal workers and military personnel. It enables them to place a small portion of their earnings into diversified stock-and-bond index funds. (p. 50) These funds are managed by an independent board with oversight by public and private sectors. (p. 50) Currently the federal savings plan has 3.7 million participants, manages assets of approximately $225 billion, and operates at a much lower cost than commercially-run funds. The Commission on Thrift wants to extend this savings and investment opportunity to all American workers who would participate through their place of employment. (p. 51)

Next, the Commission proposes to craft community-based thrift institutions to compete against payday lenders and other anti-thrifts by offering opportunities and incentives to save and by providing access to credit at low cost. (p. 51) In some cases this means creating new organizations; in others it means expanding and diversifying existing ones, especially credit unions. The Commission proposes that these thrift institutions operate as not-for-profit cooperatives. As part of this, the Commission calls for significant growth in the number of Community Finance Institutions, which currently number about 1,000. (pp. 52-53) (3)

Another component of the plan involves a change in the services provided by state lotteries. While conceding that the popularity of lotteries with the public and legislators makes abolishing them unrealistic, the Commission proposes that lotteries enable customers to gamble *and* to save. In the future you can buy a scratch off or a "savings ticket." (p. 54) The report says that a good marketing slogan for such savings tickets can be "Every ticket wins!" (p. 54) But the report gives no details on how the proposed savings component would work.

Finally, the report offers a list of additional possible strategies that should be considered to promote thrift, such as reinstating low usury caps, banning credit card companies from college campuses, instituting school savings programs, coaxing banks to offer more services to low income customers, and many others. (pp. 55-59)

It remains to be seen whether the Commission on Thrift triggers the sweeping change that it hopes for. Those who benefit from the status quo are certainly going to oppose its plan aggressively. Nevertheless, the members of the Commission are to be applauded for studying and acting on a crisis in America that begs for intelligent problem-solving.

---

1. *For a New Thrift: Confronting the Debt Culture,* Institute for American Values, 2008. References to this report here are by page number.

2. One assumes that the Commission anticipates the use of public service announcements on radio and television for this purpose. However, PSAs which are critical of advertisers who pay for air time will likely object to them, in which case the Commission will need to turn to

foundations and benefactors to provide funds to purchase ads. One also assumes that a comprehensive education initiative needs to involve schools but the report says very little about this aspect.

3. "Community Development Finance Institutions are supported by the CDFI Fund established by the U.S. Congress in 1994. To date, this fund has awarded $820 million to local financial institutions." (p. 53)

Energy – the Turning Point (July 31, 2008)

FAST FORWARD FIFTY YEARS TO the United States of American 2058. Most of the cars and trucks run on natural gas, ethanol, or batteries, not gasoline or diesel fuel. Most of the nation's electricity is generated by...

- thousands of huge solar panels arrayed across the western states,
- hundreds of nuclear power plants, and
- thousands of windmills along a 400-mile wide corridor through the central states from North Dakota and Minnesota to Texas.

A huge new transmission grid spreads energy from these sources across the nation.

In a high school science class, a teacher explains to her students that the turning point in energy policy in America was summer 2008 when the cost of a gallon of gasoline surpassed $4 a gallon and two prominent Americans – Republican T. Boone Pickens, a billionaire oil man, and Democrat Al Gore, a former vice-president – released far-reaching energy reform plans a day apart in the month of July. (1) These plans gained traction, the teacher explains, for the following reasons:

- Oil, a non-renewable source of energy, had become too expensive, and oil and coal were major causes of global pollution.
- The White House, Congress, and the American people were willing to swallow the huge one-time cost of an energy overhaul – trillions

of dollars – as a preferable alternative to sending $1 trillion a year every year to foreign oil producers.
- Despite some differences, the Pickens and Gore plans shared a commitment to energy independence for the nation and much greater use of renewable and clean sources of energy. (2)
- The authors of the plans had far-reaching influence with different but important political constituencies.
- The celebrity of the authors guaranteed extensive media exposure to their plans.
- Support for greater reliance on renewable domestic sources of energy had been growing across the country when the reports surfaced.
- Support for greater reliance on non-renewable but abundant domestic sources of energy had also been growing across the country when the reports surfaced.
- The fact that two such disparate public figures as Pickens and Gore spoke with one voice on the need for an overhaul of energy production and distribution in America made people from all backgrounds pay attention.
- And the energy overhaul had other important benefits for the nation, including the creation of tens of thousands of good-paying manufacturing and construction jobs and a surge in national pride and patriotism.

Now, back to 2008. The scenario just described is a possible future. Whether this possible future becomes an actual one depends on whether the American people and their leaders are prepared to accept the challenge of Mr. Pickens and Mr. Gore to launch a bold and expensive national initiative in the field of energy similar to the mobilization of the nation for World War II, the defeat of Hitler and his allies, the Marshall Plan, the construction of the interstate highway system, and Neil Armstrong's visit to the moon. Only time will tell.

1. For the Pickens Plan, see www.pickensplan.com and for the Gore plan, see www.wecansolveit.org. The two plans were released within a twenty-four hour period, the Pickens plan on July 17 and the Gore plan on July 18.

2. As to differences between the two plans, the Pickens Plan emphasizes wind power and the conversion of natural gas from the generation of electricity to transportation but is silent on the future of coal, solar power, and nuclear power while the Gore Plan emphasizes solar power, wind power, and electric cars and seems to call for a phase out of coal but is silent on natural gas and nuclear power. (See page 11 of the Gore Plan.) The silence of both plans on nuclear energy, which provides 75% of the electricity in France, is a serious flaw. Also, both plans are silent on various technical issues that stand in the way of implementation of their major proposals. For instance, how can we store surplus electricity generated by wind turbines until it is needed?

Whatever Happened to Jefferson and Madison? (August 14, 2008)

THE MOST RECENT WORK OF Pulitzer Prize-winning historian, Garry Wills, is *Head and Heart: American Christianities* which appeared in 2007. The chapters on religion during the Revolutionary Era show how far the United States has drifted over the generations from the plan of our founders. (1) Let's take a look at them.

Wills explains that the founders believed that to build an enduring republic they would have to minimize the impact of religion on government. They were keenly aware of the blood that was spilled in the Crusades, the Inquisition, the persecution of the Jews, and the religious wars in Europe in the 16th and 17th centuries, and they saw firsthand religious intolerance in the colonies. They also agreed with British philosopher, John Locke, (2) that human beings have a natural right to form their own beliefs on religion based on reason and conscience, that the duly-constituted government must possess a monopoly of power, that churches are subordinate to the State and its laws, and that churches may use only admonitions and exhortations, and never coercion, in dealing with their members or non-members.

Wills tell us that Jefferson and Madison led the battle to build a lasting new republic based on the separation of government and religion. Jefferson's insistence on this is found in his "Bill to Establish Religious Freedom" in Virginia, his "Letter to the Danbury Baptists," and his behavior as President. The Virginia statute disestablished the Anglican Church and ended the practice of taxing Virginians to support it. (3) In his "Letter to the Danbury Baptists," Jefferson characterized the Virginia statute, and the Constitution, as erecting "a wall of separation between Church and state." During his presidency, he refused to issue prayer day proclamations. (4)

As for Madison, Father of the Constitution, the Constitution, his essay against compulsory taxation to support churches, (5) the "Federalist Papers," and his behavior as President show his agreement with Jefferson. Madison insisted on religious liberty for all and required churches to tolerate one another. He also opposed a religious test for public office and government support for a particular church or for religion in general. Like Jefferson, he opposed prayer day proclamations. (6) He also opposed paying chaplains with public funds, tax exemptions for churches, government-endorsement of religious charities, and allowing churches to acquire extensive wealth. (7)

Thus, our founders were deeply fearful of sectarianism and they aimed to disentangle religion and government. (8) Although contemporary political leaders pay lip service to Jefferson and Madison, few follow their lead. Today most politicians pander to religious groups and their leaders. The White House sends hundreds of millions of dollars to religious charities, the Justice Department hires only applicants who pass an evangelical litmus test, atheists or agnostics are unelectable to high office if they disclose their views, pastors openly defy IRS rules about partisan political activity, forty states exempt parents who subscribe to faith-healing from prosecution for denying medical care to their sick children, embryonic stem cell research is halted, and Genesis myths trump science in many classrooms. This list goes on and on. (9) Today, religion rules. Whatever happened to Jefferson and Madison?

---

1. See *Head and Heart*, "Part Two: Enlightened Religion," Chapters 7-14, pp. 121-249.
2. Locke's writings had a powerful influence on our founders. The doctrines of natural rights, limited government, government by consent, majority rule, the separation of powers, the legitimacy of revolution or rebellion against an illegitimate government, the separation of church and state, and others, are found in his *First Treatise of Government*, *Second Treatise of Government*, and *Letter Concerning Toleration*.

3. Jefferson's "Bill for Establishing Religious Freedom" provides, in part, that:

> ...(N)o man shall be compelled to frequent or support any religious worship, workplace, or ministry whatsoever, nor shall (he) be enforced, restrained, molested, or burthened in his body or goods, nor shall (he) otherwise suffer, on account of his religious opinions or belief; ...all men shall be free to profess, and by argument to maintain, their opinions in matters of religion, and the same shall in no wise diminish, enlarge, or affect their civil capacities.
> (Quoted by Wills, p. 196)

4. Wills, p. 237.
5. "Memorial and Remonstrance." See Wills, pp. 207-222.
6. Madison reluctantly issues a prayer day proclamation during the War of 1812, a decision he later regretted.
7. Wills, pp. 242-247. On the issue of church wealth, Madison was fearful that wealthy churches would attempt to exert political influence.
8. Wills shares two "laments" by early U.S. citizens who recognized, and apparently regretted, the secular origins of our nations:

> In 1812 Timothy Wright wrote:
> We formed our Constitution without any acknowledgement of God, without any recognition of His mercies to us as a people, of his government, or even of his existence. The Convention by which it was formed never asked, even once, his direction or his blessing upon their labors. Thus we commenced our national existence, under the present system, without God.
> (Quoted in Wills, p. 223)

> In 1813 Chauncey Lee wrote:
> Can we pause and reflect for a moment, with the mingled emotions of wonder and regret, that that public instrument which guarantees our political rights and freedom and independence – our Constitution of national government, framed by such an august, learned and able body of men, formally adopted by the solemn resolution of each state, and justly admired and celebrated for its consummate political wisdom – has not the impress of religion upon it, not the smallest recognition of the government or the being of God, or the dependence and accountability of men – be astonished, O Earth! – nothing by which a foreigner might certainly decide whether we believe in the one true God, or in any God. (Quoted in Wills, pp. 223-234)

9. Other examples include vouchers and other forms of government support of religious schools, displays of nativity scenes on public property, allowance of proselytizing by Christian ministries in jails and prisons, prayer breakfasts sponsored by public officials, legislative prayers, office holders and candidates closing speeches with "God bless you and God bless America" or a variation, newly-elected presidents utilizing a Bible during their oath and adding the words "So help me God" to the presidential oath provided in the Constitution, highly publicized

efforts by office-holders to block the disconnection of life support systems from individuals in persistent vegetative states, such as Terri Schiavo, stacking public boards of education with evangelicals, evangelical opposition to bills promoting children's rights, state referenda defining marriage as the bond between one man and one woman, "In God We Trust" on currency, "One Nation Under God" in the Pledge of Allegiance, government "sex education" programs promoting abstinence only and ignoring condoms and the pill, the White House and others promoting the teaching of intelligent design alongside or instead of evolution, opposition to casino gambling by evangelicals and their political patrons in some states, the placing by the State of Utah of 12-feet crosses at the sites of state highway patrol officers who died in the line of duty, a 36-year old "Free Day Away" program at Fort Leonard Wood in Missouri where trainees may leave base provided that they participate in a religious program conducted by the Tabernacle Baptist Church of Lebanon, Missouri, incorporation of religion into the health care programs of the U.S. Department of Veterans Affairs, etc.

The Faith-Based White House (August 29, 2008)

AS THE SUN SETS ON George W. Bush's presidency, he will leave office with the distinction of bringing religion into politics more than any other President in history. This is the conclusion of Pulitzer-Prize-winning historian, Garry Wills, in *Head and Heart: American Christianities*, his history of religion in America. (1)

Wills points out that evangelicals were politicized during the 1960s and 1970s as they watched the nation sink into what they viewed as a moral abyss. (2) They were distressed over activism among blacks, women, gays, Vietnam protesters, and others, they were infuriated by court decisions on abortion, pornography, religious displays on public property, sex education in public schools, Darwinism, and prayer and Bible reading in the schools. Evangelicals counterattacked. Soon we had the Moral Majority, homeschooling, a proliferation of Christian schools and colleges, evangelical takeovers of school boards, a national network of textbook evaluators to assure that textbooks reflect "Biblical values," challenges to sex education in the schools, an assault on the Equal Rights Amendment, an explosion of Christian broadcasting, and more. (3)

Despite their efforts in the late twentieth century, evangelicals had made little progress over the years. They considered all the presidents from Nixon to Clinton huge disappointments. (4) As Wills observes,

Roe v. Wade had not been reversed. Prayer had not returned to the public schools.

Evolution had not been wrenched out of the school curriculum. The progress of the women's rights movement was growing... Gays were not going back into the closet but on to more and more TV shows and Broadway hits... (and) pornography had broken new ground on the Internet. (5)

Enter George W. Bush. Bush talked the evangelical talk and walked the evangelical walk. Bible study groups met daily at the White House. With the help of Karl Rove, an expert in "using religion as a political tool," (6) the new President packed the White House and federal agencies with born-again Christians and he consulted evangelical leaders and their organizations at every step as his administration set up its policies. (7) In the Bush White House, abortion was now murder, not a right to be protected, (8) same-sex marriage was an abomination that must be outlawed, (9) providing government grants to churches was constitutional because separation of church and state was a myth, (10) the jury was still out on evolution (11) and global warming, (12) embryonic stem cell research was immoral because embryos are human persons, (13) disconnecting Terry Schiavo's life support was murder, (14) sex education meant abstinence only, foreign aid must not be used for abortion, condoms, or the pill, and supporting Israel unqualifiedly was a Biblical imperative. (15)

Now, given the fact that a majority of Americans support few if any of these stances, and that Americans will soon elect a new president, an obvious question arises. What is the future of faith-based government? Is George W. Bush a trend-setter or merely an aberration? Based on the domestic and foreign fruits of eight faith-based years, I opt for the latter. What do you think?

---

1. The Penguin Press, New York, 2007. See pp. 353-552. References here are by page number.
2. See Wills, pp. 465-479.
3. Wills, p. 488.

4. Nixon's first Supreme Court nominee, Lewis Powell, sided with the majority on *Roe v. Wade*. Carter defended the Equal Rights Amendment and refused to join a March for Life in Washington. Reagan did nothing to outlaw abortion or put prayer back in the schools and his surgeon general promoted sex education and condoms to contain the spread of AIDS. The elder Bush supported the Hate Crimes Act and invited gay and lesbian leaders to the White House. Clinton tried to legitimate gays in the military, vetoed the ban on partial birth abortion, and had a highly publicized affair. See Wills, pp. 490-494. Wills also points out that, surprisingly, the evangelical position on abortion is not scriptural. "For those who make it so central to religion in our time," Wills writes, "this seems like an odd omission." (p. 526)

5. Wills, p. 489.

6. Wills, p. 516. In the same place, Wills writes:

> Rove shaped the hard core of the Republican Party around resentments religious people felt over abortion, homosexuality, Darwinism, women's liberation, pornography, and school prayer. Anyone who reacted strongly against just one of these things could very likely be made to oppose most or even all of the others, and be drawn into an alliance that cut across older patterns of economic, regional, or party ties. Rove made the executive branch more openly and avowedly religious than it had ever been, though he had no discernible religious beliefs himself.

> Wills says that Rove's religious indifference – he is likely an agnostic – helped him consolidate Right-wing Protestants, Catholics, and Jews. Also, Wills says, Rove Intentionally refused to woo moderates so as not to "endanger the hold on his righteous core by any gestures of reconciliation with the moderates." (Wills, p. 533)

7. Wills, p. 499.
8. Wills, p. 500.
9. Wills, p. 501.
10. Wills, p. 502.
11. Wills, p. 504.
12. Wills, p. 506.
13. Wills, p. 508.
14. Wills, pp. 509-511.
15. Wills, p. 514.

Mistakes Were Made (but not by me) (September 11, 2008)

In 2006 Oprah Winfrey endorsed a book by James Frey which was purported to be a memoir of his drug addiction and recovery. It was entitled *A Millions Little Pieces*. Oprah's endorsement made the book an instant bestseller. As time passed an investigative website called "The Smoking Gun" and a journalist named Richard Cohen showed that Frey's story was fabricated. Initially Oprah reasserted her support for Frey. (1) The fact is that Oprah had been duped but that she was intent on justifying her original decision and her credibility despite the facts. Remarkably, though, she made a 180 degree turnabout, publicly declared that Frey was a liar, apologized to the journalist, and chastised Frey in front of a national TV audience. (2)

Do most of us show the courage and candor which Oprah showed? No, say Carol Tavris and Elliot Aronson, psychologists and co-authors of a book entitled *Mistakes Were Made (but not by me)*. Their book draws from hundreds of research studies of how people deal with their mistakes. It shows that most of us, to maintain our confidence and self-esteem, routinely fail to admit our mistakes and reject information that questions our beliefs, decisions, or preferences. We thrive on self-justification at the expense of truth.

Early in the book, Tavris and Aronson cite a well-known recent example of a failure to admit mistakes. (3) The Bush administration sold the invasion of Iraq to the nation and the Congress on two principal claims, that Saddam Hussein possessed weapons of mass destruction and that he aided and abetted international terrorism. Both proved to be groundless. Not only did the White House fail to acknowledge this, but it shifted to new justifications for the invasion. (4) President Bush continues to assert his confidence in the wisdom of his decisions about Iraq to this day.

Tavris and Aronson show how bias, distortion of the past, and self-justification infiltrate all of our relationships, personal and professional. One of the most illuminating chapters is on marriage. It should be mandatory reading for all couples planning to start or end a marriage. The authors point out that stable, lasting marriages are only possible when a person is able "to put empathy for the partner ahead of defending their own territory" and able "to listen to the partner's criticisms, concerns, and suggestions undefensively." (5) Tavris and Aronson marshall persuasive evidence that successful marriages have "a ratio of five times as many positive interactions (such as expressions of love, affection and humor) to negative ones (such as expressions of annoyance and complaints)." (6) Once the "magic ratio" dips below 5 to 1, the marriage is in trouble. (7)

As one reads *Mistakes Were Made*, one wonders if people can let go of self-justification and admit mistakes. The authors insist that we can and they furnish impressive examples of public figures who have done so. They tell us that the first steps to success are being aware of the tendency to self-justify (8) and reminding ourselves regularly that we are fallible. (9) Finally, a warning. If your experience in reading *Mistakes Were Made* matches mine, you'll be surprised, and perhaps embarrassed, to find yourself in some of the stories it tells. (10)

---

1. Oprah said: "The underlying message of redemption in Frey's memoir still resonates with me…" and she blamed any problems on the publisher. See Carol Tavris and Elliott Aronson, *Mistakes Were Made (but not by me)*, Harcourt Books, 2007, p. 214. References here are by page number in this book.
2. Page 215.
3. Pages 18-19.
4. The new justifications included "getting rid of a 'very bad guy,' fighting terrorists, promoting peace in the Middle East, bringing democracy to Iraq, increasing American security, and finishing 'the task (our troops) gave their lives for.'" On the claim that the U.S. is in Iraq to

fight terrorists, a report issued by sixteen U.S. intelligence agencies concluded that "the occupation of Iraq had actually *increased* Islamic radicalism and the risk of terrorism." (p. 3)
5. Page 180.
6. Page 173.
7. Page 173.
8. They write:

> The need to reduce dissonance is a universal mental mechanism, but that doesn't mean we are doomed to be controlled by it.
> Human beings may not be eager to change, but we have the ability to change, and the fact that many of our self-protective delusions and blind spots are built into the way the brain works is no justification for not trying... An appreciation of how dissonance works, in ourselves and others, gives us some ways to override our wiring. And protect us from those who can't. (pp. 222-223)

9. Page 228.
10. *The Wall Street Journal*, on the book's cover, makes this point. It describes the book as "entertaining, illuminating, and – when you recognize yourself in the stories it tells – mortifying."

Jim Tressel, Coach *and* Author
(September 25, 2008)

JIM TRESSEL HAS BEEN KNOWN as a remarkably successful college football coach, first at Youngstown State University and now at The Ohio State University. His teams have won five national championships at the two schools combined. With the publication of *The Winners Manual for the Game of Life*, (1) he is now a coach <u>and</u> author.

The Winners Manual for the Game of Life is a self-help book that Tressel has distilled from a nearly four-hundred page handbook entitled *The Winners Manual* which Coach Tressel developed over the years and which he gives to his football teams each year as they begin preparation for a new season. He changes it slightly each year.

The heart of the handbook is "The Plan," a "step-by-step process of personal assessment and goal setting" for his players and coaches which includes "nineteen fundamentals" which Tressel has boiled down to ten in his book. (2)

Why would a busy coach with a crushing schedule take the time to write a book? It is certainly not to enrich himself. He is already wealthy and he is donating all proceeds from the book to an expansion of the library at Ohio State. His purpose, he tells us, is to help people become more productive and responsible. He writes:

I want to present ideas, principles, and truths in a way that will encourage you, lift you up when you're wrestling with life, and push you forward and motivate you to be a better person and a more vital part of whatever team you serve. (3)

As one who has known Tressel well since 1986 when he arrived at Youngstown State, I find that the book is a mirror image of Tressel the person. The Tressel whom I know is a master of time management, organization, and problem-solving who has an extraordinary gift for bringing people of diverse backgrounds together in a common cause. He relates remarkably well to people of all ages, circumstances, and vocations, and he copes with success and failure remarkably well. In my judgement, those who buy into Tressel's plan for self-evaluation and goal-setting in his book will be taking the same path that Tressel has taken for decades.

Anyone who reads *The Winners Manual* will learn that Jim Tressel is a devout Christian and that his religion shapes his approach to coaching and to life. Yet his practice of religion is refreshingly tolerant and humble. Tressel acknowledges that "non-religious people can be moral and religious people can be immoral" and he insists that "all people are to be loved, regardless of what they think or do..." even when they differ sharply with him. (4) He generously supports many non-religious charities, including colleges and hospitals. He is the antithesis of those strident and arrogant zealots who believe that they have a monopoly on morality and that God speaks directly and exclusively to them.

His coaches and players know his religious commitment but he respects their autonomy. On religious issues, he is scrupulously non-coercive. Players may attend chapel services or participate in prayer or not, as they wish. (5) In the "goals sheet" in the handbook that his players and coaches fill out in the spiritual/moral domain, about a quarter make no mention of religion at all. Many times he has held practices on Sunday.

Further, his book features quotations in the border taken from his handbook which he carefully selects to inspire his players and to encourage them to think. More than a dozen of these quotes are by atheists or agnostics.

Finally, one of his mentors, who receives considerable attention in the book, is an agnostic, and a number of essays in the handbook are by a friend who is an atheist. (6)

I invite you to read *The Winners Manual for the Game of Life* and find out whether it inspires you to improve your life. If it doesn't, I'll be surprised.

---

1. With Chris Fabry, Tyndale House Publishers, Inc., 2008. References to the book here are by page number.
2. Pages xiv-xv. The ten fundamentals are attitude, discipline, excellence, faith and belief, work, handling adversity and success, love, responsibility, team, and hope. See p. xxii and pp. 39-41.
3. Page xvi.
4. Online interview of Coach Tressel, 9-18-08.
5. Online interview of Coach Tressel, 9-18-08, and in-person interviews on 9-17-08 of Ken Conatser and Carmine Cassese, two of Tressel's long-time associates, the former an assistant coach, the latter an equipment manager.
6. Dr. Pat Spurgeon is the agnostic mentor and I am the atheist friend. In my introduction of Tressel to a huge banquet audience in 2000 which had convened to celebrate Tressel's appointment as head football coach at Ohio State, I noted that "Jim Tressel gives religion a good name."

Chris Hedges on the Radical Evangelicals (October 9, 2008)

THE RADICAL SEGMENT OF AMERICAN Evangelicals is the focus of the fourth book by Chris Hedges, a former correspondent for the *New York Times* and co-recipient of the 2002 Pulitzer Prize for reports on global terrorism. The book, entitled *American Fascists: the Christian Right and the War on America*, is a chilling expose and critique of the quest for theocracy, and its leaders, among them Francis Schaeffler, Jerry Falwell, D. James Kennedy, Pat Robertson, James Dobson, Timothy LaHaye, Rod Parsley, and others. (1) Hedges did his research for the book not only by reading publications and tuning into the broadcasts of the movement's celebrities, but by interviewing dozens of current and former Evangelicals, and attending worship services and workshops.

Hedges tells us that the radical religious right takes its cue from R.J. Rushdoony who published *The Institutes of Biblical Law* in 1973. According to Hedges, Rushdoony argues that:

> Christians are the new chosen people of God and are called to do what Adam and Eve failed to do: create a godly, Christian state. The Jews, who neglected to fulfill God's commands in the Hebrew scriptures, have, in this belief system, forfeited their place as God's chosen people and been replaced by Christians… The world is to be subdued and ruled by a Christian United States. (2)

Further, Hedges says, Rushdoony proposes to strip the federal government of all its functions save national defense, to turn over education and social welfare to Christian churches, and to replace the secular legal code with "Biblical law." (3)

According to Hedges, the radical Religious Right thrives on the disappearance of community in American culture, the despair that has set in with the loss of millions of manufacturing jobs, the plague of drug addiction and alcoholism, and various other crises. The vulnerable are systematically recruited by intoxicating preachers and their trained disciples who use virtually any tactic, moral or not, that works. (4)

And what happens to the newly saved? They join mega-churches which become the center of their lives; they tap into the huge Christian broadcasting industry for virtually all their news and entertainment; they send their children to Christian schools or home school them; they buy into the gospel of prosperity peddled by their spiritual leaders (5); they join the crusade to abolish the separation of church and state; they learn to hate gays, Muslims, abortionists and the rest of the unsaved; they embrace an agenda which seeks to "cure" homosexuals, outlaw abortion, restrict sex education to abstinence, deny global warming, and promote patriarchy in the family, the church, and the state; and they subscribe to the prophecy of the Rapture. (6) In this Rapture, "one day, without warning, the saved will be lifted into heaven and the unsaved left behind to suffer a seven-year period of torment and chaos known as the Tribulation." (7)

A mainstream Christian, Hedges charges that the militant Evangelicals have turned a religion of love and peace into a religion of hate and power. He concludes his book with an entreaty to moderate Christians and all others committed to democracy and an open society "to give up passivity, to challenge aggressively this (extremist) movement's appropriation of Christianity and to do everything possible to defend tolerance." (8)

---

1. Free Press, 2006.
2. *American Fascists*, pp. 12-13. Rushdoony, Hedges says, takes his cue from Calvin's *Institutes of the Christian Religion*, published in 1536.

3. *American Fascists*, p. 13. Hedges claims that the White House Office of Faith-Based Initiatives, established by President George W. Bush, is enacting many of Rushdoony's tenets. Hedges concedes that only a minority of the nation's 70 million Evangelicals today fully endorse Rushdoony's theocracy, but, he warns, this minority "is taking over the machinery of U.S. state and religious institutions" and he regrets that too often moderate Evangelicals defer to the radical minority. (p. 19) For a picture of the diversity among Evangelicals, see page 20.

4. *American Fascists*, p. 19.

5. The major televangelists, Hedges writes, "rule their fiefdoms as despotic potentates. They travel on private jets, have huge personal fortunes and descend on the faithful in limousines and surrounded by a small retinue of burly bodyguards. These tiny kingdoms, awash in the leadership cult, mirror on a smaller scale the America they seek to create." (p. 91)

6. At a seminar run by Dr. D. James Kennedy on how to win converts, Hedges reports the following:

> The most susceptible people, we are told in the seminar, are those in crisis: people in the midst of a divorce, those who have lost a job or are grieving for the death of a close friend or relative; those suffering addictions they cannot control, illness, or the trauma of emotional or physical abuse." (p. 56)

7. See *American Fascists*, Chapter Three, "Conversion," Chapter Four, "The Cult of Masculinity," Chapter Six, "The War on Truth," and Chapter Seven, "The New Class." On the Christian broadcast industry, Hedges counts "5,500 Christian broadcasters… who reach, according to their figures, an estimated 141 million listeners and viewers across America." (p. 129) Probably the largest company is the Christian Broadcasting Network (CBN) of Paul and Jan Crouch. See Chapter Nine, "God: The Commercial," pp. 164-181. One reason that fundamentalists oppose hate-crime legislation, Hedges says, is that, if passed, it would inhibit them from spewing hate toward homosexuals and other enemies of God in their programming. (p. 139) On the gospel of prosperity, Hedges writes that, according to fundamentalists, "Wealth, fame, and power are manifestations of God's work, proof that God has a plan and design for believers." (pp. 132-133) Hedges notes in several places that fundamentalist preachers who subscribe to the gospel of prosperity have enjoyed the generous support of many titans of American business, among them the Waltons, Amway founder Richard DeVos, Sr., and beer baron Joseph Coors. For a summary of the moral agenda of fundamentalists, see Hedges' description of a church service led by Rod Parsley, head of the World Harvest Church, pp. 158-163.

8. *American Fascists*, p. 207.

Chris Hedges on the New Atheists (October 3, 2008)

IN A BOOK PUBLISHED IN 2006, journalist and author Chris Hedges pilloried religious fundamentalists in America, charging them with corrupting Christianity, undermining the Constitution, and promoting American imperialism. (1) In his most recent book, *I Don't Believe in Atheists*, (2) Hedges shifts to the opposite side of the ideological spectrum to critique a group which he calls the "new atheists" and which he considers *secular fundamentalists*. According to Hedges, the new atheists, are as "intolerant, chauvinistic, and bigoted" as the Christian theocrats. (3) And what have these popular critics of religion said that Mr. Hedges finds so disturbing?

The new atheists, Hedges charges, are prisoners to the myth of progress. (4) They see the flow of history through rose-colored glasses, expecting the march of reason and science to unlock all mysteries, solve all problems, and usher in a post-religious global paradise bereft of gods and miracles. They ignore the fact that science is a tool for good <u>and</u> evil and that the selfish, aggressive, and destructive side of human nature is here to stay. Based on the historical record, Hedges insists, it is folly for the new atheists to believe in moral progress. In the twentieth century, for instance, with ever-more sophisticated weapons made possible by science, humans butchered 130 million other humans and maimed many millions more in various conflicts. (5)

Hedges sees other problems among the new atheists beyond their naïve optimism. "They misuse the teaching of Charles Darwin and evolutionary biology," he writes, "just as the Christian fundamentalists misuse the Bible." (6) They demonize the one billion plus Muslims in the world when only "a tiny subset (of them) are criminals and terrorists." (7) Their knowledge of the Bible and the Quran is "shallow and haphazard" and they "are blind to the underlying human truth and reality expressed through religious myth." (8) In their self-appointed roles as "the saviors of civilization," (9) they exhibit an arrogance and superiority that belies their human fallibility. (10) They fail to understand that religion is indispensable to ethics. (11) And, finally, like their religious counterparts, the new atheists hold up the United States as "the paragon of human possibility and goodness" despite the fact that it is, in his judgment, a nation in decline. (12)

In his book, I believe, Chris Hedges aims to remind seculars that they, too, are human, and to a considerable extent, he succeeds. Yet the book is not without its flaws. In the first place, the author's knowledge of atheism is limited. Most of his criticisms of the handful of new atheists he has studied don't apply to many of the most distinguished old ones, among them John Dewey, Sidney Hook, and Paul Kurtz, none of whom gets even a mention in the book. Next, his view of religion as the foundation of morality has been challenged by legions of philosophers, I believe successfully, since the time of the ancient Greeks. And, finally, he overlooks the fact that there has been moral progress, witness the abolition of slavery and the advancing liberation of women in America and elsewhere.

---

1. *American Fascists: the Christian Right and the War on America*, Free Press, 2006.
2. Free Press, 2008.
3. *I Don't Believe in Atheists*, p. 1. All subsequent references are to this book by page number.
4. Page 95.
5. Page 114.
6. Page 6.
7. Page 16.
8. Page 34.
9. Page 39.
10. Page 111.
11. Page 92.

12. Page 129. On this subject he writes:

> The failed imperialist project in Iraq, along with the maintenance of a costly military machine and the arms industry that feeds off the American state, has likewise begun to take its toll. The United States is dependent on other countries, particularly those in the Middle East, for its natural resources.
> It is hostage to foreign states, which control the country's mounting debt.
> Its infrastructure is crumbling, its social services are in decline, and its educational system is in shambles. It is rotting from the inside out. And in the midst of this decline, our secular and religious fundamentalists hold our society up as the paragon of human possibility and goodness. (p. 129)

Are American Voters Stupid?
(November 13, 2008)

CONSIDER THE FOLLOWING FACTS ABOUT the American people:

- Only two out of five of us can identify the three branches of government;
- Less than half of us know which nation dropped the atomic bomb;
- Only one-third of us know that the Congress, not the President, declares war;
- Only 30% of us know that members of the U.S. House of Representatives serve two-year terms and only 25% of us know that members of the U.S. Senate serve six-year terms;
- Most Americans continue to believe that the 9/11 terrorists came from poverty or were neglected as children despite overwhelming evidence to the contrary;
- A generation ago presidential speeches were pitched at the level of twelfth graders. Today they are pitched at the level of seventh graders;
- Even after the 9/11 Commission had stated publicly that Saddam Hussein had provided no support for Al Qaeda, a poll showed that half the population still insisted that he had;
- Only 25% of us can name more than one of the five freedoms guaranteed by the First Amendment but more than 50% of us can name two members of the Simpson family. (1)

These revelations, and many others, come from Rick Shenkman, an Emmy Award-winning reporter and historian, in his new book entitled *Just How Stupid Are We? Facing the Truth About the American Voter*. (2) The vaunted wisdom of the American people, Shenkman says, is a myth. When it comes to government and politics, we are ignoramuses – ill-informed, apathetic, and easily manipulated. (3)

Shenkman argues that while there was never a Golden Age in which the American electorate had extensive knowledge about our government and how it functions, the past sixty years has seen a persistent dumbing down of voters. Studies show that today "young Americans know far less about politics than their counterparts did a generation ago, even though they spend more time in school." (4) Ours has become a culture of entertainment and consumption dominated by television. (5) The invasion of the home by television brought superficiality, sound bites, slogans, and inane ads. By 1963 TV had supplanted newspapers as the primary source of news. (6) Newspapers had provided detail, subtlety, and nuance which were lost in TV news. With TV, images trump facts, (7) politicians are "brands" to be marketed, (8) and how people look and talk count for more than their knowledge, accomplishments, or problem-solving skills. (9) As time passed fewer and fewer Americans read about, talked about, and cared about public affairs. (10)

What does Shenkman propose to do to change all this? The most important change we need in America, he says, is to reintroduce civics as a mandatory subject in grade school, high school, and college. (11) The reading of newspapers and other news sources must be a part of this. (12) When proficiency tests are given, they must test for knowledge of government as well as knowledge of math and science. (13) All first year college students should be given weekly current events tests and those who pass with flying colors should receive federal tuition subsidies. (14) Finally, outside our schools and colleges, we need "democracy parties," social gatherings where issues are discussed in depth. (15)

Shenkman says he is trying to be "the Paul Revere of American civics." (16) I, for one, hope that he succeeds.

1. The five freedoms granted by the First Amendment are speech, religion, press, assembly, and petition for redress of grievances. The Simpson family members are Homer, Marge, Bart, Lisa, and Maggie. The facts listed here are given in Rick Shenkman, *Just How Stupid Are We? Facing the Truth about the American Voter*, Basic Books, 2008. See pages 20, 20, 24, 19-20, 136, 17, 4 and 13 respectively. Other facts reported by Shenkman are these:

> Only half the population knows that President George W. Bush favors privatizing social security. (p. 35)

> In 2006 36% of the population believed that the U.S. Government was complicit in the 9/11 terrorist attack despite the fact that there was no evidence to support such a view. (p. 130)

> On the eve of the invasion of Iraq, only one in seven Americans could find Iraq on the map. (p. 14)

> Most Americans cannot name their Congressional representative or their two U.S. Senators. (p. 24)

2. Basic Books, 2008. Other books by Shenkman include *Legends, Lies, and Cherished Myths* and *Presidential Ambition*. You can learn more about him on his blog entitled How Stupid? See http://howstupidblog.com. A good recent interview of Shenkman by Robin Lindley, a Seattle journalist, is at http://hnn.us/blogs/entries/55966.html.

3. Page 168.
4. Pages 117-118. See also page 111.
5. Page 181.
6. Page 103. Today only one out of five Americans in the 18 to 34 age group read any part of a newspaper regularly. (p. 26)
7. Page 110.
8. Page 121.
9. Page 102.
10. Schenkman says that today "The People" find politics "boring," that they are "ignorant and irrational about public affairs," and that their opinions about politics are "usually muddled." (p. 76)
11. Pages 177-178. Shenkman proposes that a non-partisan commission draw up national civics tests. (p. 180)
12. Page 179.
13. Page 178.
14. Page 179. The federal law setting up this fund, he says, can be called The Too Many Stupid Voters Act. (p. 179)
15. Page 180.
16. See the interview of Shenkman by Robin Lindley referred to above in footnote 2.

A Lesson from Scandinavia
(November 27, 2008)

DURING THE YEARS 2005 AND 2006, American sociologist Phil Zuckerman spent fourteen months in Denmark and Sweden to study these two societies. In a recent book, *Society without God: What the Least Religious Nations Can Tell Us About Contentment*, (1) he reports these findings:

- Denmark and Sweden have among the lowest rates of violent crime in the world. (pp. 28-29) (2)
- Denmark and Sweden have the lowest rates of HIV and AIDS in the world. (p. 27)
- Sweden is third and Denmark is fifth in the world in economic competitiveness. (p. 27)
- On gender equality, Denmark is second and Sweden is third in the world. (p. 27)
- On access to the Internet, Sweden is third and Denmark is fourth in the world. (p. 28)
- Denmark and Sweden are tied for the lowest infant mortality rates in the world with Norway, Iceland, Japan, and Singapore. (p. 26)

- Denmark and Sweden are tied for first place in the world with the Netherlands in the health and safety of children. (p. 26)
- Denmark ranks fourth and Sweden ranks eighth in the world in the standard of living. (p. 27)
- Political corruption is virtually non-existent in Denmark and Sweden. (p. 28)
- Denmark and Sweden are tied for first in the world in a recent international study of social justice (p. 30)(3), and
- Denmark ranks second and Sweden ranks third in the world in financial aid to poor nations. (p. 29)

Thus, according to Zuckerman, Danes and Swedes are among the most contented and generous people on the planet. But that's not all that Zuckerman has to report about these two nations. Remarkably, he notes, two of the most prosperous societies in the world are also two of the least religious. (4) Indeed, a huge majority in both countries are atheists or agnostics. Only 24% of Danes and 16% of Swedes believe in a personal God compared to more than 90% in the United States. (p. 24) Only 18% of Danes and 33% of Swedes believe in heaven compared to 80% of Americans. Only 10% of Danes and 3% of Swedes believe in hell compared to 75% of Americans. (p. 11, pp. 24-25) This is the lowest rate of belief in hell in the entire world! (p. 25)

Next, only 7% of Danes and 3% of Swedes believe that the Bible is the literal word of God compared to 33% in the United States. (p. 25) Further, Danes and Swedes have the lowest church attendance in the world with only 3% of Danes and 7% of Swedes attending regularly. (p. 25, p. 162)(5) Also, only 8% of Danes and 15% of Swedes consider it important for a politician to believe in God compared to 64% of Americans who do (p. 12), and contrary to public and private practice in America, very few Danes and Swedes pray. (p. 2) Finally, more than 80% of Danes and Swedes accept evolution while less than half of the U.S. population does. (p. 10)(6)

Professor Zuckerman sees an important lesson for us in his study of Denmark and Sweden. Contrary to what we've heard from "certain outspoken conservative Christians," (7) the sociologist suggests, a secular society need not be a scene of violence and depravity. (p. 4, pp. 17-18) Denmark and Sweden, he says, are not only "impressive models of societal health" (p. 17) but living proof that humans can survive and prosper without religion. (pp. 55-56)(8)

---

1. New York University Press, 2008. References here to this volume are by page number.
2. For instance, in Aarhus, Denmark, a city of 250,000 residents, there was a total of one murder in 2004. (p. 6)
3. This study was done by a German group of social scientists associated with an institute called Hans-Bocker Stiftung. (p. 30) Denmark and Sweden are not without problems, however. Taxes are high, there is social friction due to recent waves of immigration, children eat too much candy, rates of bicycle thefts are high, fertility rates are low, and alcohol consumption is high. (p. 34)
4. Other irreligious societies are the Netherlands, the Czech Republic, South Korea, Estonia, France, Japan, Bulgaria, Norway, England, Scotland, Wales, Hungary, and Belgium. (p. 25) Zuckerman points out that in all of these relatively secular societies the citizens freely gravitated from a religious to an irreligious perspective unlike North Korea, the former Soviet Union, China, and Albania where the governments attempted to impose secularism on the citizens. Zuckerman says that forced secularism doesn't work. See pp. 20-22.
5. Paradoxically, despite the fact that most Danes and Swedes are atheists or agnostics and don't attend church regularly, 83% of Danes and 80% of Swedes continue voluntarily to pay a tax to the National Church, which is Lutheran (p. 112), and many hold traditional events such as weddings, baptisms, confirmations, and funerals in church. Zuckerman says that Danes and Swedes, while rejecting the supernatural dimensions of Christianity – Jesus performed miracles, Jesus was God, Jesus rose from the dead, the Bible is God's revelation, the Genesis account of creation is accurate, there is an afterlife with a heaven and a hell, etc. – maintain a "cultural religion" similar to many Jews. (pp. 153-155) Oddly, in Denmark a person may be a pastor and an atheist. (p. 154)
6. Despite the fact that Danes and Swedes are irreligious, they are not hostile to religion, they shun serious discussions of it, they deem a person's views about religion a private matter, and many non-believers dislike being labeled an atheist because they take the term to imply hostility to religion. When one asks them what it means to be a Christian, they say it means being kind, helping people who need help, not hurting others, etc. As a rule they reject the supernatural components. See Chapter 8, "Cultural Religion," pp. 150-166. Also, see pp. 97-109.

7. Zuckerman lists the following examples of Christian conservatives who claim that a society that is irreligious will fail: Pat Robertson, the late Jerry Falwell, Ann Coulter, Bill O'Reilly, Laura Schlesinger, William Bennett, Rush Limbaugh, and Paul Weyrich. (p. 4, pp. 17-18)

8. American fundamentalists will no doubt object to Zuckerman's strongly favorable evaluation of Denmark and Sweden by noting that in these countries abortion has been legal for more than thirty years, prostitution is legal, and homosexuality is tolerated.

Galbraith on Global Warming and Planning (December 11, 2008)

THE MOBILIZATION FOR WORLD WAR II by the United States shows government planning at its best. During a four-year period the United States recruited, trained, and deployed eleven million soldiers; commissioned the production of countless aircraft, seacraft, trucks, jeeps, tanks, bombs, guns, and bullets; kept inflation low; and achieved full employment. (1) The result was victory over the Axis powers. By contrast, the devastation in New Orleans caused by Hurricane Katrina shows government planning at its worst. In New Orleans the levees were structurally flawed; residents remained in low lying areas of the city at great risk; and the evacuation plan ignored those without automobiles. The result was that thousands died, hundreds of thousands fled, most permanently, and New Orleans today is "largely a ruin." (2)

These are the sentiments of James K. Galbraith, an economist, in his most recent book, *The Predator State*. In this book Galbraith gives us both a devastating critique of free market economics and a plea for a recommitment by government to planning. Galbraith argues that in a "properly designed (economic) system, planning and markets do not contradict each other" and "are not mutually exclusive." (3) Markets, he says, "distribute today's resources to meet tomorrow's needs" (4) because markets do not think ahead. (5) Thus, the interests of future generations must be provided for through government planning. (6)

Although Galbraith sees a need for effective planning by government in several areas, the one which he addresses with a special sense of urgency is global warming. He cites a 2007 report on this subject by the Intergovernmental Panel on Climate Change (IPCC). This report, Galbraith insists, is a wake-up call to the governments of the world to take individual and joint action on a par with the U.S. mobilization for World War II to prevent unprecedented global disaster. (7)

According to the IPCC report, failure to act will cause carbon dioxide in the atmosphere to reach levels within the next three generations that will cause the collapse of ice sheets in the West Antarctic and Greenland. If and when half these ice sheets melt, sea levels will rise by twenty feet around the world resulting in the loss due to flooding of "every beach, every low-lying island, every coastal marsh, and nearly every coastal city on the face of the globe, as well as the ports, airports, power plants, refineries, and other seaside infrastructure..." (8) To reduce greenhouse emissions, Galbraith argues, we will have to get gasoline out of cars and coal out of power plants and replace them with new, clean energy. (9) The unfettered market will do nothing to help us. Indeed, governments will have to take control of the sources and uses of energy from private corporations. (10) "Either the problem of climate change will be planned out, by a public authority acting with public power," Galbraith writes, "or it will be planned away, by private corporations whose priorities lie in selling coal, oil, and gas-burning cars." (11)

The science behind Galbraith's proposal on climate change is well-founded despite the naysayers. Whether the more than six billion people across the world and their political leaders have the intelligence, responsibility, and courage to act in time, however, is another question.

---

1. See James K. Glabraith, *The Predator State: How Conservatives Abandoned the Free Market and Why Liberals Should Too*, Free Press, 2008, p. 172. References to this book here are by page number. Galbraith is the son of John Kenneth Galbraith, famous Harvard economist and U.S. Ambassador to India, who died in 2006.
2. Pages 168-169.
3. Pages 164-165.
4. Page 165.

5. Page 167.
6. Pages 166-167. Galbraith cites two inherent market flaws: "Even if the market is perfectly efficient, it still suffers from two ineradicable defects. The first relates to the distribution of income and power: the market conveys signals only in proportion to the purchasing power of the individuals transmitting them. The poor do not matter to the market. The second relates to representation: people not yet born do not turn up in the stores. They send no market signals at all." (p. 166)
7. The report is *Climate Change 2007: Synthesis Report*, Intergovernmental Panel on Climate Change Fourth Assessment Report, November 17, 2007. Galbraith opines that "In the IPCC, we can come as close as humanity has ever known to a trusted voice on a scientific matter." (p. 171)
8. Page 170.
9. Page 171.
10. Page 170.
11. Page 175.

Religious Illiteracy (December 26, 2008)

In a recent book on the subject of religious literacy in America, (1) Stephen Prothero, a historian of religion, argues that, paradoxically, "Americans are both deeply religious and profoundly ignorant about religion." (2) For instance, despite the fact that a huge majority of Americans are Christians, only half can name even one of the four Gospels, (3) a majority cannot name the first book of the Bible, (4) and only one-third know that Jesus delivered the Sermon on the Mount. (5) Americans are ignorant not only about Christianity but other religions as well. Only one-third of us can identify the founder of a religion other than Christianity and a vast majority of us are unfamiliar with the basic teachings of Islam, Buddhism, and Hinduism. (6)

How did Americans become so religiously illiterate? Prothero traces religious ignorance in America to two sources in the 19th century. The first is the rise of evangelicalism in the Second Great Awakening which catapulted emotion over reason and actively discouraged religious learning. The second is the growth in non-denominationalism within Protestant America, partly as a defense against waves of Catholic immigrants, which resulted in a lowest common-denominator faith and the removal of the Bible from most public schools. (7) Thus, believers, not secularists, were responsible for the flight of religion from classrooms. (8)

So how does Professor Prothero propose to overcome religious illiteracy in America? He calls for two required courses in American high schools, one in the Bible and one in world religions. (9) According to

Prothero, studying the Bible, arguably the most influential book ever written, will help students understand American history and literature while studying world religions will give students insight into religious diversity in America and help them grasp developments and events around the world. Prothero points out that, contrary to public perception, teaching *about* religion has been consistently ruled constitutional by the U.S. Supreme Court. (10)

Prothero acknowledges that his proposal faces obstacles. Teacher training will have to be revamped so that each school system has teachers qualified to teach courses in the Bible and world religions; funds will have to be found to support the new courses; and teachers, administrators, and parents will need to be educated about the distinction between teaching and preaching. Nevertheless, Prothero argues, we need to confront these problems head on because we need religiously literate citizens in today's world. (11)

I am convinced that Prothero's picture of religious illiteracy in America is accurate and that his proposal to overcome it is sensible and timely. (12) Whether it will be adopted across the nation is, of course, another question altogether. My sense is that the only hope for implementation of Prothero's plan is if President-Elect Barack Obama, who seeks to bridge the gulf between evangelicals and seculars, to defuse the culture wars, and to upgrade public education, makes Prothero's agenda his own. (13)

---

1. Stephen Prothero, *Religious Literacy: What Every American Needs to Know – and Doesn't*, HarperCollins, 2007. References here are to this book by page number. Prothero chairs the Department of Religion at Boston University.
2. Page 1. Prothero has a lot of company here. For instance, pollster George Gallup, after conducting dozens of surveys over decades, opines that the United States is "a nation of Biblical illiterates." (p. 6)
3. Page 6 and page 30.
4. Page 30.
5. Page 30. Prothero also reports that the "vast majority" of his students at Boston University did not know that the First Amendment both guarantees citizens the right to practice religion and prohibits government from endorsing religion. (p. 29) He also says that members of the

dozens of Protestant sects typically do not know what is unique to their denomination or what differentiates it from others. "Many Baptists cannot tell you how their denomination understands its signature rite of adult baptism. Many Methodists will simply shrug if you ask them about their denomination's distinctive doctrine of sanctification. And many Lutherans have no idea who Martin Luther is." (p. 33)

6. Page 33.

7. Pages 90-91.

8. Pages 89-103. The disappearance of religion from public schools is usually blamed, incorrectly, Prothero says, on late 20th century Supreme Court decisions banning prayer and devotional Bible reading in the schools (p. 88) or "diabolical secularists conspiring to banish religion from the public square." (p. 89)

9. Prothero also proposes a mandatory course in religious studies in all colleges. See pp. 139-141.

10. Page 129. For instance, see Justice Thomas Clark's majority opinion in *Abington v. Schempp* (1966). In a concurring opinion in the same case, Justice William Brennan wrote: "The holding of the Court today plainly does not foreclose teaching *about* the differences between religious sects in classes in literature or history. Indeed, whether or not the Bible is involved, it would be impossible to teach meaningfully many subjects in the social sciences or the humanities without some mention of religion." P. 129)

The constitutionality of teaching about religion in the public schools is also affirmed in *Stone v. Graham* (1980) and *Edwards v. Aguillard* (1987). (p. 129)

Prothero says that under the law teachers may neither proselytize for Christianity or crusade against it. (p. 133) He writes: "For this agenda to succeed, it is crucial that the distinction between religious studies and theology – between teaching and preaching – be maintained in required courses in higher and secondary education." (p. 141)

For the content which Prothero recommends for his proposed high school course in the Bible, see pp. 132-135.

Prothero points out that the recognition that we need religiously literate citizens and that teaching about religion is constitutional explains why thirty-five religious and secular groups, including the National Association of Evangelicals, the American Muslim Council, and the American Humanist Association, signed a statement in 1995 which endorses teaching about religion in the public schools (p. 131)

11. Prothero argues that "a student ignorant of the Bible and the world's religions cannot be said to be ready for either college or citizenship" (p. 139) and "the costs of perpetuating religious ignorance are too high in a world in which faith moves, if not mountains, then at least elections and armies." (p. 145)

12. Recently, when my course in Introduction to Philosophy was taking up the segment on the philosophy of religion, I enumerated the major religions of the world and asked students to raise their hands if they were followers of the one then mentioned. When I finished I noticed that one student had not raised his hand. I asked whether he was a secular. He replied that he didn't raise his hand because I hadn't mentioned his religion

– Catholicism. He was apparently oblivious to the fact that Christianity, which was first in the list I mentioned, includes Catholicism, Protestantism, and Orthodoxy.

13. One of the most valuable parts of Prothero's book is Chapter Six: "A Dictionary of Religious Literacy," which runs for more than eighty pages. It gives explanations of dozens and dozens of terms from the world's religions and is followed by a "Religious Literacy Quiz."

Charles Curran's Rocky Road
(January 8, 2009)

CHARLES CURRAN, ONE OF THE most influential theologians of the past half century, grew up in Rochester, New York. He decided at the age of 13 to be a priest, earned two doctorates in Rome, where he was also ordained, and accepted an appointment to the theology faculty at Catholic University of America in 1965, a campus that would serve as the stage for an epic battle between Curran and the Vatican. (1)

The battle was joined when Pope Paul VI issued the encyclical *Humanae vitae* in 1968 which affirmed the church's rejection of what it called "artificial" birth control, despite a recommendation to the contrary by a majority of a panel which the Pope himself had established to study the issue. (p. 49)(2) This prompted the young theologian to organize a protest in which over six hundred Catholic theologians signed a statement disagreeing with the Pope's position on moral and theological grounds. (pp. 50-51)(3) The Vatican was not pleased.

Curran's differences with church teaching were anchored in his strongly held belief that "...the Catholic tradition is a living tradition and the work of Catholic theology involves ongoing revision." (p. 197)(4) Curran repeatedly pointed out that the church had revised its teaching sensibly on social issues including slavery, democracy, human rights, usury, capital punishment, and others, but on sexual matters it was paralyzed in a medieval neo-scholastic worldview which was fixated solely on the biological aspects of sex. (p. 5, p. 86, p. 199) Curran was relentless in calling for reform. Within a decade, in his books, articles, and speeches, he publicly challenged the church's traditional teaching on priestly celibacy, the ordination of women, birth control, homosexuality, sterilization, divorce, abortion, premarital sex, masturbation, and euthanasia. (5)

Criticisms of Curran's work by the Vatican and other Catholic conservatives prompted his university to attempt to fire him in 1967 but school officials backed off after faculty and students rallied to his cause and staged a strike. But many years later, after he was officially condemned by the Vatican as a heretic in 1986, Catholic University managed to cut its ties to him successfully. (p. 5)(6) Despite the church's actions, Curran's book sales shot up and his influence grew. (p. 244) After short-term stays at Cornell, the University of Southern California, and Auburn, Curran accepted an endowed chair in 1991 in human values at Southern Methodist University where he remains today.

If you ask Charles Curran why he stays in a church that condemned him, he will reply that only the hierarchy, not the church, condemned him. (p. 244) The church, he insists, is all the people of God and it "…is as much mine as the pope's." (p. 246) If you ask him what sustained him during the pitched battles with the Vatican and officials at Catholic University, he will cite a confidant hope that the church will eventually change and a resilient sense of humor. (p. 251, p. 259) Fortunately, in America, dissent by a scholar is seldom punished as severely as Curran was. Let's hope that it stays that way.

---

1. References here are by page number in Charles Curran, *Loyal Dissent: Memoir of a Catholic Theologian*, Georgetown University Press, 2006. One observation which Curran made in Rome was that the Vatican was filled with ambitious priests "trying to plot their careers" which showed that the church "was not only human but sinful." (p. 13) Curran also says that any doubts that the church is imperfect should have disappeared with the pedophilia scandal in which bishops "put institutional survival and 'the good name of the church' above the needs of innocent victims." (p. 239)

2. Curran notes that after the publication of *Humanae vitae* church attendance in America dropped by 11% and fully one-quarter of the graduates of Catholic colleges left the church. (p. 53)

3. The statement concluded that Catholics "could responsibly decide to use birth control" if it is necessary "to preserve and foster the values and sacredness of their marriage." (p. 52) Later the Congregation of the Doctrine of the Faith charged that Curran's protest had robbed the encyclical "of its intended effect…" (p. 113)

4. Curran was deeply influenced in this view in Rome by one of his theology professors, Bernard Lonergan, a Canadian Jesuit. For more on Lonergan, see Joseph Flanagan, *Quest for Self-Knowledge: An Essay in Lonergan's Philosophy*, University of Toronto Press, 1997.

5. On the subject of the ordination of women as priests, Curran argues that the church's logic is flawed. It holds that women should not be ordained because all the apostles were men. This reflects the times, not divine law, according to Curran. By the church's logic, Curran notes, only Jews should be ordained priests since all the apostles were Jews. (p. 240)

6. Coincidentally, the head of the Vatican office which declared Curran unfit to teach Catholic theology – the Congregation for the Doctrine of the Faith – was Cardinal Josef Ratzinger, now Pope Benedict XVI.

Sidney Poitier's Remarkable Journey
(January 22, 2009)

SIDNEY POITIER IS THE FIRST black actor to win the Academy Award for Best Actor. He won it in 1963 for his role in *Lilies of the Field*. (1) Subsequently he received virtually every major honor which an actor can receive. (2) Poitier starred in some forty films, including *Blackboard Jungle* (1955); *The Defiant Ones* (1958); *The Bedford Incident* (1965); *A Patch of Blue* (1965); *Guess Who's Coming to Dinner* (1967); *To Sir, With Love* (1967); and *In the Heat of the Night* (1967). He also performed to critical acclaim on stage and on television and he directed nine films. (3)

Poitier's artistic success is nothing short of amazing when you consider his roots. He grew up on an island in the Bahamas without plumbing, electricity, paved roads, automobiles, or schools. He wore trousers which his mother made from flour sacks. His parents were tomato farmers whose business collapsed when the State of Florida banned tomato imports from the Bahamas in 1936. At that point the Poitier family moved to Nassau, a modern city, where Sidney attended school briefly, got in trouble with the law, and discovered race, class, and movie theaters. (4) At the age of 15 Poitier's father sent him to live with his older brother Cyril in Miami but racism there quickly drove him north to New York City. He lived in Harlem for fourteen years, many of them spent as a dishwasher. (5) His first try at acting at the American Negro Theater was a disaster. Poitier had no training, he could barely read, and he had a "thick singsong Bahamian accent." (p. 56) He then undertook a program of self-improvement. With the help of an elderly Jewish waiter, he learned to read and speak by reciting the daily newspaper. (p. 57) He took acting classes (p. 58) and absorbed much from friends and fellow actors as well as radio and movie house newsreels. (6) Eventually he landed his first stage and film roles. (7)

Despite Poitier's growing success, none of the Hollywood movie companies sought to sign him to an exclusive contract. (p. 94) Poitier considered this an asset, however, because it allowed him to "pick and choose" his projects so that none of his roles would embarrass his family or contradict his own values. (p. 94) This independence explains why he turned down a leading role in a film in which his character was intimidated into silence about a crime (pp. 64-67), why he refused to sign loyalty oaths during the height of the cold war (pp. 93-99), and why he asked for and got a script change in a scene from *The Heat of the Night* so that when a white man slapped him, he slapped back (pp. 136-137). (8)

How does one account for great artistic accomplishment by a person who grew up in a Third World culture, who had virtually no formal schooling, who had regular brushes with the law, and who couldn't read until his late teens? Poitier himself offers two speculations – that his gift for theater had genetic roots (p. 20) and that unseen mysterious forces – fate, if you will – guided him on his career path. (p. 61) Whatever the reasons, Sidney Poitier, who turns 82 next month, has given us a legacy of extraordinary films that will entertain, educate, and inspire young and old for many generations.

---

1. See Sidney Poitier, *The Measure of Man: A Spiritual Autobiography*, HarperCollins, 2008. References to this book here are by page number.
2. Among Poitier's awards are the Academy Award for Best Actor, the BAFTA Award for Best Actor in a Leading Role, the Golden Globe Award for Best Actor – Motion Picture Drama, the AFI Life Achievement Award, the Cecile B. DeMille Award, Kennedy Center Honors, the NAACP Hall of Fame Award, the Marian Anderson Award, the Grammy Award for Best Spoken Word Album, an Honorary Oscar, and Knight Commander of the Order of the British Empire (knighthood). See "Sidney Poitier," *Wikipedia*.
3. "Sidney Poitier," *Wikipedia*.

4. Poitier quit school at age 12. His aborted schooling in Nassau did play an important part in his later career because one of his teachers, Mr. Fox, became the model for his role in *To Sir, With Love*, a story about a teacher in an impoverished area of London (p. 187). In Nassau, after Poitier saw a movie, he would return home and act out all the parts. (p. 33)

5. In New York, Poitier sometimes slept in a pay toilet or on a rooftop because he could not afford an apartment. When winter set in, he decided to join the U.S. Army so that he had food, clothing, and lodging. His career in the military was short-lived. To quicken his release, he feigned psychological problems and narrowly escaped a court martial. (pp. 52-55)

6. Poitier says that his "teachers" included Paul Robeson, Dr. Ralph Bunche, A. Philip Randolph, Adam Clayton Powell, Roy Wilkins, Mary McCloud Bethune, Walter White, Whitney Young, and Langston Hughes as well as contemporaries including Harry Belafonte, Leon Bibbs, and Philip and Doris Rose. (p. 76) He writes: "By their example and my own intense effort at reading the newspapers, I picked up useful bits of information every day." (p. 77) He also acknowledges Louise, a fellow acting student, who "taught me much, not the least of which was to appreciate how much a greater command of the language can enrich one's life." (p. 79) He credits a long list of actors with helping him to hone his acting skills, including Marlon Brando, Rod Steiger, Lee Grant, Ruby Dee, Alice Childress, Frank Silvera, Spencer Tracy, and Canada Lee, among others. (p. 144)

7. His parents viewed the film, *No Way Out*, at a Nassau movie theater in 1950. (p. 60)

8. Poitier reports that the actor John Cassavetes helped to reinforce Poitier's strong feelings about roles. Cassavetes told him never to do an artistic favor for a friend. Cassavetes said "You've got to have one area of your life where there's no room for compromise." (p. 147)

Rabbi Wolpe's Rebuttal (February 5, 2009)

IN HIS MOST RECENT BOOK, *Why Faith Matters* (1), Rabbi David J. Wolpe makes the case for religion and rebuts recent critiques of religion by a quartet of prominent atheists called the New Atheists. (2) This is a book that deserves a large audience among religious and seculars because it is accessible, well-argued, and thought-provoking.

One of Rabbi Wolpe's main objectives is to defend religion from the charge that religion is the main cause of violence in the world. He argues that violence is due not to religion but to human nature. (p. 43, p. 52) All of us, whether religious or secular, he says, are prone to hostility. (p. 69) The Rabbi concedes that the Crusades, the Inquisition, and 9/11 demonstrate that religion "is capable of great evil" (p. 53), but he insists that seculars who believe that there will be peace without religion are naïve. (p. 71) He notes that most ancient tribal societies were at war continuously (p. 50) and that the great empires in history, from the Persian to the Assyrian to the Greek to the Roman, give us a "chronicle of cruelty." (p. 51)

Further, he charges, secular movements have brought explosions of violence, not peace and love. One this score he cites the excesses of the French Revolution and the millions of deaths at the hands of Mao in China, Stalin in Russia, and Pol Pot in Cambodia. (pp. 65-67)(3) Here he is right on target. On the other hand, Rabbi Wolpe is silent on a crucial issue: if humans are aggressive by nature, and God is the architect of human nature, doesn't God deserve a measure of blame for violence?

One part of Rabbi Wolpe's case for religion disappoints me – his use of Bertrand Russell as the poster child of secularism. Russell made important contributions to moral theory, logic, mathematics, and literature, but as the Rabbi properly points out, his private life was a "mess," with four marriages, "proudly proclaimed infidelities," and abandonment of his children. (p. 6) Russell prompted young David Wolpe to abandon his faith for ten years. Later, when the Rabbi discovered that his hero was irresponsible, he concluded that a life without religion is lonely, selfish, and hedonistic. (p. 61) This is a classic case of hasty generalization. Russell is as representative of secularism as pedophile clerics are representative of religion. Has Rabbi Wolpe never heard of seculars such as baseball Hall-of-Famer Ted Williams, media mogul Ted Turner, golfer Annika Sorenstam, investor Warren Buffet, actor Angelina Jolie, TV personality Andy Rooney, composer Irving Berlin, inventor Thomas Edison, computer entrepreneur Bill Gates, cyclist Lance Armstrong, and countless others, whose talent, service, and generosity have enriched lives near and far?

Rabbi Wolpe's book also includes a series of insightful criticisms of what he views as the overblown attempt by the New Atheists to explain all human behavior through evolutionary theory. For instance, he argues that if, as Richard Dawkins holds, the key to human behavior is the drive to reproduce our genes, why do wealthier families who can afford many children have so few, and why do so many women opt for abortion when adoption is available. (p. 30)

Whether you are religious or not, you'll find much of value in David Wolpe's *Why Faith Matters*.

---

1. See David J. Wolpe, *Why Faith Matters*, HarperOne, 2008, with a Foreword by Rick Warren. References to this book here are by page number. Wolpe is not alone in replying to the New Atheists. Among other replies is John F. Haught, *God and the New Atheism: A Critical Response to Dawkins, Harris, and Hitchens*.

2. He specifically identifies Sam Harris, Christopher Hitchens, Richard Dawkins, and Daniel Dennett. See Sam Harris, *The End of Faith* and *Letter to a Christian Nation*; Christopher Hitchens, *God is Not Great*; Richard Dawkins, *The God Delusion*; and Daniel Dennett, *Breaking the Spell*.

3. He also mentions Hitler's Germany as an atheist regime (p. 67) but that is debatable.

Faith Healing and Children
(February 19, 2009)

SUPPOSE A CHILD IN THE United States dies from a medically treatable condition because her parents prayed over her but did not take her to a doctor. Will criminal charges be filed against the parents? In most cases, no. American prosecutors have found it difficult to obtain convictions in such cases because the laws in most states exempt parents from prosecution for child neglect, child abuse, and manslaughter if their religion mandates spiritual healing. The statute in Wisconsin is typical. It says that a parent cannot be found guilty of a crime if "he or she provides a child with treatment (for sickness) by spiritual means alone...in lieu of medical or surgical treatment...in accordance with (a bona fide) religious method of healing." (1) Such statutes were adopted by states in the mid-1970s at the behest of the Department of Health, Education, and Welfare when it issued new regulations which exempted parents who practice spiritual healing from criminal charges. States were required to adopt this exemption to receive federal funds for child protection programs. (2) Even though HEW rescinded this exemption in 1983, exemptions remain on the books in more than forty states. (3)

Many groups have called for the repeal of these exemptions, among them the United Methodist Church, the National District Attorneys Association, the American Medical Association, and dozens of child advocacy groups. (4) Thus far, however, only Massachusetts, Colorado, South Dakota, Maryland, and Hawaii have repealed them. (5)

Those who practice spiritual healing take their cue from the Epistle of James in the Bible. Chapter 5, verse 14, asks "Are any among you sick?" and then prescribes prayer by elders and anointing with oil. (6) Historian Shawn Francis Peters says that faith-healers interpret this passage to mean that Christians should turn only to God and never to doctors to heal the sick. (7) Many who promote healing by prayer alone, Peters says, believe that prayer is superior to medical science, (8) and that it drives out the root cause of illness – Satan. (9) This abandonment of medicine by faith-healers contrasts sharply with most well-known advocates of prayer as therapeutic who call for prayer and traditional medical care. Larry Dossey, Herbert Benson, Harold Koenig, William Parker, Randolph Byrd, and Dale Matthews are among this group. (10)

In *When Prayer Fails: Faith Healing, Children, and the Law*, Peters shows that thousands of children have died needlessly in England and America due to lack of medical treatment, and that prosecutors, the public, and the media in these two countries increasingly tolerate refusal of medical care by adults on the grounds of religious liberty but increasingly object to parents denying medical care to their children. We have reached a point in America where the Congress needs to adopt a law similar to one in England which provides severe penalties if a parent fails to provide "adequate food, clothing, medical aid, or lodging for (a) child…" (11) If and when our government sends a signal that it is ready to follow the British lead, we can expect vigorous resistance from various faith-healer groups, especially the Church of Christian Science. That resistance must be overcome for the sake of the most vulnerable among us, our children.

---

1. Shawn Francis Peters, *When Prayer Fails: Faith Healing, Children, and the Law*, Oxford University Press, 2008, pp. 14-15. References to this book here are by page number.
2. Peters, p. 116. Rita Swan, head of the child advocacy group, CHILD, avers that the HEW exemption was promoted by Christian Science staff in the Nixon White House including H.R. Haldeman and John Erlichman. See Peters, p. 116.

3. Peters, pp. 112-116. Also, see "Christian Science," *Wikipedia*.
4. Peters, p. 15.
5. Peters, pp. 197-202.
6. Peters, p. 30.
7. Peters, p. 30.
8. Oddly, the playwright George Bernard Shaw, himself a religious skeptic, came to the defense of faith-healers in Great Britain who were being harassed by prosecutors by accusing the government of a double standard. He noted that "hundreds of children (in the care of doctors) die every day" but few doctors were charged with crimes. See Peters, p. 60 and p. 80.
9. Peters, p. 33, p. 72, and pp. 78-79.
10. Peters, pp. 42-44.
11. Quoted in Peters, p. 53.

John Haught and the New Atheists
(March 5, 2009)

JOHN F. HAUGHT IS A Roman Catholic theologian who specializes in religion and science and who has served on the faculty at Georgetown University for most of his career. His new book, *God and the New Atheism*, is a reply to recent assaults on religion by three popular religious skeptics – Richard Dawkins, Sam Harris, and Christopher Hitchens. (1) Let's focus on three of the many issues which Haught raises.

Firstly, Haught charges that the unholy trio has only a superficial grasp of religion. (2) For them, Haught says, religion means Biblical literalism, creationism, and terrorism, "the most extreme forms of rabid religiosity." (3) As the New Atheists "unveil religion at its absolute ugliest," he says, they altogether ignore both theology and religious moderates. (4) In doing so, he writes, they miss the nuanced interpretations of religion of "biblically informed, critically reflective, religious thinkers" such as Paul Tillich, Alfred North Whitehead, Paul Ricoeur, Bernard Lonergan, and Karl Rahner, among others. (5) Had they done their theological homework, Haught says, they would have discovered that these seminal figures long ago critiqued and repudiated the literalist, anti-scientific, and violent expressions of religion which the New Atheists ridicule so tirelessly in their books.

Secondly, Haught says that the New Atheists commit methodological errors when they proclaim, on the one hand, that "science alone can be trusted to put our minds in touch with reality" (6) and, on the other hand, that a scientific explanation makes a religious one superfluous. (7) On the first claim, while conceding the importance of science, Haught observes that we often abandon the objective, analytical stance of science to discover reality. For instance, we rely on subjective, interpersonal experience to learn that we love a person and that he or she loves us. (8) The same happens, he says, in our encounter with a work of art or with beauty in nature. (9) Indeed, according to Haught, it is in our subjective intuition that we encounter a divine "Thou" reaching out to us. (10) On the second claim, Haught argues that science does not trump religion because science and religion offer non-competing levels of interpretation. (11) Consider, he suggests, that a page in his book can be seen simultaneously as marks made by a printing press, as words used by him to convey ideas, and as the result of his publisher's request for a reply to the New Atheists. (12) Similarly, he notes, nature can be seen simultaneously without contradiction as unfolding dramas of natural selection *and* divinely inspired liberation. (13)

Thirdly, Haught argues that the New Atheists' disdain for faith is paradoxical in that the scientific enterprise is permeated by faith. For instance, he observes, scientists take it on faith that they can trust their minds, that nature is intelligible, and that truth is worth seeking. (14) Further, he adds, theology, not science, furnishes the only plausible justification of these assumptions, namely, they manifest the handiwork of a loving God. (15)

Haught's reply to the New Atheists reflects his deep knowledge of science and theology. This is why both seculars and religious should read it and why it deserves a serious response by one or more of the New Atheists.

---

1. John F. Haught, *God and the New Atheism: A Critical Response to Dawkins, Harris, and Hitchens*, Westminster John Knox Press, 2008. References to this book here are by page number.
2. Page 36.
3. Page 28.
4. Page 29.
5. Page xii.
6. Page 41.

7. Page 83.
8. Pages 45-46.
9. Page 45.
10. Page 54, page 86.
11. Page 84.
12. Pages 84-85.
13. Page 85.
14. Page 46.
15. Pages 50-52; page 97.

Christopher Hitchens on Religion
(March 19, 2009)

THE ATTACK DOG AMONG THE New Atheists is on the loose again. Christopher Hitchens has published another in-your-face critique of religion entitled *God is Not Great: How Religion Poisons Everything*. (1) Hitchens offers the reader a long list of indictments of religion, including the following:

- The teachings of religion about the origin of the cosmos and the origin and development of biological species contradict well-established science.
- All of the traditional arguments for the existence of God have significant defects.
- All of the traditional attempts to explain how the enormous suffering that afflicts sentient creatures is compatible with an all-powerful and all-good God are an exercise in sophistry.
- Religious scriptures amount to myths and fables that are contradictory, unhistorical, and, in the case of the Quran, largely plagiarized.
- Religion is patriarchal and denigrates women.
- Religion inflames tribal and ethnic hostility.
- Religions are intolerant of those who reject or question them, including seculars, heretics, and adherents of other religions.
- The moral codes which religions promote are shallow and incomplete, and in some cases, "positively immoral." (2)

- Religion inflicts physical and psychological harm on children.
- Religion finds a problem for every sensible solution in the Middle East, Africa, Asia, and elsewhere.
- And prayer doesn't work.

These are traditional criticisms of religion in the vast literature addressing it over the centuries. Most seculars endorse them. In fact, many believers endorse some of them. For fundamentalists, though, they are the teachings of Satan.

God is Not Great is similar to Hitchens' previous writings on religion. The tone is strident and dismissive. If you're looking for a conciliatory or respectful attitude toward believers, you won't find it in this book. How refreshing it would be if Hitchens had included mention of some redeeming features of religion such as these:

- A religion can change for the better. For instance, in the United States 175 years ago, thousands of clergy endorsed slavery; today none does. And for generations Protestants and Catholics in Northern Ireland carried on a bloody, senseless civil war; today a peace accord between these groups is holding up despite recent attempts by domestic terrorists to destroy it;
- Religion has contributed to important social change in some parts of the world. For instance, Gandhi's Hinduism figured prominently in the struggle for the independence of India and King's Christianity figured prominently in the U.S. civil rights struggle; (3)
- Religious organizations provide valuable humanitarian services to people in need. For instance, on the national level we have Habitat for Humanity, Goodwill Industries, Catholic Charities, the Society of St. Vincent de Paul, and St. Jude Children's Research Hospital, among others, and on the local level we have Beatitude House, Potter's Wheel, and Angela's Place, among others; and
- Thousands of American schools and colleges with religious affiliations have educated millions over the generations and many of these

colleges – Georgetown, Notre Dame, and Boston College are good examples – have deserved reputations as outstanding institutions of higher education. (And let's not forget that Harvard, Yale, and most other Ivy League schools were originally founded to train clergy.)

Finally, Hitchens mentions but downplays the harm produced by secular regimes in the past century such as Mao's China, Stalin's Soviet Union, and Pol Pot's Cambodia. (4)

If you want to read a more balanced, less rhetorical critique of religion, take a look at *The Transcendental Temptation*. This classic was published 23 years ago by philosopher Paul Kurtz, a much kinder, gentler atheist than Hitchens.

---

1. Twelve, Hatchette Book Group USA, 2007. References to this book here are by page number.
2. Hitchens, p. 205.
3. In fact, Hitchens insists that Mohandas Gandhi was only a minor force in the successful drive for independence in India and that Hinduism had little impact on his behavior. (See p. 184) Further, he informs us that Christianity provided no inspiration for Dr. Martin Luther King, Jr., in the U.S. civil rights struggle. (See p. 180) This amounts to historical revisionism.
4. Hitchens acknowledges that the excesses of communist dictators caused him to abandon the Marxism of his youth. See page 151. On the record of secular regimes, see Rabbi David J. Wolpe, *Why Faith Matters*, pp. 51-67. It is interesting to note that Hitchens has gone through multiple identities including Anglican, Methodist, Marxist, Greek Orthodox, Jewish, and most recently atheist. One wonders if he's finished. See p. 195.

Ted Kennedy's Legacy (April 9, 2009)

A TEAM OF REPORTERS AND an editor from *The Boston Globe* have published a book entitled *Last Lion: The Fall and Rise of Ted Kennedy* which gives us a thorough, objective study of Joseph and Rose Kennedy's youngest child. (1)

The reader will find much that is familiar in the *Last Lion*. Ted was born into a family of wealth and privilege in 1932 when his mother was forty-one because, as a devout Catholic, she refused to use birth control. (p. 3) Husband Joe was often away making money, courting women, including actress Gloria Swanson, or serving as FDR's ambassador to Great Britain. (p. 17) Rose agreed to ignore Joe's adultery in exchange for what some euphemistically call "retail therapy," that is, shopping to her heart's content in the United States and Europe. (p. 29) Also, Joe set up a $1 million trust fund for each of his children in the hope that lifetime financial security would free them to devote themselves to public service. (p. 17)

Further, we learn that as Ted grew up, unlike his siblings, he struggled in school. His parents transferred him so often that by age eleven he had attended ten schools. (p. 26) Despite his mediocre academic record, Ted followed his brothers Jack and Bobby to Harvard where he was suspended during his first year for cheating on a Spanish test. (p. 38) After a stint in the U.S. Army, he returned to Harvard, completed his degree, and, following the family tradition, enrolled in law school at the

University of Virginia where he and his partner eventually won the moot court competition. (p. 53) We also learn that after the death of Jack and Bobby, Ted became a surrogate father to their children with mixed results. After his first marriage failed, Ted married Vicki Reggie, a divorcee with two children, with whom he built a stable marriage which thrives today. (p. 290) We also learn much about Chappaquiddick but we still get no credible explanation of why the Senator waited nine hours to report the fatal accident to the local police. (pp. 145-168)

The reader of the *Last Lion* will also find some new and surprising information about Senator Kennedy's legislative record. During his forty-seven years in the Senate, he has authored some 2,500 bills, 300 of which are law. (p. 396, p. 403) He has played a pivotal role in the passage of virtually every law in the past half century in civil rights, health care, immigration, and education. His achievements include the Americans with Disabilities Act; Head Start; the Women, Infants, and Children program; Health Maintenance Organizations; the No Child Left Behind Law; increases in financial aid for college students and for cancer research; the Immigration Act of 1965; the Ryan White Act for AIDS research; and hundreds of others. Understandably, Senator John McCain has described Ted as "the most effective member of the Senate." (p. 387) Other members from both sides of the aisle have echoed this tribute, including Orrin Hatch of Utah. (pp. 322-337, p. 387) (2)

Although many will remember Ted Kennedy for his family's tragedies and his personal excesses, his enduring legacy to the nation is a remarkable legislative record built on his personal charm and political savvy, his intense study of proposed legislation, his readiness to reach across the aisle, and his belief that half a loaf is better than none.

---

1. Simon & Schuster, 2009. Senator John McCain's characterization of Kennedy as "the last lion in the Senate" accounts for the title of the book. The reporters are Bella English, Neil Swidey, Jenna Russell, Sam Allis, Joseph P. Kahn, Susan Milligan, and Don Aucoin, and the editor is Peter S. Canellos. References to the book here are by page number.

2. Senator Hatch tells a story about a letter he received from a senior citizen in southern Utah which said: "Senator Hatch, when we heard you might run for office, we supported you. When you actually ran for office, we voted for you. And when we heard that you were friends with Senator Kennedy, we prayed for you." (p. 332)

American Religious Identification Survey 2008
(April 23, 2009)

LAST MONTH RESEARCHERS AT TRINITY College in Hartford, Connecticut, published the results of a national survey of beliefs about religion called the *American Religious Identification Survey,* or *ARIS* for short. This is the third such survey from this group over an eighteen year span. (1) Perhaps the most startling finding in *ARIS 2008* is about the Nones. That's N-O-N-E-S. The Nones are the non-religious among us. There are twenty million more Nones today than in 1990, an increase of 138%, and the percentage of Nones has jumped from 8.2% to 15% of the population. (p. 3) Indeed, Nones are the only group on the American religious landscape which has increased in numbers and percentage in every state in the past two decades. (p. 17)

Here are some of the survey's other findings:

1. While the majority of Americans self-identify as Christian, and the number of Christians in the nation has increased since 1990 by 22 million, the percentage of Christians in the adult population has dropped by more than 10%. (p. 3)
2. Mainline Protestants dropped form 18.7% to 12.0% of the population. (p. 5) (2), and Baptists dropped from 19.3% to 12.9% of the population. (p. 5) At the same time, the number of Americans who self-identify as "generic Christians" or "non-denominational

Christians" rose from less than 800,000 in 1990 to more than 8 million in 2008. (pp. 5-6)
3. 27% of Americans say that they do not expect to have a religious funeral or service when they die. (p. 10)
4. On the subject of divorce, except for Jews and Mormons, whose divorce rates are typically low, Nones compare favorably to believers. The divorce rate for Catholics, Baptists, and Nones is 11%; other Christian groups, such as Pentecostals and generic Christians, have a higher divorce rate. (p. 13)
5. The influx of Hispanics, now the nation's largest minority, (p. 15) has contributed significantly to a huge increase in the Catholic populations of California, Texas, and Florida. (3) Over the past two decades, the Catholic population rose from 29% to 37% in California, from 23% to 32% in Texas, and from 23% to 27% in Florida. (pp. 20-22) Migration of Catholics from the northeast and the mid-west also contributed to this trend. (pp. 20-22)
6. The percentage of Catholics in New England declined from 50% in 1990 to 36% in 2008. At the same time, the percentage of Nones in New England grew from 8% to 22%. (p. 18)

Does all this mean that we are witnessing "The Decline and Fall of Christian America," as the cover of a recent issue (April 13, 2009) of *Newsweek* magazine suggests? Hardly. A significant majority of Americans remain Christian, more and larger mega-churches are built each month, Christian media reach over a hundred million of the faithful daily, Christian groups spend hundreds of millions of dollars each year to proselytize and to shape public policy, and, as is the case today, the occupant of the White House for the foreseeable future will be a person of faith.

---

1. The 1990 survey was published in 1993 under the title *One Nation Under God: Religion in Contemporary American Society*, and the 2001 survey was published in 2006 under the title *Religion in a Free Market: Religious and Non-Religious Americans*. The principal investigator for all three is Barry Kosmin, a sociologist. For the 2008 survey, see www.americanreligionsurvey-aris.org. *ARIS 2008* follows on the heels of the *U.S. Religious Landscape Survey* which was

published in February of this year. This survey found that a) 28% of Americans have left the religion of their youth for another religion or no religion, b) the fastest growing segment of the population is those who say they are religious but connect with no particular church and those who say that they are atheist or agnostic, c) more than one in ten Catholics born in the United States are no longer Catholic, and d) those embracing Protestantism – mainline, evangelical, and historically black – have declined to a bare majority – 51%. See my WYSU commentary on this survey at www.wysu.org. Click on "Public Affairs," then "Commentaries." Both surveys have been reported extensively in the media and *ARIS 2008* serves as the basis of the cover story in *Newsweek*, April 13, pp. 34-38.

2. Mainline Protestants are Methodists, Lutherans, Presbyterians, Episcopalians, Anglicans, and members of the United Church of Christ.

3. Surprisingly, the percentage of Catholics among Hispanics in America has declined from 66% in 1990 to 59% in 2008. Many Hispanics have gravitated to generic Christianity (from 8% in 1990 to 11% in 2008) and to the Nones (from 6% in 1990 to 12% in 2008). (p. 14).

Redemption at Starbucks (May 14, 2009)

MICHAEL GILL WAS BORN INTO a family of wealth and privilege. After graduating from college, he took a position with advertising giant, J. Walter Thompson. There he moved up the corporate ladder from copywriter to creative director to executive vice president. His accounts included Ford, Burger King, Christian Dior, the United States Marine Corps, IBM, and USAir. So devoted was Gill to his employer that he abandoned his family on a Christmas morning when a phone call from Ford summoned him to Detroit.

Then, after twenty-five years, the unthinkable happened. A young corporate executive whom he had mentored invited him to lunch where she announced coldly: "We have to let you go, Michael." (1) His "loyalty" had been rewarded with a "pink slip." (2) At the age of 53, with a wife and four children to support, he was suddenly out of work.

Gill tried to market himself to his old clients as a consultant but that didn't work. Then matters went from bad to worse. He had a short-lived affair which produced his fifth child, his marriage collapsed, his four older children ostracized him, he suffered an 80% hearing loss in his left ear due to a brain tumor, and, despite the $2,000 suits that he wore, he was nearly broke. Desperate and depressed, he stopped at Starbucks in Manhattan to figure out his next step. As he sat alone, a young African-American woman, who had pegged him from a distance as a man down on his luck, approached him. "Would you like a job?" she asked. She said that her name was Crystal, that she was manager of the Starbucks at 93rd and Broadway, and that she was interviewing applicants to join her team of "Partners." Thus began an improbable second career which Gill chronicles in his book *How Starbucks Saved My Life*.

Crystal's Starbucks became the stage on which Gill sought redemption. How ironic. A white Yale-educated aristocrat, the son of an editor of *The New Yorker* magazine who grew up in a mansion, got a second chance in life thanks to a compassionate young black woman who never knew her father and whose drug-addicted mother died young. It was a steep learning curve for Gill. He had to learn the names of dozens of coffee drinks and how to make them. He had to learn about the different scones, muffins, cookies, cakes, donuts, bagels, and croissants. He had to learn every job in the store. He had to learn the names of all the regular "Guests," or customers, and their favorite drinks. He had to learn to *ask* his Partners for help instead of issuing commands as he had done before. He had to overcome his life-long aversion to math so that he could work the register. He had to learn to work as a co-equal among mostly African-Americans who were much younger than he. He had to learn to treat all Guests with respect, including the homeless. He had to learn to overcome self-pity and reconnect with his children. Remarkably, with Crystal's guidance, he became productive and valued, he found dignity in work for the first time, and he was genuinely happy.

Today Michael Gills remains with Starbucks in what he calls "the best job" he has ever had. His journey of self-renewal can be a source of inspiration for anyone whose career has taken a sudden jolt. Unfortunately, in today's economy, there are millions who need it.

---

1. Michael Gates Gill, *How Starbucks Saved My Life*, Gotham Books, 2007, p. 11.
2. Page 29.

Suicide Terrorism (May 28, 2009)

SUICIDE TERRORISM IN TODAY'S WORLD began with an attack by Hezbollah against the U.S. marine barracks in Lebanon in 1983. That attack drove Israel, France, and the United States out of Lebanon and convinced many groups, including the PLO, Islamic Jihad, al-Qaeda, and the Tamil Tigers, among others, that suicide missions can be an effective tool to achieve their goals. (1) As suicide attacks proliferated, millions puzzled over what prompts a person to become a suicide terrorist. The popular speculations are that they are religious extremists, victims of poverty, impressionable youth, mentally ill, poorly educated, or low-achievers. (2) Based on a study of more than four-hundred suicide terrorists from 1980 to 2003 by Robert A. Pape and his associates from the University of Chicago, which is entitled *Dying to Win: The Strategic Logic of Suicide Terrorism*, we know now that all of these explanations are mistaken. Here are some of the study's findings:

Firstly, the role of religion as a motivation to suicide terrorism is exaggerated. Fifty-seven percent of suicide attacks around the world during the period studied were perpetrated by seculars. For instance, in Lebanon, thirty of thirty-eight known suicide terrorists "were affiliated with groups opposed to Islamic fundamentalism." (3) Further, very few of those suicide attackers who were religious were inspired to violence by their religious beliefs. (4)

Secondly, most suicide terrorists are not impressionable adolescents. Only 13% of suicide terrorists were between the ages of fifteen to eighteen.

55% were between the ages of nineteen to twenty-three and the remaining 32% were age twenty-four or older. (5)

Thirdly, suicide terrorists as a group possess a favorable socioeconomic status. They score far better on educational attainment and income than the overall population of their countries. (6)

And fourthly, "The main purpose of suicide terrorism is to use the threat of punishment to compel a target government to change policy, and most especially to cause democratic states to withdraw their forces from land the terrorists perceive as their national homeland." (7) These patriotic sentiments are typically shared across the local population and explain popular support for suicide terrorism. (8)

Based on these findings, Professor Pape issues recommendations as to how the United States can defeat suicide terrorism. His principal one is that the U.S. needs to withdraw its troops from majority Muslim nations and give up any hope of transforming them. (9) As it does this, the U.S. should "work with Iraq, Saudi Arabia, and other Persian Gulf states to ensure that they maintain the critical infrastructure for a rapid return of U.S. forces should that prove necessary" (10) and it should cultivate "the friendliest possible relations" with Iran. (11) Following this policy, Pape predicts, will "suck the oxygen out of the atmosphere that breeds anti-American suicide terrorism." (12)

Pape and his associates deserve credit for producing a fact-based study which demythologizes suicide terrorism and provides wise counsel to political leaders. I hope that the White House and the Pentagon are paying attention.

---

1. Robert A. Pape, *Dying to Win: The Strategic Logic of Suicide Terrorism*, Random House, 2005, pp. 73-74. References here to this book are by page number.
2. *Dying to Win*, p. 200.
3. *Dying to Win*, p. 205.
4. *Dying to Win*, p. 210.
5. *Dying to Win*, p. 207.

6. *Dying to Win*, pp. 212-213. The research team writes:

> "The bottom line, then, is that suicide attackers are not mainly poor, uneducated, immature religious zealots or social losers. Instead, suicide attackers are normally well-educated workers from both religious and secular backgrounds. Especially given their education, they resemble the kind of politically conscious individuals who might join a grassroots movement more than they do (resemble) wayward adolescents or religious fanatics." (p. 216)

7. *Dying to Win*, p. 27. The study repeats this finding in many places. See p. 38, p. 108, p. 126, and p. 237.
8. *Dying to Win*, pp. 48-49.
9. *Dying to Win*, p. 241.
10. *Dying to Win*, p. 247.
11. *Dying to Win*, p. 248.
12. *Dying to Win*, p. 249.

President Obama's U-Turn (June 11, 2009)

IN 1899 THE U.S. SUPREME Court issued an important decision on whether government may constitutionally grant public funds to a religious organization. In *Bradfield v. Roberts* the Court ruled that the District of Columbia could pay a hospital in Washington operated by an order of Catholic nuns to provide a secular service to the poor – health care. (1) Under this ruling, many religious groups received public funds without controversy year after year. Typically such groups did not seek to proselytize their clients, only to serve them, and used no religious test in hiring and firing. When George W. Bush was elected President, however, he created a White House Office of Faith-Based and Community Initiatives with the intent to distribute much more tax dollars to religious organizations and he issued executive orders which changed past practice. Now such groups could mix sectarian and secular activities and could use religious criteria to hire and fire. (2) Challenges to the Bush program in the courts were unsuccessful.

As a result, many who were opposed to President Bush's faith-based programs turned to candidate Barack Obama for hope and he seemed poised to deliver relief if elected. For instance, in a speech in Ohio on July 1, 2008, he said:

> First, if you get a federal grant, you can't use that money to proselytize to the people that you help and you can't discriminate against them – or against the people you hire – on the basis of their religion.

Second, federal dollars that go directly to churches, temples, and mosques can only be used on secular programs. And we'll also ensure that taxpayer dollars only go to those programs that actually work. (3)

Based in part on these affirmations, Mr. Obama won solid support from civil libertarians and other supporters of separation of church and state, including millions who identify themselves as non-religious. No fewer than 75% of the secular community voted for him. (4)

Since his election, however, Mr. Obama seems to have done a U-turn. He has left the Bush executive orders intact, he has retained the Bush White House Office of Faith-Based and Community Initiatives, and he has hired a 26-year old Pentecostal minister to run it. Seculars are disappointed and angry. For example, the current issue of *Free Inquiry*, a magazine that has a huge readership in the secular community, features no fewer than five articles critical of President Obama's early decisions on faith-based programs. (5) Seculars are not the only ones concerned. The Pew Research Center reports that 73% of Americans object to religious groups being allowed to discriminate in hiring and firing, and 61% oppose proselytizing of clients by religious groups who receive public funds. (6)

President Obama should either shut down the faith-based programs altogether or issue new rules to prevent proselytizing and discrimination in employment in them. He should also order that such programs be evaluated by the General Accounting Office or some other competent agency to determine their effectiveness. Only programs which successfully achieve their secular goals should be refunded.

---

1. See Rob Boston, "The Faith-Based Initiative 2.0: Can We Unplug It?" *Free Inquiry* June/July 2009, p. 32.
2. President Bush denied that he authorized proselytizing but his failure to require monitoring of expenditures permitted and encouraged sectarian activities.
3. Quoted in Rob Boston, p. 34.

4. Rob Boston, p. 34.

5. See pp. 26-40, *Free Inquiry* June/July 2009. The authors are Daniel Horowitz and Ruth Mitchell, who present an official position paper of the Council for Secular Humanism; Rob Boston, a senior policy analyst at Americans United for Separation of Church and State; Susan Jacoby, a specialist in American intellectual history; D.J. Groethe, an associate editor of *Free Inquiry*; and Ronald A. Lindsay, a lawyer and bioethicist who is CEO of the Center for Inquiry/Transnational.

6. Rob Boston, p. 34.

Karl Rove (June 25, 2009)

IF YOU WOULD LIKE TO learn about a contemporary admirer of Machiavelli, take a look at a book by James Moore and Wayne Slater, two long-time observers of the American political landscape, entitled *The Architect: Karl Rove and the Master Plan for Absolute Power*. (1)

Moore and Slater inform us that Rove signed on to the Republican agenda while still a student and that he left college early to pursue his passion for politics. After a time as a leader of the national Young Republicans, he became a political consultant in Texas where he established a direct-mail company and compiled a long list of generous donors to Republican candidates and causes. Although he worked for many candidates, he saw in George W. Bush, whose religion helped him defeat alcoholism, the ideal candidate for state and national office. Rove not only guided Bush to two terms as Governor of Texas and two as President of the United States but he resuscitated a dormant Republican Party in Texas and many other states. How Rove accomplished all this is the focus of Moore and Slater's book.

The authors argue convincingly that for Rove whether a tactic is legal or moral is peripheral to whether it works. Among his favorite tactics is attacking opponents though surrogates. Anne Richards in 1994, John McCain in 2000, and John Kerry in 2004, among others, were victims of this strategy. In Kerry's case, the Swift Boat Veterans for Truth, which was bankrolled by three Texas Republican billionaires, including T. Boone Pickens, sowed seeds of doubt among many voters about Kerry.

The authors also credit Rove with exploiting religion in an unprecedented way. This is all the more remarkable when you consider that Rove is an agnostic, one who holds that we can neither prove nor disprove the existence of God and should therefore remain neutral on the issue. (2) To Rove religion is simply a political tool. He concluded early in his career, based on years of careful polling, that the more regularly a person attends church, the more likely that person is to vote Republican. He therefore used religion to energize religious conservatives to register, vote, volunteer, and contribute to Bush and other Republicans. He collaborated with Ralph Reed from the Christian Coalition and hundreds of other conservative religious leaders across the nation. He convinced them that George W. Bush shares their values and that, if elected, he will appoint judges who will overturn *Roe v. Wade* and he will propose a Constitutional Amendment outlawing gay marriage.

There are fascinating paradoxes in Rove's use of the religious right's antipathy to homosexuality in campaigns. One is that many Republican homosexuals, both those who had come out and those who had not, acquiesced in this strategy as necessary to win and to advance the overall Republican agenda. Among them was Ken Mehlman, chairman of the national Republican Party. (3) Another is that Rove had homosexuality in his own family. Rove's stepfather, whom he loved and respected, eventually came out of the closet. This may have been a factor in the later suicide of Rove's mother.

You'll find dozens more surprises in *The Architect*. Whether you consider Rove a hero or a villain, the book is worth reading because Rove is without peer as a political consultant in America today. And, at the age of fifty-nine, he is likely to ply his trade for many more years.

---

1. Crown Publishers, New York, 2006.
2. See page 19 and page 22, among others.
3. See pages 63-65 et ff.

Carrie Fisher (July 9, 2009)

EXCEPT FOR THE 1950S, WHEN she and her brother graced the covers of magazines and tabloids by the dozens with her celebrity parents, Debbie Reynolds and Eddie Fisher, Carrie Fisher's first exposure to the public was in 1977 as Princess Leia in the iconic film *Star Wars* which she began filming at age 19. Between these publicity spikes Carrie has largely moved under the radar despite the fact that she has produced an impressive body of work as an actor and writer. She has appeared in twenty films, she has written three screenplays and four novels, one of which, *Postcards from the Edge*, was adapted into a film directed by Mike Nichols and starring Shirley MacLaine and Meryl Streep, and she is one of Hollywood's top script editors. In her most recent literary product, a reminiscence entitled *Wishful Drinking*, which is also the title of her one-person stage show, Carrie gives us a frank look at her, her family, and the culture of Hollywood. (1)

Having known or read about dozens of dysfunctional people, I find Carrie Fisher without peer. This woman is addicted to alcohol and drugs and suffers from bipolar disorder which causes her severe depression, mercurial mood swings, and suicidal urges. She has spent many months over the years in a succession of rehab programs and many years in therapy with a string of psychiatrists. Not long ago she underwent three weeks of electroconvulsive treatments, or ECT, which caused severe memory loss. (2) She also reports that drug usage is the norm in

Hollywood. For instance, her father smokes four joints a day, prompting her to nickname him Puff Daddy, Cary Grant experimented with LSD in the sixties, (3) and Harrison Ford had a stash of pot during the filming of *Star Wars*. (4)

Moreover, she has been unlucky in love. Carrie's first marriage, to singer/songwriter Paul Simon, ended in divorce, as did her second marriage, to Brian Lourd, father of her daughter Billie, her only child, who left her for a man. Although she candidly acknowledges an active sex life with multiple partners, including Senator Chris Dodd, she remains single.

It is difficult to avoid blaming Carrie Fisher's problems on her family and her upbringing, although she balks at this. After all, her father abandoned her mother for Elizabeth Taylor when Carrie was only two years old, leaving her mother, who was at the peak of her busy career, to raise her and her brother, and her parents practiced serial monogamy for decades. Her father showed up only once or twice a year as she grew up and her mother's husbands included two who drained her mother's assets. Also, as a child, she was abducted and raped by a boy whom she knew. Further, she quit high school at her mother's bidding to appear in minor roles in her mother's stage shows.

The culture of Hollywood which Carrie Fisher describes in *Wishful Drinking* is stacked against a child's prospects of normalcy. Hollywood attracts an inordinately high percentage of narcissists and hedonists who produce shaky bonds and at risk children, many of whom grow up to mimic their parents. This aside, *Wishful Drinking* is brilliantly written and features a type of gallows humor that is remarkable given the sad story that Fisher tells. Hopefully, Carrie Fisher has conquered her demons and can now turn her considerable talents to writing plays and novels that will entertain millions.

---

1. Simon & Schuster, 2008. References to this book here are by page number.
2. In one rehab program, Carrie met another celebrity patient – Ozzie Osbourne. (p. 141) Due to the memory loss, the following message from Ms. Fisher greets her callers: "Hello and welcome to Carrie's voice mail. Due to recent electroconvulsive therapy, please pay close attention

to the following options. Leave your name, number, and a brief history of how Carrie knows you, and she'll get back to you if this jogs what's left of her memory. Thank you for calling and have a great day." (pp. 14-15)

3. Page 133.
4. Page 132.

Richard A. Clarke on National Security
(July 23, 2009)

RICHARD A. CLARKE SERVED SEVEN presidents in important national security posts from 1973 to 2003. His new book, *Your Government Failed You: Breaking the Cycle of National Security Disasters*, (1) is two things, an expansion of his earlier criticisms of President George W. Bush's track record in national security and a wide-ranging evaluation of the current state of national security.

Clarke focuses much of his attention on the current war in Iraq. His position is that the war was a mistake from the start, "a fool's errand" in his words, (2) which provided a recruiting windfall for al-Qaeda. Beyond this, he faults both the White House and the Pentagon for poor planning and execution. Specifically he charges that:

- They sent too few troops.
- Despite warnings by the CIA and the State Department, they failed to anticipate the insurgency, an unforgivable oversight after the debacle of Vietnam.
- They failed to equip many of our troops adequately.
- They filled key positions in the interim government with inexperienced Americans.

- They used torture in violation of domestic and international law, a tactic that undercut America's moral standing around the world.
- They failed to provide adequate medical treatment to tens of thousands of wounded soldiers when they were sent home for treatment.
- And, they developed no exit strategy. (3)

Iraq aside, Clarke charges that the overall security apparatus in the nation today is "dysfunctional." (4) On the topic of terrorism, for instance, he cites extensive evidence to show that most of the same vulnerabilities that existed on 9/11 exist today. A major cause of this, Clarke argues, is that we have sixteen distinct federal intelligence agencies which collectively spend $50 billion a year. There is little coordination among these "fiefdoms," he says, and they frequently duplicate efforts. Perhaps the most dramatic example of the lack of coordination which he cites is the fact that the CIA knew that two known al-Qaeda terrorists were in the United States eighteen months prior to 9/11 but it failed to pass along this information to other intelligence agencies. (5) Clarke reminds us that the most sensible solution to this problem, the appointment of a strong intelligence czar to oversee all intelligence agencies, which the 9/11 Commission recommended, was blocked by Donald Rumsfeld when he was Secretary of Defense. (6)

Does the relatively new Department of Homeland Security offer us any hope? In a word, according to Clarke, "No." It is an organizational nightmare, placing twenty-two agencies with fundamentally different missions under one umbrella; it excludes key intelligence agencies such as the FBI and the CIA; it is underfunded; and it has become the prime target of the "Beltway Bandits," the private defense and security companies surrounding Washington. (7) Clarke is not alone in this appraisal. The Government Accountability Office issued a virtually identical one in a report in 2007. (8)

Clarke's book, while depressing, deserves serious attention by all of us. To ignore the informed views of one of the most experienced and respected veterans of national intelligence service would be a disservice to ourselves, our children, and our children's children. (9)

---

1. RAC Enterprises, 2008. References to this book here are by page number.
2. Page 188.
3. Clarke also offers a critique of the planning and execution of the war in Afghanistan in several parts of the book which includes some of these same points. For instance, see page 51, pages 175-176, and page 199.
4. Page 137.
5. Pages 164-165.
6. Pages 138-140.
7. See pages 210-235.
8. Page 225.
9. While Clarke does not minimize the ongoing dangers of terrorism, he argues that the most serious threat to national security is climate change. See page 263 and pages 272-273.

Isaiah's Resilience (August 6, 2009)

IMAGINE A HEALTH AFFLICTION THAT ends a career but not a life: a surgeon contracts Parkinson's disease, a NASCAR driver goes blind, a world class sprinter acquires rheumatoid arthritis, or an orchestra conductor goes deaf. My last example is not hypothetical. It happened to Dr. Isaiah Jackson, music director of the Youngstown Symphony from 1996 to 2006.

Isaiah, as he likes to be called, came to the Mahoning Valley with impressive credentials:

- He had studied music since the age of four.
- He had earned degrees from Harvard, Stanford, and the Julliard School.
- His mentors included Leopold Stokowski and Leonard Bernstein.
- He had served conducting apprenticeships in major orchestras in the United States and Europe.
- He had been guest conductor of celebrated orchestras in Toronto, New York, Rome, Los Angeles, Taiwan, Dallas, Cleveland, Boston, Washington, Vienna, Geneva, Australia, the Soviet Union, Prague, Stockholm, Berlin, Hong Kong, Cape Town, and Israel.
- And he had served as music director of the University of Rochester Symphony, the Flint Symphony, The Royal Ballet in London, and the Dayton Philharmonic.

Audiences of the Youngstown Symphony at Powers Auditorium found Isaiah to be a Renaissance man at once erudite, witty, charming, and charismatic, who wielded the baton with grace, confidence, and energy. As is often the case with conductors, however, Isaiah's support within the organization faded as time passed due in part to personnel decisions that he made and critiques that he delivered during rehearsals, so that he had to move on before he wanted to.

Isaiah's hearing loss came in two stages. In September 1995 he lost hearing in his right ear and in June 2004 he lost hearing in his left ear, a victim of what is called Sudden Sensory-Neural Hearing Loss. Thus, for years he led two orchestras, the Youngstown Symphony and the Pro Arte Chamber Orchestra of Boston, with partial or total hearing loss, thanks to his resilience and to state-of-the-art hearing devices. His final performance as maestro was a concert in Boston in January 2007 which featured Yo-Yo Ma as guest artist.

A lesser person would be depressed and bitter after being wrenched from the podium after a hearing loss. This is not the case with Isaiah. He remains upbeat and engaged. His spouse Helen and their three children have been remarkably supportive, he finds strength in prayer, and he maintains a demanding professional schedule in the Boston area where he and Helen live. He is president of a family music education enterprise called "Rhythm, Rhyme, Results" which produces innovative hip-hop and rap tracks to teach math, science, social studies, and language arts to middle school students. He also teaches a course entitled *The Future of Music* at Harvard, he teaches conducting classes at the Berklee College of Music and the Longly School, and he offers private conducting lessons to undergraduate, graduate, and post-graduate students.

Isaiah has enriched the lives of hundreds of thousands of young and old over a career spanning four decades. Perhaps the most important contribution that he has made, though, is showing us how to cope with personal tragedy.*

* Note: The sources of information for this commentary are Dr. Jackson in a recent online interview, a *Wikipedia* article about Dr. Jackson, several musicians who worked with Dr. Jackson, and the commentator's own experience as coordinator of Dr. Jackson's appointment as Scholar-in-Residence in the College of Arts and Sciences at Youngstown State University from 2002 to 2008.

Cell Phones – A Moral Challenge
(August 20, 2009)

I SUBMIT A SIMPLE MORAL principle for your consideration. A person who poses an avoidable and unnecessary threat of harm to innocent people should take steps promptly to end the threat.

If you embrace this principle but you use a cell phone while driving, you should stop doing so because cell phones distract drivers and significantly increase the likelihood of accidents. This is clear from the extensive laboratory and road research on drivers and cell phones which was reported this summer in a series of articles in *The New York Times*. (1) Here are some of the revelations in this series:

- In 2003, in order to "avoid antagonizing members of Congress," the National Highway Traffic Safety Administration suppressed research that showed that cell phone usage by drivers was becoming a "serious and growing threat on America's roadways."
- Drivers significantly overestimate their ability to multitask.
- Cell phones are now the number one distraction for drivers in the United States.
- Drivers who use cell phones cause far more fatalities than drivers distracted by all other causes combined.
- Drivers who use cell phones are four times as likely to cause a crash as drivers who do not use them.

- Cell phone users who are sober perform in laboratory tests with the same driving efficiency as drivers who are legally drunk.
- Headsets and other hands-free phones do not materially reduce the risks of a crash because the conversation itself takes a driver's attention off the road.
- Cell phone distractions cause at least 2,000 traffic deaths a year and 330,000 accidents a year.
- In the United States at any given moment 12% of drivers are using cell phones to talk, text, or e-mail.
- Drivers who text while driving often focus on their screens instead of the road for stretches of more than five seconds.
- Finally, truck drivers who text while driving are twenty-three times more likely to have an accident than when they are not texting.

One of the ironies surrounding the use of cell phones while driving is that a high percentage of the very same people who acknowledge that using cell phones while driving is dangerous admit that they continue to do so anyhow. This includes people who caused accidents in the past because they were distracted by their cell phones. (2)

Despite the proven dangers of cell phone usage by drivers, there is no imminent prospect of legal reform. Cell phones are so popular that legislators are reluctant to take a stand for safety over convenience. This year one-hundred seventy bills restricting cell phone usage while driving were introduced in the various states but only ten were adopted. One reason for this is that legislators themselves typically use cell phones while driving. Another is that the cell phone industry lobbies effectively against bans. Moreover, where there are legal restrictions, enforcement is usually lax; for instance, taxi drivers in New York City largely ignore the city's ten-year old ban on the use of cell phones by cabbies and usually the police don't interfere. (3)

So, be proactive. Protect yourself, your passengers, and drivers and passengers in other vehicles. Pull over to a safe spot before you use your cell phone. It is the responsible thing to do. If you wait for government to cower you into doing so, you may wait a long, long time. Meanwhile, thousands of people will suffer or die needlessly. And you or a loved one could be one of them.

---

1. See *The New York Times*, July 19, 2009, July 21, 2009, July 28, 2009, and August 4, 2009.
2. For instance, see the case of Christopher Hill in *The New York Times*, July 19, 2008.
3. See *The New York Times*, August 4, 2009.

John Stuart Mill on Women's Rights
(September 3, 2009)

THE 19ᵀᴴ CENTURY BRITISH PHILOSOPHER John Stuart Mill is recognized in modern philosophy chiefly for two reasons. He refined the Utilitarian tradition of philosophy established by Jeremy Bentham and he reemphasized the primacy of individual liberty and self-determination against the inroads of the majority in democratic societies. One part of Mill's contribution has been largely overlooked, however. It is his call for legal and social equality for women in an 1861 volume entitled *The Subjection of Women*. (1)

Mill lived in an era when women were subordinate to men by law and custom. They were expected to marry, rear children, and devote themselves to their families. In most cases they could not pursue a formal education, own property or amass wealth, vote, serve on juries, practice a profession or trade, seek a divorce, even from an abusive husband, or travel alone. Women lived in the shadow of their *de facto* masters, their husbands.

Mill's case for women's equality reflects his Utilitarian roots. The subordination of women, he argues, is not only "wrong in itself" but "one of the chief hindrances to human improvement." (p. 7) By denying women the same opportunities as men, he says, society not only impedes the development of roughly half the population but denies itself the benefit of their talents. (pp. 88-89) Why is such a foolish practice followed? Mill asks. Because, he says, our customs and laws are a carryover of the law of the strongest. (pp. 10-11) The fact that men are typically superior to women in physical strength leads to the presumption that men are superior to women in all areas, despite the fact that there is no proof to support this claim. (p. 10) In this respect, Mill says, the predicament of women parallels that of slaves. (p. 11, p. 18)

Mill argues that the progress of society requires that all people, men and women, not be imprisoned in the "fixed social position" in which they are born but instead be given opportunities to develop their talents and to pursue their desires as long as they pose no threat to the rights of others. (pp. 22-23) To the naysayer who doubts the potential of women to match the achievements of men in literature, science, government, medicine, education, and the arts, Mill retorts that this is self-serving speculation. The only way to measure the potential of women is to free them from domestic bondage, give them the same opportunities as men, and observe the results. (p. 22, p. 26, p. 62, p. 74) History confirms that Mill's confidence in the outcome was prescient. To the skeptic who opines that the liberation of women will destroy marriage and the family, Mill answers that a marriage which is attractive to women, one based on equality and mutual respect instead of subordination, will prosper indefinitely. (pp. 33-34) To those who argue that authority to make decisions in any organization must ultimately rest in a single person, Mill replies that this is certainly not the case in successful partnerships in business, and that even if it were, this does not mean that the controlling voice on a given matter must be the husband's. (p. 45)

In a nutshell, then, Mill argued nearly 150 years ago that the liberation of women will produce two important results. It will benefit society by triggering the contributions of women in many fields and it will benefit women by granting them the autonomy that is essential to happiness. In my view he was right on both counts.

---

[1]. The edition used here is Prometheus Books, Great Books in Philosophy Series, 1986 (ISBN 0-87975-335-8). References here to this volume are by page number.

Is Socialism Coming? (September 24, 2009)

IN THE UNITED STATES TODAY health care reform is front and center. President Obama has stumped for reforms in dozens of appearances across the nation, an address to the Congress, and no fewer than five televised news shows last Sunday. On a daily basis the media report the latest wrinkles in a spate of health care proposals under discussion in the Congress and speculate on the political prospects of the President's preferred "public option."

In the health care debate, as in the government bailout of failing banks and two major U.S. auto producers, some critics of the White House invoke the "S" work – *socialism*. They warn that America is abandoning its historic commitment to limited government, private ownership, and the free market in favor of a welfare state, public ownership, and a planned economy. Such critics, including those attending TEA (Taxed Enough Already) parties, seem to share Ronald Reagan's distrust of government. Government, they believe, is the problem, not the solution. Government, they tell us, is inept, it covets more and more power, it steals from producers to support parasites, it threatens our liberties, and it saddles future generations with enormous debt. (1) Setting aside the voices of dissent from the radical fringe – the birthers, the conspiracy theorists, those who vilify the President as a liar, and those who construe his pep talk to the nation's students as socialist propaganda – let's engage the central issue: Is the United States abandoning capitalism for socialism?

Let us understand that under socialism the government owns and administers the productive apparatus of society and provides all the good and services, and by contrast, under capitalism individuals and companies own and administer the productive apparatus of society and provide all the goods and services with the possible exception of law enforcement and national defense. Now, where can we find examples of these two systems in practice? The fact is that we can't because the dominant economic system in the world today is a mixed one. A mixed economy incorporates elements of socialism and capitalism, although the mix differs from nation to nation. When a good or service is provided by a public source in a society, there is a socialist component; when a good or service is provided by a private source in a society, there is a capitalist component.

Thus, if you want to see socialist components in the United States, look no farther than the Grand Canyon National Park, Social Security, Head Start, Medicare, Medicaid, the U.S. Postal Service, food stamps, police and fire departments, Youngstown State University, the Canfield public schools, the Public Library of Youngstown and Mahoning County, and the Mill Creek MetroParks. (2) Similarly, if you want to see capitalist components in the United States, look no farther than Disney World, the stock market, McDonald's, Wal-Mart, Amazon.com, Microsoft, Omaha Steaks, UPS, ESPN, Grove City College, Farmers National Bank, the Exal Corporation, and Handel's Ice Cream.

It seems clear to me that the U.S. is not abandoning capitalism for socialism. Rather, it continues to blend elements of both systems. Although the specific jurisdictions of the public and private sectors in America will change in the future as they have in the past, our economic hybrid is here to stay for the foreseeable future.

---

1. See, for instance, the recent statements of the Atlas Society, a group which seeks to perpetuate the ideas of Ayn Rand, an advocate of laissez-faire capitalism.

2. One of the ironies in recent weeks is a mother objecting to her child hearing a talk in his public school by President Obama because she wanted to shield her boy from "socialist propaganda." Public schools are a socialist component in America. If Americans were pure capitalists, there would be only private schools.

Religion in the Public Schools
(October 15, 2009)

MILLIONS OF DOLLARS ARE SPENT on litigation annually over disputes about religion in the public schools. A great many of these lawsuits could be avoided if school officials and parents had a better understanding of the key laws and court decisions governing this area. Fortunately, a book has just been published which can promote such an understanding and help all parties comply with the law and minimize litigation. It is entitled *Religion in the Public Schools: A Road Map for Avoiding Lawsuits and Respecting Parents' Legal Rights.* The author is Anne Marie Lofaso who teaches in the College of Law at West Virginia University. (1)

Religion in the Public Schools deals with all the hot button legal issues in our public schools, including:

- prayer, moments of silence, meditation, and invocations,
- dress codes,
- Bible study groups,
- censorship of student publications,
- use of school facilities by non-curricular and non-school groups,
- alternatives to evolution such as creation science and intelligent design,
- courses on religious scriptures or world religions,

- requests to accommodate religious holidays and religious dietary practices, and
- the right of students to opt-out of material in classes to which they or their parents object, among others.

Let's focus here on just one of these – prayer in the public schools.

Professor Lofaso points out that decisions by the U.S. Supreme Court and lower courts place strict limits on prayer in school because of the Establishment Clause in the U.S. Constitution which prohibits government entities from endorsing or promoting religion. She writes:

> Under Supreme Court decisional law, it is unconstitutional for public school officials to write prayers for recitation by students, select prayers for recitation by students, start each day with a reading from the Bible, set aside moments for silent prayer or meditation if the purpose of such a moment is clearly to foster prayer, invite outside clergy to graduation to give a prayer or an invocation, or develop a selection process for students to vote on which students may give a prayer...before high school football games over the school's public address system. (2)

Even prayer at school board meetings is unconstitutional. (3) Does any prayer on school property pass constitutional muster? Yes! An individual student may pray on his or her own at any time "before, during, or after the school day." (4) Further, prayer which is initiated by students and which is voluntary, such as early morning prayer meetings around a flagpole or a pregame prayer, is permissible provided that school officials, including coaches, do not promote or lead it. (5)

Professor Lofaso's book should be required reading for future public school administrators and teachers who are matriculating in the nation's colleges of education. It should also be read and kept for reference by superintendents, principals, members of boards of education, attorneys who practice public school law, teachers, and parents. It is thorough, accessible, clear, and extensively documented. Indeed, *Religion in the Public Schools* is a model of discipline-related public service for which Anne Marie Lofaso deserves the gratitude of everyone with an interest in public education.

---

1. 2009, Americans United for the Separation of Church and State. ISBN 978-0-615-31001-5. References to this book here are by page number.
2. Pages 26-27.
3. Page 33.
4. Pages 37-38.
5. Page 38. "Where the conduct is genuinely student-initiated activity and not fostered or supported by public school staff, that conduct is constitutionally permissible." (Page 37) At the same time, though, there is no consensus among the courts whether teachers and other school representatives may legally participate in such student-initiated prayer meetings. See pages 38-39.

Tiger's Two Lives (August 19, 2010)

RECENTLY TIGER WOODS POSTED AN 18-over par 268 at Firestone, a course where he had won seven times. He did worse than all eighty golfers save one. The world's undisputed top golfer for years, Woods enjoyed an image as a mature, responsible father and husband. He was a hero to millions of young people and corporations paid millions of dollars a year for his endorsement. Suddenly, as revelations about his private life hit the news, Woods' world imploded. A loving, faithful husband turned out to be a playboy. His image in shreds, his market value collapsing, his personal and professional life in turmoil, Woods became the star in an American tragedy of his own making. Whether Woods can recover his game and his adulation remains to be seen. Meanwhile, Woods has plenty of company.

Consider these parallels. A famous Christian evangelist rails against homosexuality from the pulpit at a Sunday service, then boards a plane for a dalliance with a male prostitute. A county prosecutor enriches himself by reducing or dropping charges against criminal suspects for the right price. A banker selects appraisers who agree to artificially inflate their appraisals to that he can give huge loans to select customers at great risk to his bank. A legendary motorcycle builder who is married to a wealthy, famous, and beautiful actress, takes a time-out at work two to three times a day to enjoy sex with his mistress. A U.S. Senator who cultivates an image of love and support for his cancerous wife fathers an illegitimate child with another woman during a protracted affair. A political wunderkind who shocks the political world by beating a heavily favored opponent for state Attorney

General joins his cronies after work for regular bouts of sex and alcohol with young women in his employ. A popular Governor who is among the top prospects for his party's presidential nomination regularly leaves his family and his state to cavort with a South American lover. Like Tiger Woods, all of these individuals, and thousands more, ruined their reputations and careers through reckless and imprudent actions.

What can one say about people who self-destruct? Some excuse them on grounds that they were victims of broken families, or abusive parents, or sex addiction, or malicious journalists, or political enemies, or the devil, or fate, or a divinity with a plan.

In my view, these are simply rationalizations. The individuals referred to succumbed to temptations for instant gratification, for short-term pleasure and excitement, the future be damned. They all failed to take the long view. Had they taken the long view, they would have understood that happiness and success require self-restraint, prudence, and loyalty, that a fulfilling life requires earning and keeping the respect of oneself and one's family and associates, that the fact that you *can* do something does not mean that you *should* do it, and that in today's world there are very, very few secrets. In other words, they would have cultivated practical and moral wisdom. In this respect, Tiger has a long way to go.

Chris Hedges on American Culture
(September 16, 2010)

THOMAS JEFFERSON AFFIRMED THAT A democratic republic can survive and prosper only if the citizens are literate and well-informed. This is why he proposed tax-supported schools in every community and founded the University of Virginia. So, how is the America of 2010 faring by Jefferson's standard? We don't have Jefferson to ask but we do have Chris Hedges. In his seventh book, entitled *Empire of Illusion: The End of Literacy and the Triumph of Spectacle*, Hedges, a recipient of the 2002 Pulitzer Prize for his reporting on global terrorism, takes a sober look at literacy in America. (1) His book is fundamentally a literacy report card and he gives the United States an F.

Consider these facts which Hedges cites:

- 7 million Americans are illiterate and the number grows by 2 million a year;
- 30 million Americans cannot read a sentence;
- Among those who read, 50 million read at the 4th or 5th grade level;
- In 2007, 80% of U.S. families did not buy or read a book; and
- One-third of those Americans who graduate from high school never read a single book after high school for the rest of their lives, and

42% of those who graduate from college never read a single book after college for the rest of their lives.

These jarring facts lead Hedges to indict our schools and colleges for training students to be compliant, money-driven careerists instead of critical thinkers who value autonomy and curiosity and who see the need to challenge the idols of the tribe.

If Americans care little today about the pursuit of knowledge through books, magazines, and newspapers, what *do* we care about? Hedges claims that most of us care about entertainment in order to escape from reality. Certainly TV serves this purpose. The average American watches TV four hours a day and in the average household the TV is on for six hours forty-seven minutes a day. But TV is not alone. Professional wrestling, celebrity worship, pornography, and many other diversions supplement it.

Let's focus on pornography. Hedges points out the following:

- Over 13,000 porno films are produced in America a year;
- There are 4.2 million porno websites. This amounts to 12% of the total number of websites;
- One out of four daily search engine requests, or 68 million a day, is for porno material;
- In 2006, the pornography industry raked in a staggering $97 billion worldwide. This is more than the combined revenues of Microsoft, Google, Amazon, eBay, Apple, NetFlix, Earth Link, and Yahoo!;
- Approximately 80% of all porn dollars spent by Americans go to AT&T Broadband, Comcast, and Direct TV, which is owned by General Motors; and
- The principal users of Internet porn are between the ages of twelve and seventeen.

Hedges says much more than I can report on here on topics such as corporate influence in politics and journalism, NAFTA, Ivy League colleges, and others. *Empire of Illusion* is worth your time, as are his other books, especially the ones on American evangelicals and the new breed of in-your-face atheists. Few can match his analytical powers.

---

1. Nation Books, 2009. All the data cited in this commentary are taken from this book.

Ayaan Hirsi Ali's Jeremiad
(October 14, 2010)

BORN IN 1969, SHE LIVED in Somalia, Saudi Arabia, Ethiopia, and Kenya. A devout Muslim, she attended a madrassa, wore a hijab, supported the fatwa against Salman Rushdie, (1) underwent a cliterodectomy at age six, (2) and dutifully endured beatings by family members for alleged moral lapses. (3) Fast forward to 2010. Soon to turn forty-one, having lived in the West since 1992, Ayaan Hirsi Ali is today a secular and a stern critic of Islam. Her most recent book, *Nomad: From Islam to America*, subtitled *A Personal Journey Through the Clash of Civilizations*, is a wake-up call to the West, a jeremiad which prophesies a bloody, violent future for the planet unless Islam is transformed, the human rights of Muslim women are recognized, and Westerners come to their senses.

What exactly are Hirsi Ali's issues with the faith of her youth?

Firstly, she says that Muslims have a naïve, literalist, and unhistorical understanding of the Quran. The Quran, she insists, was written by humans over hundreds of years and not, as Muslims believe, dictated to Mohammed by God's messenger. (4) She sees a desperate need for the historico-critical method that was applied to the Bible in recent generations to be applied to the Quran.

Secondly, she says that Islam is misogynistic. Women in most Muslim countries are the literal property of their fathers and enjoy few rights compared to men. They are subject to beatings, disfigurement, or death for real or imagined improprieties.

Thirdly, Islam is theocratic, she says. In most Muslim societies, the church trumps the state. Anyone who dares to raise questions about Islam or the prophet Mohammed is persecuted. Curiosity and skepticism are heresy.

Fourthly, Islam poses a long-term threat to Western institutions, she insists, because Muslim immigrants in the West settle in enclaves and refuse to integrate physically, psychologically, or politically. Immigrants carry their tribal culture with them, she says. (5)

They home school their children or they establish private religious schools, often with government subsidies, they follow Shari'a instead of the civil law, and they abuse public welfare benefits.

And what does Hirsi Ali propose as a remedy? First and foremost, she argues that Westerners need to become vocal about gender discrimination in majority-Muslim countries. She calls out Western feminists and multiculturalists for their silence about the violations of the human rights of Muslim girls and women. (6) Further, she proposes that the Christian Church, especially the Vatican, stop pursuing dialogue with Muslims and work to convert them instead. How ironic. For Hirsi Ali, an atheist, Christianity and the Christian God are far preferable to Islam and Allah. (7) Also, Western governments need to stop allowing Muslim immigrants to create ghettoes insulated from the wider society, they need to stop subsidizing madrassas, and they need to help Muslim immigrants become engaged citizens.

It is no surprise that Hirsi Ali requires round-the-clock security. Although many find her message offensive, we ignore it at our peril.

---

1. See "Ayaan Hirsi Ali," *Wikipedia*.
2. Ayaan Hirsi Ali, *Nomad: From Islam to America - A Personal Journey Through the Clash of Civilizations*, Free Press, 2010, p. 20. Most of the information in this commentary is drawn from this volume.
3. *Nomad*, p. 55

4. *Nomad,* p. 206.
5. *Nomad,* p. 79.
6. *Nomad,* p. 224. Hirsi Ali also criticizes Muslim women who attend colleges in the West, many of whom confront her at her public appearances, for their naivete. She writes: "If (they) lived in Saudi Arabia, under Shari'a law, these college girls in their pretty scarves wouldn't be free to study, to work, to drive, (or) to walk around." (p. 133)
7. *Nomad,* p. 238, p. 244.

Lou Holtz (November 18, 2010)

IN HIS AUTOBIOGRAPHY, ENTITLED *Wins, Losses, and Lessons*, (1) Coach Lou Holtz recounts two incidents in his senior year of high school which were a turning point in his life. In the first incident, Lou's high school coach visited his parents and urged them to send him to college to earn a degree so that he could become a football coach. The coach explained to them that Lou had a special gift for learning and teaching football and that he would excel in that profession. This came as a shock to Lou's parents. On the one hand, he had been a weak student all along and, on the other, they were already struggling to make ends meet and taking on the additional burden of college expenses could be overwhelming. In the second incident, in a neighborhood grocery store in East Liverpool, Lou overheard two of his brother's friends bemoan his parents' decision to enroll him at Kent State University. They agreed that it was a terrible waste of money because Lou simply wasn't college material. Holtz writes that the vote of confidence by his coach and the insult by his neighbors steeled his resolve to succeed at Kent.

And succeed he did. He declared a major in history, he joined ROTC, and he earned his degree with a 3.0 GPA. But he didn't turn into a bookworm. During his Kent years, Lou joined a fraternity, worked part-time as a janitor, coached the freshman football team at Ravenna High School to a perfect 11-0 record, fell in love with a coed named Edie, played linebacker for Kent State for two years at a scrawny 165 pounds, helped coach the Kent State freshman football team, and hitchhiked home regularly to visit his family and friends. He also formed strong views about how to coach. He decided that good teachers and good coaches have three things in common: they "know their subject inside and out," they are able to present their knowledge in a "cohesive and interesting way," and they "have enthusiasm." (2)

Although Lou and Edie parted ways, Lou found a new love, Beth Barcus, and in summer 2011 they will celebrate their golden wedding anniversary. Lou's career took him, Beth, and their four children to twelve stops in his first forty years of coaching. Among the highs was a national championship at Notre Dame in 1988; among the lows was a debacle with the New York Jets in 1976 and getting fired at Arkansas in 1983. (3) Incidentally, at Arkansas Lou was successfully represented by a young Attorney General named Bill Clinton in a lawsuit against him by three players. Now retired from coaching with a long list of career accomplishments and soon to turn 74, Lou spends his time as an ESPN college football analyst, a motivational speaker, an amateur magician, and a golfer, and he continues to practice his Catholicism.

Can one find any flaws in Lou Holtz's autobiography? I find two. The first is that he works both sides of the philosophical street. In some places he tells us that God has a plan for each of us that we cannot alter. (4) In others, he proclaims that whether a person succeeds or fails is entirely up to that person. (5) The second is that, despite his frequent emphasis on the importance of religion in his life, he ducks the strongest challenge to religion – the problem of evil. How do we explain has an all-powerful and all-good God allows so much suffering to afflict humankind, young and old?

---

1. Lou Holtz, *Wins, Losses, and Lessons: An Autobiography*, Harper Paperback, 2007.
2. *Wins, Losses, and Lessons*, p. 29.
3. In *Wins, Losses, and Lessons*, Holtz often expresses his admiration for Notre Dame and the privilege it was to coach there for eleven years, but, somewhat uncharacteristically, he criticizes Kevin Rooney, the school's Director of Admissions, during Holtz's years there. Holtz admits that he was so angry with Rooney that he didn't speak to him during his last eight years at Notre Dame. According to Holtz, Rooney hurt his recruiting by turning down many academically

qualified prospects and he permitted an official scholarship offer to be made only in the spring, months after competitor football programs had already extended theirs. The Notre Dame administration supported Rooney on these matters with a single exception. See pp. 231-233.
4. See *Wins, Losses, and Lessons*, p. 45, pp. 51-52, p. 67, p. 175, p. 228, p. 284.
5. See *Wins, Losses, and Lessons*, p. 31, p. 39.

Krista Tippett (January 6, 2011)

KRISTA TIPPETT IS KNOWN TO regular NPR listeners as host of a weekly program about religion which first aired nationally in 2001 and which is produced and distributed by American Public Media. Recently she changed the name of the program from "Speaking of Faith" to "Being." Her work as an interviewer has brought her three major journalism awards, including a Peabody. In a book entitled *Speaking of Faith*, she tells us about the circuitous path that she has taken personally and professionally. (1)

Born in Oklahoma in 1969, Krista grew up under the stern rule of her grandfather, a fundamentalist Baptist minister. When she left Oklahoma to attend Brown University, however, she also left behind the religion of her youth. A history student, she did a summer abroad program in Communist East Germany, and after graduation, she returned to Europe as a stringer for the *New York Times* and several other publications. Subsequently, she entered diplomatic service, initially as an assistant to the senior U.S. diplomat in East Berlin and later as an assistant to the U.S. ambassador to Germany. At this stage of her life, geopolitics was her passion.

After resigning her diplomatic position, Krista spent two years of self-assessment on the island of Mallorca off Spain, where her faith was resuscitated. There, she says, she rediscovered the Bible as neither "a catalogue of absolutes," nor "a document of fantasy," but, instead, a statement of truth in "multiple forms" and "multiple layers." (2)

Soon after Mallorca, Krista married a Scotsman, Michael Tippett, with whom she had two children, and from whom she eventually divorced. (3)

She later took a Master of Divinity from Yale. She also worked in New Haven as a chaplain on an Alzheimer's floor of a hospital. Afterwards, Krista ran a global oral history project on religion at St. John's Abbey in Minnesota where she developed the approach to interviewing for which she has become famous. (4)

Over the years, under the influence of theologians Reinhold Niebuhr, Dietrich Bonhoeffer, and Karen Armstrong, among others, Krista reached three important conclusions which helped to shape her life and her radio program. They are these: firstly, although religious people obviously do evil things, religion inspires far more good than evil; secondly, a religion should be interpreted and judged not by its extremists, a minority who practice "a radically superficial" and literalist version of their faith, but by its moderates who compose a significant majority; and thirdly, because every religion provides to its followers a genuine path to the truth for them, all of us need to respect and value religions other than our own.

Tippett also reveals her own demons in *Speaking of Faith*. These include bouts of clinical depression, significant weight loss, and insomnia. (5) She also candidly acknowledges her most troubling theological puzzle – reconciling the enormity of suffering in the world with God's goodness.

Critics accuse Tippett of relativism, fuzzy thinking, and "irrationality disguised as profundity." (6) Nevertheless, if Tippett's growing NPR audience – she is now on 240 stations – and her popularity as a speaker are any measure, her admirers far outnumber her detractors. (7) Hundreds of thousands find that her program broadens and deepens their grasp of religion and religious diversity in today's world.

---

1. Krista Tippett, *Speaking of Faith*, Viking, 2007. This is the first of two books by Tippett and she is writing a third.
2. During the Mallorca period, and for some time afterwards she tells us that she chose not to read newspapers because they were filled with so much bad news.
3. In her book she tells us next to nothing about how she came to marry or divorce, about her two children, or about her estrangement from her parents. She needs to write a book entitled *Speaking of Me*.
4. See "Krista Tippett," *Wikipedia*.

5. Tippett claims that these personal struggles have helped her to be a more effective interviewer and to see the humanity in people from diverse backgrounds.

6. See the blog "Rationally Speaking" maintained by Massimo Pigliucci, professor of philosophy at the City University of New York. As for me, I have two issues with Tippett. In her effort to empathize with diverse religious practitioners, she is silent about irresponsible and foolish aspects, as in the case of faith healers who deny medical treatment to their children; and, to my knowledge, she has never interviewed a secular critic of religion. On the latter point, perhaps over the years she invited seculars and they declined.

7. Tippett's program is also heard internationally via the web and a podcast.

Richard P. Stevens, Humanitarian and Globetrotter (February 17, 2011)

A NUMBER OF HIGH PROFILE Americans have worked to improve life for Africans. Among them are Angelina Jolie, Brad Pitt, George Clooney, and Oprah Winfrey. Their generosity has received plenty of attention by news organizations. By contrast, Americans who are not celebrities but have undertaken humanitarian projects in Africa and elsewhere have done so with little fanfare. One example is philosopher Robert Paul Wolff. In 1990 he established University Scholarships for South African Students, a foundation which has helped over twelve hundred young Africans earn college degrees. Another example is close to home – Richard P. Stevens of New Castle, Pennsylvania. (1)

Born in June 1931, Stevens followed World War II via maps of the world which he collected. As he learned about distant places, he vowed to visit them when he was older. He listened intently to the radio as Edward R. Murrow reported from London on the war. In high school he organized a group which he called the Junior Defense Army to recycle materials for the war.

Early on, this curious and perceptive child also detected flaws in American society linked to race. He observed that there were no people of color in his church, his neighborhood, or his grade school, that his parish priest never addressed racial discrimination from the pulpit, and that a local hotel and the cafeteria at the local YMCA were off limits to blacks. He also found it odd that his parish would support missions to spread Catholicism among people of color thousands of miles away but not at home. (2) All of this prompted Stevens to set his mission in life – to help people of color near and far.

After completing a doctorate in history at Georgetown University, Stevens accepted a faculty position at Lincoln University in southeastern Pennsylvania. Lincoln is a historically black institution whose graduates include writer Langston Hughes and Supreme Court Justice Thurgood Marshall. He soon took the first of a series of leaves from Lincoln to teach in Africa at half his Lincoln salary. (3) In Africa he saw apartheid first hand and joined efforts to abolish it at considerable personal risk. He also met thousands of young people in his classes and during his extensive travel across the continent. He helped scores of students complete their education in Africa or take up permanent residence in the United States. His extended family of beneficiaries includes college presidents, corporate executives, entrepreneurs, university professors, ambassadors, cabinet ministers, and an attorney general. Stevens continues to open his house to former students and their families for short or long stays.

Over the years Stevens has become so knowledgeable about Africa that the U.S. State Department and the Congress sought his counsel. He returned to African many times, including a stint as a visiting professor in the Sudan where he strove to substitute critical thinking for rote memorization of the Quran by his Muslim students. (4)

Today Richard Stevens, humanitarian and globetrotter, lives in Chevy Chase, Maryland, where he shares a house with a family from the Sudan. Few people of any race can match his record of service and dedication to people of color.

---

1. The main source of information for this commentary is Richard P. Stevens, *A Journey Into The World: Reflections of An Itinerant Professor*, iUniverse, 2010.
2. Stevens also wondered why during World War II our government locked up Japanese Americans but not Italian Americans or German Americans.
3. When Stevens informed his fiancée of his plans, she broke off the engagement.

4. Africa was not the only focus of Stevens' attention. He spent over a year helping to launch a new university in Kuwait and assisting young people in Central and South America to pursue higher education in the United States. After seeing the impact of drug cartels during his many visits south of the border, Stevens concluded regrettably that the only solution to crime, corruption, and political instability there lay in the legalization of drugs in the United States.

Marlo Thomas (March 17, 2011)

DANNY THOMAS (1) IS ONE of America's most popular and famous entertainers and the pride of Lebanese-Americans. But in 1986 he learned that he was not the only show business success in his family. On the same night that year, Danny's son and daughter made history – each received a Grammy. Tony Thomas won as producer of the Best Comedy Series, *The Golden Girls,* (2) and Marlo Thomas as Best Dramatic Actress in a TV movie, *Nobody's Child.* (3) These are a few of the hundreds of facts that we learn in Marlo Thomas' new memoir – *Growing Up Laughing: My Story and the Story of Funny.* (4) *Growing Up Laughing* offers us an intimate portrait of Danny Thomas and his remarkable family, (5) in-depth interviews by Marlo Thomas of twenty-three of America's most famous comedians, (6) and hundreds of jokes, mostly one-liners, inserted between the chapters. (7)

Here are some of Marlo's revelations about her family in *Growing Up Laughing*:

- Danny Thomas' spouse, Rose Marie Cassaniti, a Sicilian-American, was a gifted singer. At age 19 she had a 15-minute radio show called "The Sweet Singer of Sweet Songs." In fact, she first met Danny when he auditioned to be the announcer on this program. After she and Danny married, she abandoned her career, although she continued to sing at family events. Danny and Rose Marie's daughter, Terre, was also a singer and actress, but like mom, she too abandoned her career after marriage.

- Many of Danny Thomas' stories on stage were embellishments of stories told him by his barber – Harry Gelbert. When Danny used one of Harry's stories as the basis for one of his own, he always gave Harry credit. (8)
- When Danny Thomas was struggling as a young comic, he prayed to St. Jude, patron of hopeless causes, to help him, promising that if he would, Danny would one day build a shrine in his honor. Once Danny made it, he kept his promise. He founded St. Jude Children's Research Hospital in Memphis in 1962 and dedicated years to raising funds for it. (9)
- Marlo discoverer that in the sixteen marriages in her family the husbands ruled the roost. When their wives had complaints, the men replied "Where's she gonna go?" Marlo felt that the women suffered, in her words, "the everyday drip, drip of dissolving self-esteem." "Marriage," she concluded, "is like living with a jailer you have to please" and she vowed that she would never marry. Her parents nicknamed her "Miss Independence." When she was offered a role in *That Girl* as a wife, she refused it, demanding instead that she be a single, independent woman, to which ABC acquiesced. At the same time, she read Betty Friedan's *The Feminine Mystique*, she met and befriended Gloria Steinem and Bella Abzug, and she co-founded the Ms. Foundation. Her no-marriage vow collapsed, however, when she met Phil Donahue as a guest on his show in Chicago in 1977. They married in 1980 and remain married today.
- At Danny Thomas' funeral in 1991, Roger Williams played Danny's favorite piece, "Autumn Leaves," two presidents – Gerald Ford and Ronald Reagan – spoke, and Milton Berle and Bob Hope gave eulogies. In his remarks Bob Hope quipped that Danny Thomas was so religious that "he had stained glass windows in his car."

Growing Up Laughing is a touching reminder that our nation is filled with remarkably talented immigrant families who crossed an ocean to start anew. How fortunate we are that they did so. (10)

Commentaries

1. Danny Thomas is the stage name of Amos Alphonsus Muzyad Yakhoob which was later Anglicized to Amos Jacobs.
2. In addition to *The Golden Girls*, Tony Thomas' TV credits include *Nurses, The Practice, Soap, Benson, Beauty and the Beast, Empty Nest, Herman's Head,* and *The John Laroquette Show*, among others. His film credits include *The Dead Poet's Society* and *Final Analysis*, among others.
3. Marlo's competition in this category included Vanessa Redgrave and Katherine Hepburn. Marlo's reputation soared with her TV sitcom *That Girl*, which ran from 1966 to 1971, but she has also appeared in over 100 films, TV series and specials, and live theater productions, and she has authored five books. In addition to her Grammy, she has received four Emmys, a Golden Globe, and a Peabody, and she is an inductee into the Broadcasting Hall of Fame.
4. Hyperion, 2010.
5. When Marlo grew up in Beverly Hills, her dad's buddies frequented their house for dinner and after dinner banter. Among the regulars were Milton Berle, Sid Caesar, Carl Reiner, Jan Murray, George Burns, Bob Hope, and Don Rickles. Danny's two best friends were Sid Caesar and Milton Berle. When the three of them were in their seventies, they formed an act called "Legends of Comedy" and played all the major night clubs and casinos for over a year.
6. Those interviewed include Alan Alda, Joe Behar, Sid Caesar, Stephen Colbert, Billy Crystal, Tina Fey, Larry Gelbert, Whoopi Goldberg, Kathy Griffin, Jay Leno, George Lopez, Elaine May, Conan O'Brien, Don Rickles, Joan Rivers, Chris Rock, Jerry Seinfeld, Jon Stewart, Ben and Jerry Stiller, Lily Tomlin, Robin Williams, and Steven Wright.
7. Some of the jokes inspire groans, others belly laughs. Here's a sample:

- "If a man speaks in a forest and no woman can hear him, is he still wrong?"
- "What are the three words a woman never wants to hear when she's making love?" "Honey, I'm home."
- "I just got back from a pleasure trip. I took my mother-in-law to the airport."
- Two Beverly Hills women are shopping on Rodeo Drive when one of them notices a child in a baby carriage. "Oh, look at that beautiful baby!" says the first woman. "Aww, how adorable," says her friend. "Oh, my God, that's *my* baby." "How do you know?" "I recognize the nanny."
- "Elizabeth Taylor has more chins than a Chinese phone book."
- "Women like silent men. They think they're listening."
- "What's the difference between a Rottweiler and a Jewish mother? Eventually, a Rottweiler let's go."
- "I'm writing a book. I've got the page numbers done."
- "Marriages don't last. When I meet a guy, the first question I ask myself is: Is this the man I want my children to spend their weekends with?"
- "When I eventually met Mr. Right, I had no idea that his first name was Always."
- "My husband said he needed more space. So I locked him outside."
- "Two peanuts were walking down the street and one was a-salted."

- Mice infested a synagogue. Everyone was terrified. "Don't worry," said the rabbi, "I'll take care of it." The next day all the mice were gone. An older man asked the rabbi, "How did you get rid of all the mice?' "Easy," the rabbi said, "I Bar Mitzvahed them. As everyone knows, once they're Bar Mitzvahed, they never come back."
- "Fund-raising is the second oldest profession in the world."

8. Harry Gelbert's son, Larry, became a comedy writer whose credits include M*A*S*H*.

9. Danny Thomas was helped immensely in fund-raising for St. Jude's by dozens of his show business friends. In fact, most of them continued to help St. Jude's after Danny's death.

10. When one counts the dozens of awards that Danny, Tony, and Marlo received for their achievements in show business, it is clear that the Thomas family is the single most honored family in the history of American entertainment. (Danny won four Emmys for his TV series, *Make Room for Daddy*, as well as many other awards.) See footnotes 2 and 3.

James A. Haught, *Fading Faith* (April 14, 2011)

IN A NEW BOOK ENTITLED *Fading Faith – The Rise of the Secular Age*, (1) James A. Haught proposes that there is a significant decline in religion in the developed nations. (2) In France, for instance, less than 7% of adults attend church regularly. In Denmark and Sweden the figure drops to 5%. Across Europe only 15% of adults attend church. In England, the percentage of people attending Sunday school dropped from 50% in 1900 to 4% in 2000. In a recent poll in England which asked people to identify the most inspirational figures in history, only 1% named Jesus; 65% named Nelson Mandela. In Ireland, the Archdiocese of Dublin ordained only one priest in 2004 and none in 2005. The pattern is much the same in Canada, Australia, Japan, New Zealand, and Israel. (3)

At first glance it would seem that the United States is an exception to this trend. After all, faith-based programs continue in the White House. Few seculars win elections. (4) Mega-churches proliferate. Religion-driven referenda, such as prohibitions against gay marriage, pass by huge margins. Religious schools get thumbs up from the U.S. Supreme Court on vouchers and tax credits. Contributions to religious groups continue to increase. (5) Sectarian prayers begin the meetings of countless public bodies and we have a National Day of Prayer. Faith-healers who deny traditional medical care to their sick children are immune from prosecution by law in dozens of states. Finally, 45% of Americans reject evolution in favor of divine creation. (6)

According to Haught, however, America is not an exception to the secular trend. He cites the following:

- NONES, those who have no religious affiliation, have grown to 45 million and are the second largest segment of the adult population in America after Catholics;
- NONES make up 30% to 40% of young Americans;
- Since 1990, 20 million Catholics left the church. Today, 10% of American adults are lapsed Catholics.
- In the past fifty years in the United States, 20,000 Catholic priests left the priesthood and the number of Catholic seminarians dropped from 10,000 in 1965 to 3,400 in 2002;
- One out of four Americans says that "religion has no place in their lives" and one-half report that they seldom or never attend church (7);
- In the past fifty years the seven main Protestant sects in American lost 10 million members. The Methodist Church, in fact, lost an Average of 1,000 members per week for nearly fifty years;
- The percentage of Christians in the U.S. population has declined by 10% since 1990. (8)

Is Haught right about rising secularism in America? In my judgment, he is. Although the decline in religion in America is less severe than in Europe, the trend is clear. On the other hand, there is no guarantee that it will continue. In 1965 Harvard theologian Harvey Cox predicted the demise of traditional religion in American in a book entitled *The Secular City*. Soon after its release, there was a dramatic religious resurgence. Perhaps another one is around the corner.

---

1. Gustav Broukal Press, 2010. Haught is editor of *The Charleston Gazette*, West Virginia's largest newspaper. *Fading Faith* is his ninth book. He has won twenty national journalism awards.

2. Haught acknowledges that religion remains strong in the Third World, in Muslim nations, and in immigrant communities in Europe and North America.

3. Haught, pp. 11-16. In Canada from 1990 to 2000, the Anglican Church lost half its members, the United Church of Christ lost 39%, and the Presbyterian Church lost 35%.

4. Some secular candidates camouflage their views lest they incite opposition from believers. One Ohio legislator that I knew, an agnostic, gave the invocation at the legislative prayer breakfasts.

5. In 2004 Americans contributed some $88 billion to religious groups.

6. One can add to this list. For instance, the Ten Commandments grace many public buildings, including City Hall in Youngstown, Ohio, crosses and Christmas nativity scenes are found on public property in many communities, and creationist literature is sold in some national parks.

7. This is from a 2009 survey by *Parade* magazine. See Haught, p. 25.

8. Yet it remains high. Around 76% self-identify as Christians, even though many of these have no official connection to a Christian sect or attend church regularly. Haught draws most of the points reported here mainly from reports by the Pew Forum on Religion and Public Life, and Trinity College's American Religious Identification Survey (ARIS), two highly respected sources.

Nathan Leopold's Atonement
(May 19, 2011)

THE YEAR WAS 1924. THE place was Chicago. Nathan Leopold, Jr., was 19 years old. His buddy, Richard Loeb, was 18. (1) They were children of wealth and privilege. They were also brilliant. Leopold's IQ was 210; Loeb's was 160. They finished college while still teenagers. Although the boys often flaunted the law, it was not until they read the philosopher Nietzsche that they turned truly vicious. To prove that they were Nietzschean supermen (*ubermenschen*), they planned a "perfect crime." They kidnapped and murdered a neighbor, 14-year old Bobby Franks, and disposed of his body in a culvert south of Chicago where Leopold routinely went birding. Their crime turned out to be far from perfect, however. Detectives found a pair of eyeglasses near the body which they traced back to Leopold. Both boys were picked up by the police and interrogated. After their alibi unraveled, they confessed. Death by hanging seemed a foregone conclusion. To the shock and outrage of millions near and far, however, Judge Caverly sentenced them to life plus ninety-nine years. Their brilliant counsel, Clarence Darrow, had saved them from the gallows. (2)

Once in prison, Leopold began to reflect on his crime and his life. He soon concluded that he had been an arrogant, emotionally impaired, self-indulgent fool. He vowed to atone for his failures by dedicating the rest of his life to help others as much as he could. And atone he did.

- He became a teacher. He learned Braille to help a blind prisoner learn to read. He taught a variety of subjects to small groups at first, and then, with the warden's permission, he established the Stateville Correspondence School that enrolled hundreds of prisoners. Once these students were paroled, their recidivism rate was half that of non-students.
- Next, Leopold worked on a project with a team of sociologists from universities in the region. Their goal was to work out a formula to predict the prospects of success of parolees. Leopold authored or co-authored a series of journal articles about this project. (3)
- Further, Leopold worked in the prison hospital as an X-ray technician. He was also a member of a small team which used a mobile X-ray unit to take chest X-rays of all the inmates in Stateville and Joliet, the two Illinois state prisons.
- Finally, Leopold also served as a supervisor and volunteer during a World War II research project at Stateville to find a cure for malaria which was killing thousands of American soldiers in the Pacific theater. (4) He recruited 481 inmate volunteers to become infected with malaria so that the effectiveness of various drugs could be tested. He had himself infected, got very sick, and lost 14 pounds in six days but survived. He worked on this project 16 to 20 hours a day for 3 ½ years. And it was successful. It produced a cure for malaria labeled SN-7618. (5)

After four turndowns, Leopold was finally paroled in 1958 after 33 years in prison. His parole was supported by dozens of scientists and scholars, by poet Carl Sandburg, and, according to surveys, by 75% to 85% of the general public. He had eight job offers waiting for him. He accepted one as an X-ray and lab technician in Puerto Rico. He got married there and died there at peace with himself in 1971. (6)

---

1. The primary source of information for this commentary is Nathan F. Leopold's autobiography: *Life Plus Ninety-Nine Years*, Doubleday & Company, Inc., 1958.
2. During the trial Leopold and Loeb did little to help their own cause. They whispered to one another and giggled repeatedly. In the three-month trial Darrow built his defense on the testimony of psychologists and psychiatrists who brought Freudian analysis into the courtroom, probably for the first time. Darrow persuaded Judge Caverly that Leopold and Loeb were "broken machines" whose genetics and upbringing planted in them a compulsion to commit the crime.
3. In at least one of these articles Leopold used a pseudonym – William F. Lanne (p. 261).
4. Time constraints prevent me from mentioning Leopold's other service activities in the body of the commentary. Along the way he served as the prison librarian, building a collection of over 16,000 volumes; an extraordinary linguist, he translated science articles from foreign languages (e.g., French, German, and Dutch) for American scientists; an accomplished ornithologist and an expert on the Kirtland Warbler, he donated his huge ornithological collection to the Field Museum in Chicago; though a follower of Judaism, Leopold befriended prison chaplains of all faiths and helped them in their prison ministries; and he recruited hundreds of prisoners to donate their eyes upon their death for corneal transplants but a little known Illinois law which required next of kin to approve the donation put an end to the Eye Bank program.
5. *Life* magazine ran a story on the Stateville malaria project and Chicago radio station WGN did an on-site broadcast on it as well. About half the inmate volunteers were granted early parole. Some twenty-two journal articles were published about the malaria project. Despite the fact that Leopold's skills as a statistician were central to the research, he got no explicit mention in any of them. In that there were 300,000 known malaria cases a year independently of World War II, Leopold felt that the project had a long-term benefit for humankind. (pp. 305-338)
6. Leopold's transition from malefactor to benefactor proves, I believe, that some criminals can be successfully rehabilitated, that some criminals who show no remorse for their crime initially can develop it later, that some prisoners can make important contributions to society during their incarceration, and that some parolees who had been jailed for heinous crimes can live responsible, law-abiding lives on the outside. Those who are skeptical about the prospects of rehabilitation will say, no doubt, that Leopold is the exception that proves the rule.

The Class of '61 – Fifty Years Later (July 7, 2011)

ON A RECENT WEEKEND, THE Ursuline High School Class of 1961 gathered at a reunion to celebrate the fiftieth anniversary of our graduation. During four events – a social Friday night, a tour of the school Saturday afternoon, a banquet Saturday night, and a brunch Sunday – we got reacquainted with one another, we reminisced, and, of course, we gauged the impact of the years on one another. If I had to pick one word to characterize the weekend, it would be *change*.

The change in us was obvious. With few exceptions, our thin bodies were gone. In fact, one plump gentleman, whom I did not recognize across the room, waved a photo of a stick of a boy as he approached people. It was his picture from the year book. Further, dozens of heads sported white or gray hair or none at all. A blind person could tell our ages by simply eavesdropping on our conversations. All of them led inexorably to two topics – our grandchildren and our health afflictions.

Similarly, our school had changed a lot. The nuns and priests who taught us and ran the school were largely gone, replaced by laity. The classroom where many of us learned an invaluable skill – how to type – was now a computer lab. Further, the enrollment had gone down over the half century, from over, 1,200 students in 1961 to just over 400 today, while the tuition had gone up, from $110 a year to $6,500 a year.

During the weekend my classmates and I talked a lot about other changes, for good or ill, since we graduated. Here's a partial list of what arrived and what departed.

1. The arrivals since 1961 include CDs, the Super Bowl, AIDS, satellite radio and TV, cruise control, bar codes, cell phones, caller-ID, computers, the Internet, Google, Microsoft, kindles, iPods and iPads, YouTube, Facebook, HD TV, the GPS, Wal-Mart, the ubiquitous "Made in China" label, microwaves, MRIs, telemarketers, right-turn-on red, the Youngstown freeway, malls, international terrorists, drug trafficking, reality TV, a decline in marriage, an explosion of cohabitation, GM Lordstown, the Exal Corporation, V&M Star, Turning Technologies, the Covelli Center, Botox, and Viagra.
2. The departures since 1961 include Idora Park, the Toddle House, the Broadway Diner, the 20th Century Restaurant, the Mural Room, the Ringside, the Brass Rail, Strouss-Hirschberg's, McKelvey's, Livingston's, General Fireproofing, Youngstown Sheet & Tube, U.S. Steel, Republic Steel, the car dealerships on Wick Avenue called "The Wick Six," the Ohio and Tod Hotels, the Warner, Palace, State, Paramount, Strand, and Regent theaters and the Park burlesque, nearly all drive-in theaters, a single digit divorce rate, a busy airport, and the car bombing known as the "Youngstown tune-up." (1)

Finally, I want to mention the classmate who was the undisputed center of attention at the reunion. At 67 years of age, he is the father of six-year old triplets. He transports them and their young mother in a stretch limousine which he bought on eBay. Although his new family has reenergized him, there is a downside. His retirement is on indefinite hold.

---

1. The "Youngstown tune-up" refers to an explosion due to a bomb planted inside a car, usually under the hood. In the war between two factions of organized crime between 1955 and 1963, there were 75 Youngstown tune-ups. This prompted a cover story on Youngstown in *The Saturday Evening Post* in 1963 entitled *Murdertown USA*.

Rob Bell on Hell (July 14, 2011)

ROB BELL IS A CHARISMATIC 40-year old pastor of the Mars Hill Bible Church in Grandville, Michigan, which attracts over 10,000 people for Sunday services. (1) Although Bell was well-known in religious circles before the publication this year of his latest book, (2) *Love Wins*, this book has catapulted him into a pastoral rock star. (3) His celebrity was sealed when *Time* magazine did a cover story on him in the April 25th issue this year.

Love Wins stirred up a theological hornet's nest. One of its critics, a prominent Baptist seminary president, attacked it as "theologically disastrous." (4) So, what did Bell say which ignited such an indictment? In a word, he claims that what most Christians believe about heaven and hell is wrong! He writes:

> A staggering number of people have been taught that a select few Christians will spend forever in a peaceful, joyous place called heaven, while the rest of humanity spends forever in torment and punishment in hell with no chance for anything better... This (teaching) is misguided and toxic and ultimately subverts the contagious spread of Jesus's message of love, peace, forgiveness, and joy that our world desperately needs to hear. (5)

To show how the prevailing notion of hell has gripped people, Bell recounts a story about an art show in his church in which one artist included in her exhibit a quotation by Gandhi, a Hindu. Bell was shocked to find a note attached to the quote by a visitor which said: "Reality check: He's in hell." The idea that a loving God could consign one of the world's greatest peacemakers to hell struck Bell as absurd. Similarly, Bell reasons, it is inconceivable that a loving God could condemn any other compassionate and responsible person, even an atheist, to eternal torment. (6) Bell says that those Christians who would close heaven to non-Christians fail to understand that Jesus offered a message of love, peace, and forgiveness to the *entire* world and not merely to *one* tribe, culture, or religion. (7)

But Bell doesn't stop there. For Bell, heaven and hell are not distant places somewhere "out there" where people go forever after they die. Heaven and hell, he insists, are conditions in the *here and now*. You are in heaven when you freely embrace God's love and you are in hell when you don't. (8) Those who embrace God's love, Bell says, shower love on others, especially those who suffer, and those who reject God's love are indifferent or cruel to others. (9)

Love Wins has many shortcomings.

- It fails to deal with two philosophical conundrums: Firstly, why does a loving and powerful God allow tsunamis, floods, cancer, AIDS, starvation, dementia, and crime? And, secondly, are divine omnipotence and human free will reconcilable?
- Next, it makes selective use of the Bible.
- Further, it fails to explain what happens at death if, as Bell says, heaven and hell are in the here and now; and
- Finally, it lacks the technical arguments that one looks for in a serious discussion of religion.

Nevertheless, Bell's book is a bold assault on conventional religion from within which will inspire discussion and debate for a long time and prompt a great many Christians to take a fresh look at their beliefs and practices. (10)

---

1. Bell's church, according to Jon Meachem, emphasizes discussion rather than dogmatic teaching. See Jon Meachem, "Is Hell Dead?" *Time*, April 25, p. 38.
2. In 2007 Bell was named No. 10 in a list of "The 50 Most Influential Christians in America" as chosen by the readers of "The Church Report.com." See Rob Bell, *Wikipedia*. Bell has

written several books, conducted successful speaking tours in the United States and abroad, and made appearances in a series of short films entitled NOOMA.

3. HarperOne, 2011. The subtitle is *A Book About Heaven, Hell, and the Fate of Every Person Who Ever Lived.*

4. The critic is R. Albert Mohler, Jr., president of the Southern Baptist Theological Seminary. See *Time*, April 25, 2011, p. 40. Another attack came from The Evangelical Alliance, the oldest organization of Evangelicals in the world, through its spokesperson, Derek Tidball, former Principal of the London School of Theology. Tidball charged that the book is "full of confusing half-truths" and that it "lacks clarity." See Karen Peake, the online edition of *Christian Today*, March 30, 2011. Also, *Love Wins* was so suspect in the Bible Belt that a young pastor in North Carolina who recommended it lost his job. See *Time*, April 25, 2011, p. 40.

5. *Love Wins*, Preface, viii. Also, see p. 95. According to Bell, the view that heaven is reserved for Christians is not "a central truth of the Christian faith" and to reject it is not "to reject Jesus." (Preface, viii)

6. *Love Wins*, pp. 1-4. Also, on p. 151, Bell writes: Jesus wants us to be "growing progressively in generosity, forgiveness, honesty, courage, truth telling, and responsibility." (p.51) Further, on p. 97, he writes: "God wants all people to be saved and to come to a knowledge of the truth."

7. Bell writes: a) Jesus came for Jews *and Gentiles*, that is, "everybody else." (p. 149); b) "…Jesus is bigger than any one religion" (p. 150); c) Jesus aims to save, rescue, and redeem "everybody" (pp. 150-151); and d) "(Jesus) is for all people, and…he refused to be co-opted or owned by any one culture." (p. 151)

8. See *Love Wins*, p. 117, p. 169, p. 170, and p. 194. This is typical: "…Every single one of us is endlessly being invited to trust, accept, believe, embrace, and experience (God's love)." (p. 194) Even if you reject God's love, Bell insists, God, through Jesus, sustains love for you and forgives you without your asking. Thus, for Bell, the welcome mat to heaven is always out. See pp. 188-189. Although Bell does not explicitly endorse universalism, the doctrine that all people are saved, he seems to endorse it implicitly.

9. Bell holds that countless people suffer "hells on earth." Examples are a molested child, a raped woman, a drug addict, a victim of dementia, etc. (p. 78) He sees this incongruity among Christians: "Often the people most concerned about others going to hell when they die seem less concerned with the hells on earth right now, while the people most concerned with the hells on earth right now seem the least concerned about hell after death." (pp. 78-79)

10. Hopefully, NPR and PBS will soon focus attention on Bell and his book in their programming.

When Marriage Disappears (July 28, 2011)

When Marriage Disappears is the title of a recent study on the status of marriage in America. (1) According to the study, marriage is "stable" in only one segment of our society – the highly-educated – which comprises about 30% of the population. (p. ix) (2) In the rest of society, marriage is on life support for five reasons – the divorce rate is high, the number of unwed mothers continues to grow, cohabitation has skyrocketed, fewer children live with both of their parents, and satisfaction with marriage is declining. (p. 14) Let's focus on each trend.

Divorce: Over the past fifty years, the rate of divorce has nearly doubled. In 1960, the number of divorces per 1,000 married women was 9.2; today it is 16.4. (p. 69) Given the steady increase in divorces over this period, the percentage of divorced persons in society has also increased. In fact, it has quadrupled. (p. 71) In 1960, the percentage of divorced men in society was 1.8; today it is 8.5. In 1960, the percentage of divorced women in society was 2.5; today it is 10.8. (p. 70) (3) Those who marry today for the first time face a probability of divorce or separation between 40 and 50 percent. (p. 71)

Unwed Mothers: Since 1960, the percentage of births overall to never-married women in America jumped from *one* in twenty births, or 5.3%, to *eight* in twenty births, or 40.6%. (p. 91) Since 1982, taking race into account, the percentage of births to never married least-educated *white* women increased from 21% to 43% and the percentage of births to never-married least-educated *black* women increased from 77% to 96%. At the same time, the percentage of births to never-married moderately-educated *white* women rose from 5% to 34% and the percentage of births to never-married moderately-educated *black* women rose from 48% to 75%. (p. 56)

Cohabitation: In 1960, less than half a million unmarried couples cohabited; today around seven million couples do. (p. 75) Also, about 40% of those cohabiting couples today are raising one or more children. (p. 92) Further, since 1988, the percentage of unmarried couples who cohabit has gone from 51% to 75% among the least-educated; from 39% to 68% among the moderately-educated; and from 35% to 50% among the highly-educated. (p. 22)

One Parent Household: Over the past half century, the percentage of children living with a single parent has risen 17%. (p. 89) Today, 20% of white children and 51% of black children live with a single parent. (p. 89)

Declining Satisfaction: Since 1973, satisfaction with marriage among married couples has declined 7%. (p. 65) In a recent survey, in response to the statement, "Marriage hasn't worked out for most people that I know," 53% of the least-educated, 43% of the moderately-educated, and 17% of the highly-educated, agreed. (p. 40) Also, since 1976, approval by high school seniors of childbearing outside of marriage and cohabitation before marriage has increased significantly. (p. 102) (4)

As if to add insult to injury, for supporters of traditional marriage, the study concludes on a pessimistic note, saying that there are no signs yet of a cultural shift that could lead to a "reversal of the nation's recent retreat from marriage." (p. 106)

---

1. Published in 2010, it is a collaboration of the Center for Marriage and Families at the Institute of American Values and the National Marriage Project at the University of Virginia. ISBN 978-1-931764-22-3. The study reports data gathered by the U.S. Census Bureau and the General Social Survey as well as dozens of other researchers.

2. The study defines the affluent or highly-educated as those with college degrees, the moderately-educated as those with high school degrees but not four-year college degrees, and the least-educated as high school dropouts.

3. Another way to see the decline of marriage through the increase in divorce, the increase in cohabitation, and the deferral of marriage, is to look at the trend in the percentage of adults in intact first marriages. Over the past forty years, the percentage of adults in intact first

marriages declined precipitously. Among the highly-educated, it dropped 17 points (from 73% to 56%); among the moderately-educated, it dropped 28 points (from 73% to 45%); and among the least-educated, it dropped 28 points (from 67% to 39%). (p. 21)

4. From 1976 to today, approval of childbearing without marriage rose among senior boys from 41.2% to 55.9% and among senior girls from 33.3% to 55.8%, (p. 102) and approval of cohabitation before marriage rose among senior boys from 44.9% to 68.8% and among senior girls from 32.3% to 63%. (p. 103)

Michael Shermer, Skeptic (January 19, 2012)

MICHAEL SHERMER IS A PSYCHOLOGIST, historian of religion, columnist for *Scientific American*, and public intellectual. (1) His most recent book is entitled *The Believing Brain: From Ghosts and Gods to Politics and Conspiracies – How We Construct Beliefs and Reinforce Them as Truths*. (2) It draws from extensive research over the past thirty years. According to Shermer:

> We form our beliefs for a variety of subjective, personal, emotional, and psychological reasons in the context of environments created by family, friends, colleagues, culture, and society at large; after forming our beliefs we then defend, justify, and rationalize them with a host of intellectual reasons, cogent arguments, and rational explanations. (3)

In a nutshell, "Beliefs come first, explanations for beliefs follow." (4) Shermer calls this theory "belief-dependent realism." (5)

Shermer is not merely repeating what we've heard from other psychologists for decades, namely, that all of us are victims of a variety of cognitive biases. (6) What he argues is that one bias, *the confirmation bias*, is "the mother of all biases." (7) The confirmation bias is our tendency to seek and find evidence which supports our existing beliefs and to tune out (or reinterpret) evidence which does not. (8) According to Shermer, it explains why so many people prefer unsubstantiated or discredited claims (e.g., ESP) to well-established ones (e.g., evolution). (10)

Shermer sees the origin of cognitive biases in the way our brain functions. The brain, he proposes, is a "belief engine." (11) It generates beliefs as it looks for patterns, real or imagined, and causal agents, real or imagined. For this we have evolution to thank. He writes:

> Our brains evolved to connect the dots of our world into meaningful patterns that explain why things happen. These meaningful patterns become beliefs, and these beliefs shape our understanding of reality. (122)

Once beliefs are formed, we look for evidence to confirm them. As we find what passes for evidence, our confidence in the beliefs deepens. (13) Simultaneously, we tend to form coalitions with those who share our beliefs and demonize those who don't. (14)

Is Shermer endorsing epistemological relativism? Is he saying that all beliefs are equal and "everybody's reality deserves respect"? He is not. On the contrary, he insists that there is a reality out there but that "it is rarely obvious and almost never foolproof." (15) So, how do we discover reality? What is the antidote to belief-dependent realism? It's called science. Shermer sees science as a human baloney-detection machine which tells us the difference between "what we would like to be true and what is actually true." (16) Science is "the best tool ever devised" for finding truth (17) and "the only surefire method of proper pattern recognition." (18) And why is this? Mainly because science demands skepticism. In science "a claim is *un*true unless proven otherwise." (19)

The Believing Brain sends us two important messages:

- We're not the rational and objective creatures that we like to think we are, and
- If we hope to acquire knowledge – true, justified belief – we need to value skepticism much more than we do.

Commentaries

---

1. Shermer is founder and editor of *Skeptic* magazine, producer and co-host of the TV series *Exploring the Unknown*, founder and head of the Skeptics Society, which has 55,000 members, director of a speakers series at the California Institute of Technology, a blogger (Skeptic.com), a prolific author, turning out a new book every two years or so, a regular lecturer on campuses across the nation, an interviewee on TV documentaries, a guest on a variety of TV shows, among them Donahue, Oprah Winfrey, Penn and Teller, Dennis Miller, Larry King Live, the Colbert Report, Dateline, 20/20, and Nightline, and an adjunct professor at The Claremont Graduate School. Also, Shermer was a competitive long-distance bicyclist from 1979 to 1989. During that same decade, he co-founded the Race Across America, a 3,000 mile event in which he competed five times. He also produced a series of documentaries on cycling. A neck disorder common to long-distance bicyclists is named after him – Shermer's Neck. (See michaelshermer.com and Michael Shermer, *Wikipedia*.
2. Times Books, 2011, 385 pages.
3. *The Believing Brain*, p. 5. He restates this thesis in many parts of the book. This is from page 36:

> The Enlightenment ideal of *Homo rationalis* has us sitting down before a table of facts, weighing them in the balance of pro and con, and then employing logic and reason to determine which set of facts supports this or that theory. This is not at all how we form beliefs. What happens is that the facts of the world are filtered by our brains through the colored lenses of worldviews, paradigms, theories, hypotheses, conjectures, hunches, biases, and prejudices we have accumulated through living. We then sort through the facts and select those that confirm what we already believe and ignore or rationalize away those that contradict our beliefs.

4. *Ibid.*, p. 5.
5. *Ibid.*, p. 5, p. 21.
6. Shermer discusses the self-justification bias, the framing effect, the sunk-cost bias, the status quo bias, the endowment effect, the anchoring bias, and others, which he says, are offspring of the confirmation bias. See Chapter 12, "Confirmation of Beliefs," pp. 256-279.
7. *Ibid.*, p. 259.
8. *Ibid.*, p. 259.
9. *Ibid.*, p. 259.
10. *Ibid.*, pp. 2-4. In the same pages, Shermer cites a 2009 Harris Poll of 2,303 Americans which revealed that more people believe in angels (72%) and the devil (60%) than believe in evolution (45%). Surveys elsewhere show similar trends. For instance, in England, a 2006 *Reader's Digest* survey of 2,006 people found that 43% believe they can read other people's minds, over 50% believe they had a dream or premonition of an event that later occurred, nearly 70% said they could feel when someone was looking at them, 62% said they could tell who was calling them before they picked up the phone, 20% said they had seen a ghost, and 26% said they could tell when a loved one was in trouble.
11. *Ibid.*, p. 5.

12. *Ibid.*, p. 5.
13. *Ibid.*, p. 5.
14. *Ibid.*, pp. 6-7.
15. *Ibid.*, p. 2.
16. *Ibid.*, p. 7.
17. *Ibid.*, p. 7.
18. *Ibid.*, p. 62. Shermer is quick to point out that scientists, as the rest of us, are subject to "the whims of emotion and the pull of cognitive biases…" (p. 6) This is why scientists must critique their own and one another's findings.
19. *Ibid.*, p. 135.

John Dewey on Religion (February 9, 2012)

THE YEAR WAS 1934. IN his new book, *A Common Faith*, (1) John Dewey assured his readers that traditional religion was drifting into oblivion and it would soon be a matter of interest only to history buffs. Given Dewey's stature, this assessment deserved attention. After all, Dewey was one of the world's leading philosophers and psychologists, he revolutionized the theory and practice of education, he published forty books and more than seven-hundred journal articles, and he served as president of both the American Philosophical Association and the American Psychological Association. Today, however, some four generations later, we can say with confidence that Dewey's crystal ball was cloudy.

Where did Dewey go wrong? He assumed that just as the automobile had supplanted the horse and buggy, so science would supplant religion. The writing was on the wall, so to speak. Astronomy had discredited "ascent into heaven." Geology had discredited creation in six days. Biology had dispatched the soul and the afterlife. Anthropology, history, and literary criticism had shown that revered religious figures and their deeds, if founded in fact at all, were embellished to the point of fiction. (p. 31) And psychology had shown that mystical and religious experience had a natural explanation. (p. 31) As a result, Dewey expected that more and more educated people would abandon religion and its supernatural cast (God, salvation, grace, prayer, heaven, hell, the sacraments, clergy, revelation, the devil, etc.). (p. 30) (2)

To help believers cope with their loss, Dewey proposed a secular makeover of religion. This involves two changes. The first change is that religious experience will no longer be a mystical encounter with a higher power but a courageous and persisting devotion to desirable social goals. Dewey writes:

> Any activity pursued in behalf of an ideal end against obstacles and in spite of threats of personal loss because of conviction of its general and enduring value is religious in quality. (p. 27)

Thus, a saint will no longer be a hermit who mortifies the flesh but an activist who collaborates with others near and far to improve life on the planet. (pp. 27-28) The second change is that the term "God" will no longer apply to a deity but, in Dewey's words, to "the unity of all ideal ends arousing us to desire and action." (p. 42)

To some extent, Dewey was on target:

- In the West, religion has subsided;
- In Europe and the United States, the percentage of believers has dropped while the percentage of seculars has grown, (3) and church membership and attendance has declined sharply, especially among the young; (4) and
- Most scientists are atheists or agnostics.

At the same time, however:

- Huge numbers of educated, scientifically literate people have not abandoned religion;
- The loss in mainline Protestant churches in America has been offset by the gains in Pentecostal ones;
- The principal beneficiary of charitable giving in America is our churches;

- The great majority of Americans report on surveys that they believe in God and that they will never vote for an atheist candidate for public office; (5) and
- Religion continues to grow dramatically in most parts of the world outside Europe and America.

Thus, despite his brilliance, John Dewey, like many before and after him, severely underestimated the staying power of religion.

---

1. It was published by Yale University Press in 1934, runs for a mere 87 pages, and is based on his Terry Lectures at Yale University.

2. A) Dewey acknowledged, though, that some believers – "fundamentalists" – are immune to science. (p. 63)

B) Dewey felt that the decline in religiosity in society was reflected in the increase in the role of secular institutions vis-à-vis religious ones. (pp. 61-62) (For example, Super Bowl XLVI, played on Sunday, February 5, 2012, captured a record TV audience of 111.5 million and produced billions of dollars in wagering. Super Bowl Sunday is not the only Sunday when religion takes a back seat to secular institutions.)

C) Dewey also rejected the view advanced by some believers that science and religion are not really at odds because they are distinct paths to truth, the former illuminating the natural realm, the latter illuminating the spiritual one. (p. 34) He wrote:

> "There is but one sure road of access to truth – the road of patient, cooperative inquiry operating by means of observation, experiment, record and controlled reflection." (p. 32)

For Dewey, the method of science is the only reliable path to knowledge and religious claims are no longer tenable. (p. 34) Dewey would have been highly critical of the late Harvard paleontologist, Stephen Jay Gould (1941-2002), who supported the compatibility of science and religion in his book *Rock of Ages*, published in 1999. Gould referred to science and religion as "non-overlapping magisteria."

3. The percentage of atheists in America may be as high as 20%, depending on which study one uses. Virtually all studies show that the percentage in Europe is much higher.

4. The Pew Forum in recent years has published a series of studies which confirm these trends. Also, a Gallup poll in 1937 showed that 73% of Americans reported church membership; a recent one shows a drop to 63% to 65%. Of those claiming church membership, only one-third report regular church attendance.

5. A March 2007 *Newsweek* poll reveals that 62% of Americans wouldn't vote for an atheist.

Bertrand Russell - Prophet (March 8, 2012)

IN 1929 BERTRAND RUSSELL PUBLISHED a book entitled *Marriage and Morals* (1) which brought an outcry from traditional moralists. What did he say which infuriated so many? Here are nine of his key points.

1. Russell points out that early in civilization, it was believed that spirits, not men, impregnated women. When this myth prevailed, women had a relatively benign status. Once fatherhood was understood, this changed. Men forced women to withdraw from society as virtual prisoners "to make sure of the legitimacy of their children." (p. 27) Moreover, as time passed, men practiced polygyny because their wives and children were valuable property. (p. 132)
2. Patriarchy brought a double standard. Virtuous males could have sex before and after marriage with multiple partners except for another man's wife. Virtuous females, however, had to abstain from sex before marriage and restrict sex after marriage to their husband. (p. 47)
3. Christianity, according to Russell, brought two new factors into the picture. The first, following St. Paul, is the view that all sex is lustful and that celibacy is the highest calling. Those who cannot abstain, however, St. Paul advises, should marry, "for it is better to marry than to burn." (2) The second is the view that the sole purpose of marriage is procreation. (p. 52) Indeed, sex without

the intent to propagate is sin. (pp. 53-54) These novelties, Russell says, furthered the subordination of women and divorced sex from romance, intimacy, and pleasure.

4. In modern times, Russell observes, women are rebelling successfully against asceticism and the double standard. They demand that the moral freedom which is permitted to men must be permitted also to them. (p. 84) The old inducements to virtue among women – the fear of hell-fire and the fear of pregnancy – no longer work. Russell tells us that former fell victim to "the decay of theological orthodoxy" and the latter to contraceptives. (p. 84)

5. Russell says that it is time to retire the stork. Sex education should move from the alley to the school and the home. (p. 102, p. 195) At the same time, obscenity laws which prohibit sex education and the distribution of art and literature should be repealed. (pp. 93-117)

6. Sexual experience prior to marriage, including cohabitation in some cases, should be encouraged to foster sexual learning, sexual fulfillment, and economic benefits, and to help people understand the distinction between sex and love. (pp. 78-92, pp. 165-166)

7. Given the fact that women outnumber men, and that as a result many women will never marry, unmarried women should be deprived neither of sexual intimacy nor the role of a parent, if they so choose. (pp. 86-88)

8. It should be easy for couples without children to divorce but not so easy for couples with children to do so. (p. 142, p. 163, pp. 234-235) Russell argues that married couples with children should strive for a "lifelong" bond for the sake of their and their children's happiness. This will require both partners to learn how to balance family, on the one hand, and career and money, on the other. (pp. 118-122, pp. 142-144)

9. Russell predicted that patriarchy in the West would gradually collapse and that the influence of father over mother and child would decline sharply. Indeed, he anticipated that there would be a great many absentee fathers. (p. 187) (3)

Whether you agree with Russell or not, one thing is certain. For good or ill, the West has moved significantly in his direction. Though he would bristle at the suggestion, Bertrand Russell was a prophet.

---

1. Liveright Publishing Company, 1929. References to this volume here are by page number.
2. I Corinthians, Chapter 7, Verse 9. Quoted by Russell, p. 45.
3. Other key points in *Marriage and Morals* include these:

   a) As sexual relations in and out of marriage improve, prostitution should decline because it causes physical and psychological harm. (p. 149)
   b) An occasional affair of a married person should be tolerated by the partner and should not put the marriage in jeopardy. (p. 230)

Abundance (June 28, 2012)

PEOPLE WHO GUSH WITH HOPE and optimism about the future are few and far between. One of them is Peter Diamandis, a fifty-one year old aerospace engineer and medical doctor, who gives us an upbeat assessment in his book, *Abundance: The Future Is Better Than You Think*. (1)

The key to a prosperous planetary future, according to Diamandis, is to "raise global standards of living," with special focus on the worst off, mainly Africans, whom he calls the "bottom billion." Abundance, he holds, starts with satisfying the basic needs of everyone on the planet, a goal toward which, he claims, significant progress has already begun. While Diamandis expects the developed nations and the United Nations to support the quest for abundance, he argues that three other ingredients are essential.

The first is Do-It-Yourself "maverick innovators" who relish a challenge and who work in small groups, usually independent of government and universities, to develop technological marvels. Since technology matures exponentially, Diamandis argues, it has a "staggering potential" to improve global standards of living. He gives dozens of examples of Do-It-Yourselfers who have changed the world. For instance, Dean Kamen built a device that purifies water with miniscule amounts of energy; Burt Rutan inaugurated private space travel; Chris Anderson invented the drone; and a small group of friends in California, who dubbed themselves the Homebrew Computer Club, spawned twenty-three companies, including Apple. (2)

The second is a new breed of wealthy and generous benefactors who are committed to improving the world. Most of them earned fortunes early in life, mainly in computers and mobile phones. He calls them *techno-philanthropists*. For instance, Bill Gates of Microsoft is spreading vaccine around the world to combat malaria, and Jeff Skoal of eBay has awarded $250 million to eighty-one entrepreneurs working to improve life on five continents. (3)

The third is significant cash prizes, sponsored by techno-philanthropists, foundations, governments, and corporations, to induce competition among teams of Do-It-Yourselfers to tackle formidable global challenges. Diamandis cites many historical examples of the success of such prizes. For instance, the lure for Charles Lindbergh's New York to Paris flight in 1927 was a $25,000 prize. Diamandis is convinced that such incentives can produce technological breakthroughs to bring the entire world safe water, abundant food, electricity, toilets and sewers, basic health care, housing, education, modern banking and transportation, and hundreds of low-cost products.

Diamandis's message is refreshing, even inspiring, but he may be written off as a modern-day Dr. Pangloss, the pie-in-the-sky optimist in Voltaire's *Candide*, unless he overcomes a major hurdle – funding. Although his X PRIZE Foundation has attracted sponsors of cash prizes for six projects so far, it hopes to secure funding for more than eighty others. One wonders how much nations stricken with debts and deficits can help. Hopefully, many more of the world's wealthy, including the one-thousand billionaires, will step up to the plate.

---

1. Free Press, 2012, 386 pages. Steven Kotler, a science journalist, assisted Diamandis with the book, and is listed as a co-author. Diamandis established the International Space University to promote space explorations, the X PRIZE Foundation to provide incentives for discoveries that can benefit millions of people, and Singularity University to offer courses, degrees, and conferences about problems facing the world and their potential solutions. He took undergraduate and graduate engineering degrees from MIT and a M.D. from Harvard.
2. Also, Tony Spear came up with the proposal to use air bags to cushion the landing of an unmanned rover on Mars, which worked, and Craig Venter fully sequenced the human genome in less than one year for less than $100 million. By contrast, the U.S. Government spent ten

years and $1.5 billion to do this. Venter is now developing synthetic life that can manufacture ultra-low-cost fuels.

3. Techno-philanthropists also subsidize dozens of organizations such as Camfed, led by Ann Cotton, which has educated over a quarter million girls in Africa, and the Acumen Fund, led by Jacqueline Novogratz, which has invested $75 million in seventy companies in South Asia and Africa to deliver affordable health care, water, housing, and energy to the poor.

Free Will on Trial (July 19, 2012)

As I collapse into my recliner to watch a network newscast, I recall the ones available, and then, without coercion, I consciously select the one I want. In other words, my choice is free. Or is it? Let's see if an experiment will tell us.

Suppose that Sue, a scientist, instructs me to look at pictures on a screen and to press a button with my right or left hand within five seconds after a sailboat appears. Suppose, further, that while I'm doing this, Sue uses a neuroimaging device to track the activity in the prefrontal cortex of my brain. After the sailboat appears a dozen times, she shows me that brain waves in the two hemispheres revealed which button I would press *before* I consciously chose to do so.

In fact, variations of this experiment have been performed hundreds of times by dozens of researchers with similar results. (1) And what does this research tell us?

According to many scientists, it tells us that free will is an illusion. Among them is Sam Harris, a neuroscientist. Harris writes:

> Some moments before you are aware of what you will do next – a time in which you subjectively appear to have complete freedom to behave however you please – your brain has already determined what you will do. You then become conscious of this 'decision' and believe that you are in the process of making it. (2)

Thus, for Harris, my choice to watch Diane Sawyer on ABC last night was triggered by unconscious events in my brain beyond my control. Indeed, all our choices, he insists, are the product of "background causes of which we are unaware and over which we exert no conscious control." (3)

What are we to make of this? Here are three points that we should consider.

Firstly, the research done so far deals with simple choices covering a few seconds. Many of our choices, however, are complex and drawn-out. They often involve careful reflection on options, evaluation of likely results, and sometimes confusion, stress, and reassessment. The research on simple choices may not apply to complex ones.

Secondly, as philosopher Albert Mele argues, even if an action begins before we are conscious of it, our conscious self may still retain the power to "approve, modify, or...cancel...the action." (4) In this connection, all of us can probably recall instances when we suppressed urges toward anger, violence, or a banana split.

Thirdly, whether choices are free or not, people need to be held accountable. If behavior reflects nature and nurture, as science tells us, then we must structure an environment which promotes civility. This means three things: punishment of wrongdoers to deter them and others from crime; rehabilitation of those wrongdoers for whom there is hope; and long-term imprisonment, or perhaps death, for those hardened criminals for whom there is no hope. A serial murderer must be stopped whether he or she acts freely or compulsively. (5)

Finally, if the sharp exchanges about these issues in the scientific and philosophical literature today are a clue, there is no end in sight to the centuries-old debate over free will versus determinism.

---

1. Benjamin Libet pioneered this research in the 1980s. For information about Libet and subsequent research, see Sam Harris, *Free Will*, Free Press, 2012, pp. 8-9, and pp. 69-76, and the "Neuroscience of Free Will," *Wikipedia*, pp. 1-15.
2. Harris, p. 9.
3. Harris, p. 5

4. *Wikipedia*, p. 8. The power of the conscious self to veto an unconscious impulse or urge is sometimes called "free won't." Libet, arguably the first to link conscious choices with unconscious causes experimentally, claimed that the conscious self retains this power. Sam Harris, however, challenges it. (After this commentary aired, Michael Shermer, who writes the *Skeptic* column in *Scientific American*, critiqued Sam Harris's position. See Michael Shermer, "Free Won't," *Scientific American*, August 2012, p. 86.)

5. Harris, a determinist, concedes the need for deterrence, rehabilitation, and, to some extent, retribution. See pp. 56 et ff.

Jim Abbott (September 13, 2012)

In September 1967 in Detroit, Mike Abbott and Kathy Adams, recent high school graduates, welcomed Jim, their first child, into the world. Their wedding, fifteen days later, was subdued because Jim was born without a right hand. (1) With the help of their parents, Mike and Kathy overcame their doubts about their ability to raise a child with a handicap and they helped Jim cope with challenges galore – putting on his clothes, tying his shoes, (2) blending in with peers, coping with jokes and insults, and opting for perseverance over self-pity. (3)

Early on it became clear that baseball was Jim's best sport. He excelled as a pitcher. He had a fast ball called a "cutter." As it approached the plate, it dropped sharply toward right hand batters. But he had to overcome a major hurdle. A pitcher is also a fielder. If he was to succeed, he had to learn to switch his glove quickly after a pitch from his right side, where he pinned the glove against his chest with his right arm, to his left hand, so that he could catch grounders, especially bunts, and throw out the runner. Virtually every team he pitched against early in his career tried to bunt early in the game to test his fielding skills. With the help of coaches, however, Jim mastered the glove transfer technique and opponents eventually abandoned the bunt strategy.

As the years passed, Jim had remarkable success:

- In three years at the University of Michigan, Jim won 26 games and lost 8, with an Earned Run Average of 3.03;

- In 1987 he won the Sullivan Award as the top amateur athlete in the nation and in the same year, as a member of the U.S.A. national team, he became the first U.S. pitcher to defeat Cuba in Cuba in twenty-five years; (4)
- In the next year – 1988 – Jim was named the Big Ten Conference Male Athlete of the Year, he pitched the entire game in the U.S. victory over South Korea in the gold medal game at the Olympics, (5) and the California Angels, the first of five teams for which he would pitch, drafted him in the first round as the eighth player selected;
- In 1991, Jim won eighteen games and finished third in the voting for the American League Cy Young Award; and
- As a member of the New York Yankees, Jim pitched a no-hitter in Yankee Stadium on September 4, 1993, against a Cleveland Indians team with formidable hitters, including Jim Thome, Manny Ramirez, Albert Belle, Kenny Lofton, Sandy Alomar, Jr., and Carlos Baerga. (6)

Alas, the speed of Jim's cutter faded during his ten years as a pro so that his success was measured. (7) His crowning achievement, however, was off the mound. At ballparks across the nation, year after year, before and after games, win or lose, he met with thousands of disabled children and their families, and every season he answered stack after stack of letters from them. He was as much an inspiration to them as they were to him. (8)

Today, Jim Abbott, at age 45 and married with two daughters, is a motivational speaker who gets rave reviews from audiences, to the surprise of no one who crossed his path over the years. It is difficult to imagine a person better suited to give hope to people, young or old, facing challenges. (8)

---

1. Jim Abbott and Tim Brown, *Imperfect: An Improbable Life*, Ballantine Books, 2012, p. 40. References to this book here are by page number. Most of the information in this commentary comes from this book, Abbott's website (jimabbott.net) and *Wikipedia*.
2. Abbott's third-grade teacher, Mr. Clarkson, actually figured out a way for Abbott to tie his shoes by himself and he taught this technique to him. (pp. 62-63)

3. Abbott reports that he encountered hundreds of people worse off than he was. For instance, as a child his parents took him to Mary Free Bed Hospital in Grand Rapids, Michigan, to be fitted for a prosthetic arm with a mechanical hand with a hook. There he saw and met children "with no legs, or no arms and no legs, or various combinations thereof." (pp. 53-54) Abbott later abandoned the prosthetic device. Abbott opines that "There was more heroism in an afternoon at Mary Free Bed than there is in a decade of baseball games." (p. 56)

4. Fidel Castro met Abbott and his teammates during this seven game series. Later, when Abbott was a pro, Castro contacted him with a request for a signed baseball, which Abbott granted.

5. Baseball was then a demonstration sport but is no longer played in the Olympics.

6. To add to this, in his senior year in high school, Jim won ten games with three no-hitters. He had an Earned Run Average of 0.76 and struck out two batters per inning on average. He also hit .427 with seven home runs and thirty-six RBIs.

7. Abbott finished his professional pitching career with a record of 87-108 and a 4.25 Earned Run Average. (p. 251)

8. Pp. 182-187.

Popular Beliefs: A Critique by Guy P. Harrison (October 18, 2012)

DID YOU KNOW THAT 27% of Americans between the ages of 18 and 25 have doubts that NASA astronauts really landed on the moon? (1) And that 4 of 10 parents in the United States refuse to give their children one or more traditional vaccinations for fear of autism? (2) These are two of the surprising revelations in a new book by science writer, Guy P. Harrison, entitled *50 popular beliefs that people think are true*. In this book Harrison examines dozens of beliefs which, despite their hold on millions, lack one important ingredient – evidence. (3)

Let's focus here on beliefs about the Moon landings and vaccinations.

According to NASA doubters, the Moon landings were a NASA hoax to embarrass the Soviet Union during the Cold War. Their case consists of three points: one – photographs of the astronauts on the Moon show no stars in the background as they should; two – there should be a crater under the lunar landing module caused by its descent but photos show none; and three – the flag placed on the Moon by the astronauts should not have been waving, as it did for a time, because there is no wind on the Moon. Harrison rebuts each:

- The stars in the sky behind the astronauts were absent for a reason that any experienced photographer understands, he says. When the camera's exposure was set to highlight the astronauts, it lost the faint light of stars in the sky behind them. (4)

- The reason that there was no crater under the lunar landing module, he explains, is that the module's powerful engine was "throttled back, way back, on descent…" to ensure a safe landing. (5)
- Next, the reason that the flag waved, he points out, is due to "vibrations and twisting caused when the astronauts drove the flag pole into the Moon surface. (6)

Beyond this, Harrison makes two further points: if the Apollo program were a hoax to embarrass the Soviets, their extensive intelligence apparatus surely would have discovered and publicized it, and given the fact that thousands of people were involved in the Apollo program, at least one participant would have confessed by now but none has. (7)

Next, do vaccinations for measles, whooping cough, and other health threats pose a risk of autism for children, as many believe? Harrison's answer is a decisive "No!" He points out that extensive, continuing research shows no link between vaccinations and autism (8) and he complains that parents who refuse to vaccinate their children put them and others at needless risk because "vaccinations have probably saved more lives than any other form of medicine in history." (9)

Fear of vaccinations began, Harrison explains, with publication of an article in 1988 in *The Lancet*, a British medical journal, by Andrew Wakefield, a doctor, which claimed that the measles vaccination causes autism. Despite the fact that Wakefield's research was subsequently discredited by research teams around the world, *The Lancet* later retracted his article, and Wakefield lost his medical license, the fear that his article triggered persists. (10)

Harrison's *50 popular beliefs that people think are true* reminds all of us that we are susceptible to speculation and myth, (11) and that the only responsible basis of our beliefs is evidence. I hope that it gets the huge, multinational audience that it deserves.

---

1. See Guy P. Harrison, *50 popular beliefs that people think are true*, Prometheus Books, 2012, pp. 97-98. References here to this book are by page number. Harrison points out that many doubters have been influenced by a "pseudo-documentary" entitled *Conspiracy Theory: Did We Land on the Moon?* which first aired on the Fox network in 2001.

2. P. 235.

3. Among the beliefs that Harrison evaluates in *50 popular beliefs...* are: there is an afterlife; psychics can read our minds; intelligence is innate and fixed; a Bible code reveals the future; all humans live many times (reincarnation); some people have extrasensory perception; psychic detectives solve crimes; Nostradamus predicted many current events centuries ago; there are miracles; space travelers visited Earth thousands of years ago; UFOs are visitors from other worlds; a flying saucer crashed near Roswell, New Mexico, in 1947; aliens have abducted humans; the position of the planets at the time of one's birth determines one's personality (astrology); the Holocaust never happened; global warming is a myth; TV news gives us an accurate picture of the world; biological races are real; alternative medicine works; faith healers cure the sick; my religion is the only true one; the Biblical account of creation is true; Biblical prophecies have come to pass; prayer works; archaeologists have discovered Noah's Ark; holy relics possess supernatural powers; there are ghosts; Bigfoot lives; there are angels; there are witches who can harm us; a lost city of Atlantis is buried in an ocean; there is a heaven and a hell; the Bermuda Triangle is an especially dangerous area for planes, ships, and boats; the U.S. Government keeps aliens in Area 51 in Nevada; the end of the world will occur on December 21, 2012; and the Rapture will occur soon.

4. Pp. 85-86. Harrison, by the way, is an award-winning photographer.

5. P. 96.

6. P. 97.

7. Pp. 92-93.

8. P. 237, p. 240.

9. P. 235.

10. Harrison also explains that many governments have taken steps to placate fearful parents. For instance, some have removed or reduced to trace amounts in vaccines a mercury-containing preservative called thimerosal and some have replaced the so-called "vaccine cocktail" with single vaccines. Despite this, the incidence of autism continues to climb, as does that of measles and other diseases, especially among the unvaccinated. (pp. 236-237, p. 240)

11. Harrison points out that all of us, including "intelligent and educated people," are tempted to believe without proof. For instance, renowned scientist, Jane Goodall, is a Bigfoot believer.

The Invisible Gorilla (October 25, 2012)

IN 1997 TWO PSYCHOLOGISTS DESIGNED an experiment in which they directed a group of volunteers to view a film that lasted less than a minute in which people assembled in a circle pass a basketball to one another. The viewers were asked to count the exact number of passes. Because they focused their attention on the movement of the ball, over half of them failed to notice something that they didn't expect. Midway through the film, a person dressed in a gorilla suit walked through the circle, stopped, faced the camera, beat its chest, and walked off, spending a full nine seconds in the film. The experiment has been repeated hundreds of times with the same results. (1)

Recently, the two psychologists, Christopher Chabris and Daniel Simons, published a book which expands on the gorilla experiment. Entitled *The Invisible Gorilla: How Our Intuitions Deceive Us,* (2) it demonstrates that all of us are victims of six illusions – attention, memory, confidence, knowledge, cause, and potential.

In the illusion of attention, highlighted in the gorilla experiment, we assume that we see far more of our visual field that we actually do. (3) In this connection, the authors urge people to discontinue the use of cell phones, both hand-held and hands-free, while driving because studies show that using a cell phone while driving dramatically impairs our ability to perceive unexpected events. (4)

In the illusion of memory, we assume that we remember the past far more accurately than we actually do. (5) For instance, a former basketball player at Indiana University vividly remembered that Coach Bobby Knight had choked him in a rage of anger at a practice but a videotape of the event which surfaced later contradicted the player's story. (6)

In the illusion of confidence, we assume that self-assured people are competent people. (7) Studies, show, however, that "the confidence that people project, whether they are diagnosing a patient, making decisions about foreign policy, or testifying in court" is no guarantee that they are as well-informed as they believe. (8)

In the illusion of knowledge, we assume that we know more about a topic than we usually do, whether we're talking about a bicycle, a toilet, a car, or a computer. If we're pressed for explanations, we usually come up short. (9)

In the illusion of cause, we mistake correlation with causality. (10) For instance, because many autistic children are first diagnosed soon after their vaccinations for measles, mumps, and rubella, many parents refuse to have their children vaccinated, despite the fact that dozens of studies with hundreds of thousands of children show that there is no causal link between autism and vaccinations. (11)

Finally, in the illusion of potential, we assume that "simple tricks can unleash the untapped potential" in our minds. (12) For instance, many parents play classical music to their babies to enhance their IQ, despite the fact that there is no scientific evidence to support such a belief. (13)

In a nutshell, then, Christopher Chabris and Daniel Simons challenge all of us to be on the lookout for the invisible gorillas, the everyday illusions that haunt us. To succeed, of course, we must first acknowledge that they exist.

---

1. This experiment demonstrates "inattention blindness," our tendency to miss unexpected objects in our surroundings because our attention is directed elsewhere. When this film was shown at a conference that I attended in Las Vegas in January 2005, most of the audience, myself included, missed the gorilla.
2. Broadway Paperbacks, 2009. References here to this book are by page number.
3. P. 7.
4. P. 25.
5. P. 241.
6. P. 73.

7. P. 231.

8. P. 82. In fact, the authors contend that "the most incompetent among us tend to be the most overconfident." (p. 95) An example of unjustified confidence that the authors use is George Tenet's answer to President George W. Bush's question as to whether Saddam Hussein really had weapons of mass destruction. Tenet replied: "It's a slam dunk." As it turned out, Tenet was wrong. (p. 95)

9. Pp. 121-123.

10. P. 231.

11. Pp. 174-176, p. 179. The authors note that "Despite the now-overwhelming evidence that vaccinations are not at all associated with autism, 29 percent of people in our national survey agreed with the statement 'vaccines given to children are partly responsible for causing autism.'" (p. 183)

12. P. 242.

13. Pp. 185-197.

Guy P. Harrison on Religion
(November 8, 2012)

AFTER YEARS OF INTERVIEWING HUNDREDS of believers of more than a dozen religions around the world, Guy P. Harrison has written a book entitled *50 reasons people give for believing in a god* (1) in which he strives to be a kinder and gentler religious skeptic than the so-called "new atheists." (2) Harrison writes:

> This (book) is a respectful reply to the friendly people around the world who shared with me their reasons for believing... My fifty replies to common justifications for belief can be read as friendly chats designed to do nothing more than stimulate critical thinking. (p. 14)

Let's take a look at three of the reasons which believers gave Harrison and his replies.

Firstly, believers say, it is obvious that god exists. After all, god is everywhere, god made everything, god answers prayers, and god runs the universe. But how can god's existence be so obvious, Harrison asks, when you consider that between 500 million and 750 million people on our planet are non-believers and that 93% of the elite scientists in the United States are non-believers? And how do you explain that beliefs about god in the two largest religions – Christianity and Islam – contradict one another? Christians insist that Jesus is god and the Bible is god's revelation while Muslims insist that Allah is god and the Quran is god's revelation. (pp. 17-22) (3)

Secondly, believers claim that "Society would fall apart without religion." (p. 295) If this is true, Harrison replies, then we would expect to find the least religious nations to be "bastions of crime, poverty and disease" and the most religious ones to be "models of societal health" but this isn't the case. He cites reports by the United Nations and research by social scientists which show that indicators of societal health are highest in the least religious nations and lowest in the most religious ones. The most secular nations – Sweden, Norway, Australia, the Netherlands, and Canada – lead the world in life expectancy, adult literacy, per capita income, educational attainment, and the status of women, and have the lowest rates of homicides, AIDS, and HIV. By contrast, the worst performing nations on these same indicators are among the most religious ones. (pp. 295-301)

Thirdly, believers say that the age of their religion is evidence of its merit. "A lie or a mistake," they declare, "could not have endured for so long." (p. 303) The problem with this justification, Harrison argues, is that *many* religions are old and *many* are not. If age is pivotal, he notes, we should all be Hindus because Hinduism is at least 6,000 years old and has roots in prehistory, and we should abandon "relatively recent religions" such as Christianity, Islam, Mormonism, and Scientology. (pp. 303-307)

During his travels and interviews, Harrison made important discoveries. One is that, when it comes to religion, comparison shopping is non-existent. Nearly all believers follow the religion of their parents and their geographical region. Another is that most followers of a given religion have little or no knowledge of other religions. (4)

It remains to be seen whether Harrison's *50 reasons people give for believing in a god* will spur the self-assessment and critical thinking that he hopes for in religious circles. That aside, the book is a helpful and informative

353

guide to the deeply felt convictions of believers around the world and one observer's measured response to them.

---

1. Prometheus Books, 2008, p. 14. References to this book here are by page number.

2. The "new atheists" include Sam Harris, Richard Dawkins, Daniel Dennett, and the late Christopher Hitchens. Many readers, both religious and non-religious, have judged their work to be arrogant, dismissive, and insulting. For instance, see John F. Haught, *God and the New Atheism*, Westminster John Knox Press, 2008, and Chris Hedges, *I Don't Believe in Atheists*, Free Press, 2008.

3. Harrison also notes that half the world's population rejects both Jesus and Allah.

4. Harrison also mentions a third, namely, most believers rely on faith and have little interest in formulating or evaluating arguments. (p. 13)

Eben Alexander's Journey into the Afterlife (November 15, 2012)

THERE IS A NEW CONVERT to the belief that consciousness is not produced by or dependent on the brain. He is Eben Alexander, M.D., a distinguished neurosurgeon who spent much of his career on the Harvard medical faculty and who has authored 150 publications and delivered over 200 papers. (1) And what prompted this conversion? It was Dr. Alexander's near-death experience in 2008 at age 54 while in a seven-day coma when he battled the rarest of illnesses – bacterial meningitis caused by *E. coli*. (2)

During his coma, the neocortex of Dr. Alexander's brain, which is "responsible for memory, language, emotion, visual and auditory awareness, and logic," shut down completely, he says, making conscious experience impossible. Nevertheless, inexplicably, he began a spiritual journey that took him to three destinations. The first was a dark, Jell-O like, red-brown "muck," a mud pool with a rhythmic, pounding sound, that he calls "the Realm of the Earthworm's Eye." The second, which he calls the "Gateway," featured a bright light, captivating music and song, and an angel guide, a beautiful woman with high cheekbones, blue eyes, and golden-brown hair. Here, with his companion, he found himself in clouds flying over trees, fields, streams, waterfalls, and people. (3) The third, which he calls the "Core," was the culmination of his journey. In the Core, which he describes as "an orb-like ball of light," he encountered God, the all-powerful, all-loving, all-knowing Creator, who gave him this message:

- God loves him and all others unconditionally;
- Evil is necessary on earth because without it human free will and human growth are impossible; (4) and
- Love will triumph over evil.

Remarkably, after his visit to the spiritual world, Dr. Alexander's "triple intravenous antibiotics" defeated the *E. coli* and, slowly but surely, he awoke from the coma, rediscovered his earthly self, which had been absent during his journey, and eventually resumed his professional practice. But he was now a changed person with an urgent mission: to share his journey with others – lay people, medical professionals, and scientists – to teach four lessons. They are that God loves all of us unconditionally, we are "spiritual beings currently inhabiting our evolutionarily developed mortal brains and bodies," we "get closer" to our genuine spiritual selves "by manifesting love and compassion" on earth, and the materialistic worldview embraced by most scientists is "mistaken." Scientists, he hoped, would learn, as he did on his journey, that: "The physical side of the universe is as a speck of dust compared to the invisible and spiritual part." (p. 82)

Although Dr. Alexander is convinced that his spiritual journey could not have been a hallucination, (5) there are, as you would expect, plenty of skeptics, neurosurgeons among them. He invites skeptics near and far to do what he failed to do before his transformative journey, that is, to keep an open mind and to investigate the voluminous and ever-growing body of research on near-death and out-of-body experience. Only time will tell if skeptics will accept his invitation and, if they do, whether their doubts will fade. (6)

---

1. Eben Alexander, M.D., *Proof of Heaven: A Neurosurgeon's Journey into the Afterlife*, Simon & Schuster Paperbacks, 2012, p. 20. References to this book here are by page number.

2. When the antibiotics which Dr. Alexander received didn't seem to have an impact, his condition deteriorated to a point that his doctors saw only two possible outcomes – death or survival in a persistent vegetative state.

3. Along the way, the angel guide, whom he calls "the Girl on the Butterfly Wing," revealed to him that he is loved unconditionally and that after his visit to the spiritual world, he would return to the earthly one.

Commentaries

4. Philosophers will point out that there are at least two fundamental problems with this claim. The first is that it is not clear how an all-powerful God can bestow power on humans via free will and still remain all-powerful. The second is that, assuming free will exists, it helps to explain moral evil, that is, suffering caused by humans (e.g., murder, rape, burglary, identity theft, etc.) but not natural evil, that is, suffering caused by nature (e.g., hurricanes, tsunamis, tornadoes, etc.). The latter suffering remains God's doing and seems incompatible with the unconditional love which Alexander attributes to God.

5. Alexander examines and dismisses a series of neurological hypotheses to explain his experience while in a coma. See pp. 140-146 and Appendix B, pp. 185-188.

6. A testimony to the importance of Alexander's case comes from Raymond A. Moody, Jr., M.D., Ph.D., whose *Life After Life* in 1975 brought NDEs to public attention. Moody writes: "Dr. Eben Alexander's near-death experience is the most astounding I have heard in more than four decades of studying this phenomenon. (He) is living proof of an afterlife."

Race One and Race Two
(November 29, 2012)

THERE ARE TWO BASIC AND opposed interpretations of the term "race" which I will label Race One and Race Two. Let's clarify each one.

According to Race One, race is *biological*. Nature divides the human species into a variety of distinct biological groups which we can identify by their physical features such as "skin color, hair type, body stature, blood groups, (and) disease prevalence." (1) Race One tells us that all of humanity fits into one of several "gigantic boxes." (2) Although the exact number of these boxes has fluctuated over the years, a popular and recurring number is six – Asians, blacks, whites, Latinos, Native Americans, and Pacific Islanders. (3) Further, Race One tells us that "each race is loaded with unique abilities and limitations, as well as personality and moral tendencies." (4) This is because each race has "genetic determiners" (5) which set the potential for its members in all areas of human endeavor.

Next, Race Two. According to Race Two, race is *cultural*, not biological. It is a "social construct," not a product of nature. According to science writer Guy P. Harrison in his book *Race and Reality*, the claim that nature produces distinct biological groups is a myth which has no scientific credibility. (6) He cites a 1998 statement on race by the American Anthropological Association which makes these points, among others:

1. In the United States people have been "conditioned" to perceive races as "natural and separate divisions within the human species" based on physical features;
2. "(T)he vast expansion of scientific knowledge" in the twentieth century has shown, however, that humans are not divided into biologically distinct groups and that the "folk" view of races is a "myth";
3. Evidence from genetics, especially DNA, shows that there is significant variations *within* so-called racial groups, about 94%, but very, very little *between* them, about 6%; in other words, people of the same race differ from one another *more* than they differ from people of another race;
4. "(P)hysical variations in the human species have no meaning except the social ones that humans put on them"; and
5. To understand the behavior of any group of humans, we must look primarily to their culture. 97)

Thus, for Race Two, "All human beings living today belong to a single species, *Homo sapiens*, and share a common descent… There is great genetic diversity within all human populations" but races as genetically uniform groups simply do not exist. (8)

If biological race has no merit, why, one wonders, does the notion of race persist? It persists, according to Harrison, because race feeds the human proclivity to build psychological fences between in-groups and out-groups, between those who are similar to us in some way and those who are not, whether it be physical features, language, religion, geography, gender, sexual preference, standard of living, beliefs, customs, or something else. (9) Some of these fences are relatively innocent; they pose no danger to peace, tolerance, and co-existence, but others are not so innocent, as events past and present demonstrate so clearly. (10) Thus, we all have a stake in whether Race One, the voice of tradition, or Race Two, the voice of science, prevails.

1. Evolutionary biologist Joseph L. Graves, Jr., who rejects what I have labeled Race One and endorses what I have labeled Race Two, cites these features as the key factors in alleged biologically determined, static races, in Guy P. Harrison, *Race and Reality: What Everyone Should Know About Our Biological Diversity*, Prometheus Books, 2010, p. 45. References to Harrison's book here are by page number.
2. P. 33.
3. P. 36.
4. P. 33.
5. P. 44.
6. Race One, Harrison writes, "rests on a foundation of mistakes, lies, ignorance, pseudoscience, and delusion." (p. 15)
7. Quoted in Harrison, p. 23.
8. The quotation is from a statement by the American Association of Physical Anthropology, cited in Harrison, p. 25
9. This is one of the main themes that runs through *Race and Reality*.
10. In the United States, for instance, Race One first produced slavery, then segregated neighborhoods, schools, churches, parks, restaurants, and clubs, and a legal system with a double standard – one for whites and one for blacks.

John Stossel, Gadfly (December 13, 2012)

WE BEGIN WITH A QUESTION. Who is the TV investigative reporter whose career spans forty-three years, who has won no fewer than nineteen Emmys and five National Press Club awards, and who is a libertarian who celebrates free markets and denigrates government? If you answered, "John Stossel," you're right on the money. (1) Although it is now six years old, Stossel's book, *Myths, Lies, and Downright Stupidity*, (2) remains the best distillation of his body of work over the years. Let's focus on parts of his discussion of two topics in the book – the media and public schools.

Stossel pulls no punches with his journalistic peers. Many, he says, are scaremongers. They file stories that instill fear because "fear sells." What's more, he insists, when it comes to science and economics, reporters are "clueless." Of the many examples that he cites, here are two.

We often get news stories about potentially fatal carcinogens in thousands of food products due to pesticides. To evaluate these stories, Stossel interviewed the scientist who invented the tests to screen for carcinogens in food. He is Dr. Bruce Ames of the University of California at Berkeley. In the interview, Dr. Ames assured Stossel and the TV audience that worries about food causing cancer are silly because the level of pesticides in them is so low.

Next, virtually every time that gas prices go up, reporters sound the alarm that they are "going through the roof." "Hold on," Stossel objects. If reporters took the time to figure out how to adjust gas prices for inflation, they would discover that the cost of gas in recent years is actually cheaper than it was eighty years ago.

As for America's public schools, Stossel charges that they are failing by any reasonable standard. Why? They are government-run monopolies which perform like any other monopoly – poorly. To make his case, Stossel cites data from international tests which show two things: U.S. students of all age groups place far down the list from their peers in many other nations, including those which spend much less per-pupil than we do, and the longer students spend in our public schools, the worse they perform in such tests. (4) There is only one way to salvage education in America, according to Stossel – competition. To achieve this, he proposes, government should give all parents vouchers so that they can select their child's school, secular or religious, or opt for home schooling. "Vouchers," he is confident, "will make all schools better." (5) Thus, for Stossel, we need government-funded but not government-run schools.

Are Stossel's attacks on reporters justified? And are vouchers the key to improving our schools? Certainly, when it comes to news, accuracy takes a back seat to speed and audience impact in many cases, (6) and some reporters lack the knowledge to tackle some assignments competently. But, should we blame only reporters for these problems? How about management? As for vouchers, we've had many years of experience with voucher-driven competition and there is little evidence that they have triggered overall improvement across the nation.

A few years ago John Stossel moved from ABC, where he worked for twenty-eight years, to Fox News. (7) Despite this move, he remains an irreverent and often infuriating gadfly who finds a way to offend virtually everyone sooner or later.

---

1. When Stossel graduated from Princeton in 1969 with a degree in political science, he had a stutter which he overcame with the help of a clinic in Roanoke, Virginia. After stints as a TV news reporter in Portland, Oregon, and New York City, Roone Arledge hired him at ABC in 1981 where he won national acclaim.
2. Hyperion, 2006. The subtitle is *Get Out the Shovel – Why Everything You Know is Wrong*. References to this book here are by page number.
3. *Myths, Lies, and Downright Stupidity* has twelve chapters in which Stossel defends or disputes no fewer than 228 claims.

4. *Myths,* pp. 108-109.

5. *Myths,* p. 135. As long as parents receive the vouchers and choose their child's school, even if religious, vouchers do not violate the separation of church and state, according to Stossel.

6. The saying in the news industry is "If it bleeds, it leads."

7. Stossel joined Fox News in 2009. At Fox News, he writes a blog called "John Stossel's Take," hosts his own prime time news show on Thursdays, and appears as a weekly guest on *The O'Reilly Factor.* He also writes a syndicated newspaper column.

Juan Williams – Part One
(December 27, 2012)

IN A BOOK ENTITLED *MUZZLED: The Assault on Honest Debate*, (1) former National Public Radio correspondent, Juan Williams, gives us his account of why NPR fired him and the message which he believes it sends us about political dialogue in the United States. I'll deal with his firing in this commentary and its implied message in the next one.

Williams worked at NPR from 1999 to 2010 (2) but that wasn't his only job during those years. He also worked at Fox News, (3) wrote for the *Washington Post*, the *New York Times*, the *Wall Street Journal*, and *Time* magazine, among others, gave dozens of talks a year, and published six books.

According to Williams, although NPR managers issued complaints about his work elsewhere from time to time, his one connection that rankled them the most was Fox News. (4)

The tipping point came on a Monday in late October, 2010, in one of Williams' weekly appearances on *The O'Reilly Factor*, during which Bill O'Reilly, Mary Katherine Ham, and Williams had a discussion about O'Reilly's appearance a few days earlier on ABC's *The View*. On that program, O'Reilly said that a Muslim community center should not be built near the site of the World Trade Center because Muslims had launched the attack on 9/11. This outraged two of the five co-hosts who stormed off the set. (5) O'Reilly asked Williams and Ham to tell him if he had misspoken on *The View*. In his reply, Williams said three things:

- The 9/11 terrorists were in fact Muslim extremists; (6)
- O'Reilly's anxiety about Muslims is shared by many Americans. In fact, Williams admitted, he himself is nervous in airports when he sees people dressed in Muslim garb; (7) and
- O'Reilly "should choose his words carefully when he talks about the 9/11 attacks so as not to provoke bigotry against all Muslims" because "the vast majority of (them) are peaceful people with no connection to terrorism…" (8)

The very next day, Ellen Weiss, vice president of news at NPR, phoned Williams to fire him, telling him that his remarks about Muslims in airports had violated NPR's editorial standards, outraged Muslims who worked at NPR, and triggered an avalanche of complaints from across the nation. (9) Williams protested, arguing that she had taken his statement out of context, denied him due process, and used a double standard by punishing him but not other NPR correspondents for controversial comments. Williams was referring to Cokie Roberts, who said that Glenn Beck is "un-American" and a "terrorist," and Nina Totenberg, who opined that Senator Jesse Helms deserved "to get AIDS from a transfusion." (10)

NPR's dismissal of Williams drew strong criticism from most journalists, dozens of prominent public figures, (11) and huge numbers of NPR listeners. Within a few months, NPR's top two executives, Vivian Schiller and Ellen Weiss, resigned under pressure. (12) Meanwhile, Williams accepted a generous new contract for an expanded role at Fox News.

I conclude with a question. The story which Williams tells in *Muzzled* makes it abundantly clear that he was on thin ice at NPR for a long time because of his extensive work outside NPR. Yet when he lost his job, justifiably or not, he says that he was "stunned." (13) Why did the pink slip come as such a shock?

Next time we'll take a look at what Williams says his firing tells us about our nation.

---

1. Crown Publishers, 2011. References here to this book are by page number.
2. Williams was first host of a daily afternoon talk show and later senior correspondent and senior news analyst.
3. Williams actually worked for Fox before he worked for NPR.
4. NPR management brought plenty of complaints to Williams over the years. NPR objected to a Williams' statement on Fox in which he referred to Michele Obama as a "Stokely Carmichael in a designer dress" after she said that her husband's success in the primaries made her proud of the U.S. "for the first time in my adult life." NPR also objected to Williams' book, *Enough*, in which he supported Bill Cosby's critique of black leaders. NPR also chided him for an op-ed in the *New York Times* in which he criticized teacher unions for "blocking school reform efforts." Coincidentally, NPR management had been pressuring Mara Liasson to quit Fox. For these and other details, see pp. 13-22.
5. The two co-hosts, Whoopi Goldberg and Joy Behar, later returned to the set after O'Reilly "apologized for not being clear that he meant the country was attacked not by all Muslims but by extremist…Muslims." (p. 5)
6. Pp. 5-6.
7. P. 6.
8. P. 7.
9. Pp. 12-13. Williams believes that the complaints received by NPR were orchestrated by the Council for American Islamic Relations.
10. P. 27.
11. One defender of Williams was Sarah Palin. This surprised Williams because he had been skeptical of her qualifications to be the Republican vice-presidential candidate. Palin, like many others, called for an end to government subsidy of NPR. Near the end of *Muzzled*, by the way, so does Williams. See p. 277.
12. Schiller's departure was due not only to backlash from the firing of Williams but a clandestine video recording of comments of an NPR fund-raiser who made "disparaging remarks about the conservative and Tea Party movements and constituencies." (pp. 29-30)
13. P. 12.

Juan Williams – Part Two
(December 28, 2012)

IN A BOOK ENTITLED *MUZZLED: The Assault on Honest Debate*, (1) former National Public Radio correspondent, Juan Williams, gives us his account of why NPR fired him and the message which he believes it sends us about the nation. In my last commentary I dealt with the firing; in this one I'll focus on the message.

In a discussion on *The O'Reilly Factor* in 2010, Williams told Bill O'Reilly that although he knows that "the vast majority of Muslims" "are peaceful people with no connection to terrorism," he still feels queasy in airports when he sees people dressed in Muslim garb. (2) In saying this, Williams felt that he was being frank and honest, and trying to draw O'Reilly, with whom he routinely differs, into a serious conversation about Muslims in America. Nevertheless, his candor cost him his job at NPR.

To Williams, an award-winning and respected veteran of the Washington scene for more than twenty-five years, his punishment illustrates that genuine political dialogue – trying to engage a person whose views differ from yours on an important issue in the mutual pursuit of truth – is virtually impossible in the nation today because Americans and their leaders are so polarized. Political positions, he says, are settled and inflexible. One is either a liberal or a conservative. Moderates are an endangered species. (3) Seeking common ground with the other side is betrayal, (4) loyalty is the supreme virtue, and dogma trumps fact. Politicians and media moguls pander to their partisan constituencies and demonize opponents. (5) As a result, Williams laments, our government is paralyzed and our problems go unsolved. (6)

Next, Williams charges that polarization has a partner – hypocrisy. Take the spiraling national debt, for example. Republicans blame it on the skyrocketing costs of entitlements – Medicare, Medicaid, and Social Security – while Democrats blame it on tax loopholes favoring the rich. (7) Yet Williams cites impressive evidence from recent decades that shows that both parties are guilty of driving up the debt. (8) Everyone in Washington understands, he points out, that "government is a huge driver of the overall economy" because "most private sector jobs in the United States are tied to federal spending…" (9) As a result, all the members of Congress who want to get reelected work tirelessly "to increase spending to benefit their supporters" in and out of their districts and states. (10) At the same time, the powerful lobbying industry demands their "clients' share of the treasury" with remarkable success year after year. (11)

Arguably the most sacred of the sacred cows, Williams says, is defense spending, which exceeds $700 billion a year. Anyone who dares to raise questions about an item in the defense budget, including the need for a military presence in any of hundreds of locations abroad, is attacked as "unpatriotic" or "weak on national defense." (12)

Despite all this, Williams observes, Republicans and Democrats blame one another "for the yearly budget shortfalls that add to the debt…" (13) They "use the wizard's tactics," he says, "to distract American taxpayers while pushing their hands deep into the federal treasury." (14)

In conclusion, I give Juan Williams high marks for diagnosis. Politically, the nation is sick, very sick. What we need now is treatment. On that subject, however, Williams is silent.

---

1. Crown Publishers, 2011. References here to this book are by page number.
2. Pp. 6-7.

3. Williams gives this data on the decline of moderates in the Congress:

> ...(T)he percentage of moderates (in the House) decreased from 30 percent in 1976 to 8 percent by 2002. In the Senate the proportion of members who identified themselves as moderates in the same period fell from 41 percent to 5 percent. (p. 75)

4. As an example, President Obama was attacked by members of his own party as a "traitor" and a "sellout" when he cut a deal with Republicans in which "he agreed to extend the upper-income tax cuts in exchange for adding several months of benefits for the unemployed, as well as funding for scholarships, tax exemptions for businesses to buy equipment, and jobs programs." (pp. 119-120)

5. Williams has harsh words for "provocateurs" in the media who entertain and influence their target audiences. Whether on Fox or MSNBC or AM talk radio, they make it more and more difficult for "voices of moderation and calm persuasion" to be heard. (p. 225) See Chapter 8, "The Provocateurs," pp. 210-242, for his critique of Rush Limbaugh, Glenn Beck, Michael Moore, Arianna Huffington, Al Franken, and others. In this chapter he reveals the annual income of some of these talk radio and TV personalities. For instance, in 2010, Rush Limbaugh earned $59 million.

6. See Chapter 2, "Defying the PC Police," pp. 32-58.

7. P. 119.

8. Chapter 5, "Tax Cuts, Entitlements, and Health Care," pp. 119-151.

9. P. 131.

10. P. 131.

11. Pp. 131-132.

12. P. 134. Williams charges that all legislators, despite their protestations about the deficit, work to preserve military bases and to protect military contractors in their areas.

13. P. 133.

14. P. 132. The following is a good summary of Williams' charge of hypocrisy:

> All the wizards and their distracting tricks of political spin cannot hide the fact that politicians on every side – Republicans, Democrats, Independents, Tea Partiers, and socialists – feed at the federal trough. They brag to their constituents about 'bringing home the bacon' from Washington. They put earmarks on legislation for personal projects such as the infamous 'bridge to nowhere' in Alaska. Then, during campaigns, they shamelessly attack one another over high taxes and endless spending. All the candidates tell the voters their hands are clean, while blaming the other side for the huge yearly budget shortfalls that add to the debt, create financial burdens for future generations, and create the risk of inflation and overall economic instability. It is great political theater, but our tickets to this production are ruinously expensive. (p. 133)

Sam Harris on Guns (January 3, 2013)

IN THE WAKE OF THE massacre at Newtown, Connecticut, millions of Americans are asking what can be done to prevent such carnage in the future. Sam Harris is one of them. A best-selling author and gun owner, Harris recently published an essay on his blog entitled "The Riddle of the Gun" (1) in which he tries to show that enhancing public safety is much more difficult than most of us appreciate.

Here are some of the points he makes:

- The proliferation of firearms in the nation has not produced an increase in violence. Although Americans own over three hundred million firearms, many states recently legalized concealed carry, four millions new guns are sold every year, and the federal law banning assault weapons expired in 2004, the rate of violent crime has actually gone down twenty-two percent in the past ten years.
- Gun violence is highest where gun ownership is lowest – in our cities. Thirty percent of city-dwellers own guns compared to sixty percent of country-dwellers but the incidence of gun violence in the cities far exceeds that in the country. Much of the violence in the cities is drug and gang-related. (2)
- Although mass shootings draw extensive media coverage, they account for relatively few murders. Since 1982, there have been 565,000 homicides in the United States but less than one-tenth of one percent of those killed – 543 – were victims of mass shootings. (3)

- The weapon used in "the vast majority of murders" in the United States, including mass shootings, is not the AR 15 rifle that was used in Newtown and which many people want to ban. It is the handgun. Rifles of any type figure into only three percent of murders in the nation. What's more, the handgun is the weapon "best suited for being carried undetected" into public places and it is the one that gets a thumbs up in the courts. On two occasions, in 2008 and 2010, the U.S. Supreme Court ruled that the Second Amendment prohibits banning handguns; and
- Although no one has seriously proposed banning hunting rifles, a hunting rifle, according to gun experts, significantly expands a world-be killer's range. The scope on a hunting rifle enables a shooter to mow down victims at a distance of hundreds of yards.

Thus, according to Harris, we face this predicament: the two types of weapons most suitable for mass murder – handguns, due to ease of concealment, and rifles, due to range – are also "the most common," "the least stigmatized," and the least likely to be banned.

Given this, can anything constructive be done, according to Harris? Although he admits that preventing school shootings is probably impossible, he supports mandatory training and background checks for all gun owners, and he endorses the National Rifle Association proposal to station trained police officers in our schools. (4)

This prompts a question. If trained police officers are our only realistic hope to prevent mass slaughter, why does Harris stop with our schools? How about other sites where large numbers of people gather? Further, will there be enough trained police to go around? And, if there are, how will we pay for them?

---

1. For Harris' blog, see samharris.org/blog. Harris, a neuroscientist, came to prominence with the publication of two critiques of religion, *The End of Faith* in 2004, and *Letter to a Christian Nation* in 2006. He is often labeled "a new atheist," along with Richard Dawkins, Christopher Hitchens, and Daniel Dennett, due to the tone of their books in contrast to more moderate critics of religion such as Paul Kurtz, Michael Shermer, and Carl Sagan.

2. Thirty percent of city dwellers own at least one firearm; forty-two percent of suburbanites own at least one; and sixty percent of residents in the countryside own at least one. Overall, forty-seven percent of Americans own a firearm.

3. By contrast, it is estimated that 100,000 Americans die each year from doctors and nurses failing to wash their hands properly.

4. Ironically, Harris is a critic of the NRA, believing that it wields far too much political influence.

Etiquette in Today's World (March 5, 2013)

In recent years, I have seen dozens of instances where people were riveted to the cell phones despite the fact that they were in the company of friends and family. Just last week I watched two children at a restaurant with their mother who spoke on her cell phone during the entire meal and said very little to her children. Is this good manners? According to Philip Galanes, who writes an advice column for the Sunday *New York Times*, it isn't. Recently Galanes published a book on how to deal with problems caused by modern technology entitled *Social Q's: How to Survive the Quirks, Quandaries, and Quagmires of Today*. (1) Let's take a look at his recommendations on five problems.

Problem One: You're walking in heavy pedestrian traffic. A person walking toward you is on a collision course with you because he or she is preoccupied with a cell phone. Should you speak up and issue a warning? Recommendation: No! You should keep your mouth shut, practice the walking version of defensive driving, and walk on by. Saying something could turn an inconvenience into a confrontation and since more and more walkers e-mail, text, and tweet every year, taking on the role of a traffic cop could turn your future walks into needlessly hazardous trips.

Problem Two: Should you text or e-mail a friend or relative with whom you have a grievance? No! Don't text or e-mail to deal with personal conflicts. Face-to-face conversations or, if necessary, cell phone conversations are far better to deal with them. If you feel you must text or e-mail, wait at least two hours before your send the message.

Problem Three: Should you use your cell phone while in the company of others at a meal, a meeting, or another social event? Recommendation: No! Put your cell phone on silent mode or vibration in such situations. If you get a message that you simply must respond to, excuse yourself and keep your absence a matter of seconds, not minutes. Doing otherwise tells those around you that they don't count for much in your life.

Problem Four: You're on Facebook. To whom should you send messages? And which requests to be "friends" should you agree to? Recommendation: You should send messages to and befriend only people whom you know personally and whose company you enjoy, at least most of the time. (As an aside, most Facebook enthusiasts whom I know violate this admonition daily.)

Problem Five: Should you use an online dating service to find a companion? Recommendation: No! Face-to-face contact is the safest way to find a companion. Many who advertise themselves on online dating services are already married, they embellish their achievements and credentials, and they use photos that are out of date.

One issue that Galanes does not deal with is using a cell phone while driving. Research shows that people who do this drive with the competence of an alcohol-impaired driver and cannot respond to unexpected road problems as well as non-users. If you talk, text, or tweet while you're driving, you place the safety of yourself, your passengers, and the occupants of other vehicles at risk.

I hope that Philip Galanes will write a sequel on manners as technology changes. What you and I do routinely may be neither mannerly nor moral.

---

1. Simon & Schuster, 2011.

Elyn Saks (March 15, 2013)

Elyn Saks was born to wealthy, supportive Jewish parents in Miami in the 1950s. Bright, curious, and hard-working, she excelled in her studies. At Vanderbilt, where she majored in philosophy, she won Phi Beta Kappa honors and graduated first in her class. Elyn then accepted a Marshall Fellowship to Oxford where she earned a master's degree in philosophy. Her next stop was Yale Law School where she edited the *Yale Law Journal* and earned a *Juris Doctor*. (1)

After law school, Elyn both practiced and taught law in Connecticut for three years. Then, in 1989, she accepted an offer to join the faculty at the University of California School of Law. At USC she earned faculty tenure, served as the law school's associate dean for research for five years, and won appointment to an endowed chair. She is the Orrin B. Evans Professor of Law, Psychology, and Psychiatry and the Behavioral Sciences. At last check, Elyn's publication record includes four books, all enthusiastically received, and dozens of chapters in books and articles in law journals.

And, by the way, while doing all this at USC, Elyn also managed to earn another degree – a Ph.D. in psychoanalysis at the New School for Psychoanalysis. As a result, in addition to teaching at the USC School of Law, she also teaches psychiatry and the law at the USC School of Medicine and at the University of California, San Diego.

In 2009 Elyn received the prestigious MacArthur Foundation Fellowship, the so-called "genius award." (2) She used the $500,000 prize that accompanies the award to establish the Saks Institute for Mental Health Law, Policy, and Ethics at USC. (3)

Obviously, by any reasonable standard, Elyn Saks is a remarkably successful person. What makes her truly special, however, is the fact that she has built such an impressive career while battling schizophrenia! Schizophrenia is...

> ...a brain disease which entails a profound loss of connection to reality. It is often accompanied with delusions, which are fixed but false beliefs - such as you have killed thousands of people – and hallucinations, which are false sensory perceptions – such as you have just seen a man with a knife. (4)

For most of her life, Elyn kept her illness a secret and learned how to mask her flights from reality. Until, that is, the flights failed to end and she was forced into treatment in and out of institutions. One lesson that Elyn learned the hard way over the years is that she had to surrender her stubborn resistance to medication because every time that she quit taking her meds, she suffered relapses.

About ten years ago, against the advice of her husband and some friends, she decided to publicly acknowledge her psychosis in the hope that her story would inspire others with mental illness. (5) This resulted in a candid memoir entitled *The Center Cannot Hold: My Journey Through Madness*, which appeared in 2007.

In my judgment, Elyn Sak's life teaches us two lessons. One is that a rich and satisfying life is still possible for many victims of mental illness. The other is that if Elyn Saks can meet the crushing challenge of schizophrenia, then those of us who are *not* mentally ill should be able to meet the much less intimidating challenges that we face in our own personal and professional journeys.

---

1. As a law student, Elyn also published an article called a "Note," entitled "The Use of Mechanical Restraints in Psychiatric Hospitals," in the *Yale Law Journal* in 1986. Praise for this article which she received from a practicing attorney at the Bazelon Center for Mental Health Law, which Elyn characterizes as "the premier public interest law firm representing people with mental illness," was a source of great pride and encouragement to her. See Elyn R. Saks, *The*

Center Cannot Hold: My Journey Through Madness, Hyperion, 2007, p. 213. References to this book here are by page number.

2. The MacArthur Foundation website explains that twenty to twenty-five exceptionally creative and productive individuals receive the award in a typical year. The $500,000 stipend which the award carries comes with no strings attached.

3. According to the USC School of Law website, the Saks Institute brings together USC faculty from seven departments – law, psychiatry, psychology, social work, gerontology, philosophy, and engineering – to focus on one important mental health issue a year.

4. Saks, p. 168. Saks adds that schizophrenia is "the most severe of the psychotic disorders." (p. 328) For a schizophrenic, "the wall that separates fantasy from reality dissolves…" (p. 111) A schizophrenic's mind is not "split" but "shattered" (p. 328) and schizophrenia should not be confused with mood disorders (such as bipolar illness). Schizophrenia is a "thought disorder," not a "mood disorder." (p. 329) Mood disorders are characterized by "manic depression and depression." (p. 329) People with mood disorders can function normally with more success than people with cognitive disorders. Among recent persons with mood disorders are journalists Mike Wallace and Jane Pauley, writer William Styron, and psychologist and writer Kay Redfield Jamison. (p. 329)

Saks estimates that "only one in five people with schizophrenia can ever be expected to live independently and hold a job." (p. 288)

5. Saks, p. 333. Since Elyn published *The Center Cannot Hold*, many functional schizophrenics across the nation have come forward, not only to acknowledge their illness, but to volunteer for scientific studies. See the *New York Times*, October 22, 2011.

Religion – Can We Take a Fresh Look? (May 9, 2013)

THE VAST MAJORITY OF PEOPLE across the world are religious. And when it comes to religion, comparison shopping is the exception. Most of us embrace the religion or sect which is popular where we grow up. If you live in Utah, you're likely to be a Mormon. If you live in Saudi Arabia, you're likely to be a Muslim. If you live in India, you're likely to be a Hindu.

In the past two decades, dozens of books have appeared which encourage religious people to take a fresh look at their beliefs and practices. Nearly all have been written by secular authors, some of whom abandoned their faith and all of whom hope that books will prompt believers to have a conversion experience. The two most recent are John W. Loftus, *The Outsider Test of Faith: How to Know Which Religion is True*, and Guy P. Harrison, *50 simple questions for every Christian*. (1)

Loftus distinguishes between an "insider" and an "outsider" perspective in faith. When it comes to our own religion, according to Loftus, we take the insider's approach. We believe confidently without proof. When it comes to another religion, however, we take the outsider's approach. We are skeptics who demand proof. The challenge which Loftus throws out to believers is to apply to their own religion the same skepticism which they apply to other ones. He is hopeful that doing this will result in a significant retreat from faith.

Harrison walks much the same path as Loftus. He accuses Christians of a double standard. He writes: "If Christians only applied the same reasoning that they use on other gods and other religions (to their own), they might feel differently about Christianity…" (*50 simple questions*, p. 263) A major problem in the United States which Harrison highlights, and which extensive research supports, is prejudice by believers against non-believers. He argues that most Christians consider atheists and agnostics to be immoral and untrustworthy and that seculars are in a place where women, blacks, and gays were decades ago. (*50 simple questions*, p. 264)

Loftus and Harrison have written well-argued books. There is no question that many believers are more skeptical of other religions than their own and that many distrust non-believers. My own judgment, however, is that these authors will have little success in shrinking the ranks of believers in the United States or altering their attitudes toward non-believers. Here's why:

- The authors don't appreciate that, despite the popularity of religion in our culture, religious ignorance in America is rampant. Most believers are not so much skeptical of other religions as ignorant of them. Indeed, as Dr. Prothero from Boston University has demonstrated in his research, many believers are ignorant of important elements of their own religion.
- The primary audience of secular critics of religion is secular readers; in other words, Loftus and Harrison are preaching to the choir;
- The United States has not experienced the same rise of secularism as has occurred in Europe; although young people today in the U.S. are less religious than their elders, religion here remains deeply ingrained in our culture;
- Public attitudes toward atheists and agnostics have softened a bit in recent years but the overall picture hasn't changed dramatically and I don't expect a sea change soon. How many Americans know or care that Angela Jolie, George Will, Warren Buffet, Bill Gates,

Ted Turner and hundreds of other respected public figures are non-believers? And how many Americans are ready to vote for an atheist or agnostic candidate for public office?

* Religion in America remains a faith-based belief system, it is a product of social conditioning, and most believers consider faith indispensable to living a responsible life. I know of no evidence that this will change any time soon.

---

1. Both books were published by Prometheus Books, a secular press, in 2013. Loftus is a former Christian minister and Harrison is a science journalist. Reference to their books here is by page number.

Tom Flynn on the State of Religion in America (June 6, 2013)

Free Inquiry is a magazine which serves seculars in the United States and many other nations. Although seculars often disagree, the current issue (June/July 2013) highlights an especially wide gap over the state of religion in America between Tom Flynn, the magazine's chief editor, (1) and Jim Haught, the magazine's senior editor and a frequent contributor. (2) In this commentary I will focus on Flynn's view and in my next one on Haught's.

Flynn argues that religion in the U.S. is alive and well and that seculars who believe otherwise are mistaken. (3) A prime piece of evidence that he offers is the media coverage of what he calls "the papal succession extravaganza" – the resignation of Pope Benedict XVI and the election of Pope Francis I. He points out that it was a lead story for thirty-one straight days, often marginalizing other important events near and far. This happened, he says, because the media know that "faith still matters" to "vast numbers" at home and abroad.

Further, Flynn argues, "religion and religious institutions are (as) influential in culture…and politics as…they are in the domain of faith." To support this, he cites the following:

- President Obama continues the faith-based programs started by his predecessor which grant public funds to support religion;

- Recently the Indiana Supreme Court ruled that the nation's largest state-sponsored voucher program, granting parents tax dollars to enroll their children in religious schools, is constitutional;
- The nation's original motto – *e pluribus unum* – "from many one" – was replaced by "In God We Trust";
- Despite protests and litigation, countless public bodies open their sessions with prayer, and many governments allow crosses and nativity scenes on public property and display the Ten Commandments in public buildings; and
- Two states have passed legislation recently banning abortion long before the *Roe v. Wade* standard of 24 weeks and others are planning to do so.

Flynn also responds to surveys cited by seculars who claim that religion is dying. They show that today one of five adult Americans and one of three in the eighteen-to-twenty-five age group are non-religious. So what? he asks. "Do the math" and you will see that *four* out of *five* adults and *two* out of *three* young people remain religious! The fact is, Flynn insists, "Religious believers are still very much in the majority, and they are still enormously powerful."

Although he doesn't summon other evidence to buttress this conclusion, probably due to space limitations, there is much that he could. It includes chaplains in legislatures and the military, the fact that contributions to religion far exceed those to any other recipient, the prohibition of same-sex marriage in dozens of states, the refusal of many schools to teach evolution, the exemption from prosecution in dozens of states of faith-healers who deny traditional medical care to their sick children, the relentless promotion of the agenda of the Religious Right in the courts by legal groups with combined budgets that exceed $100 million a year, and the fact that a significant majority of Americans say that they will never vote for an atheist or agnostic for president. (4)

Personally, I think Flynn is a realist and that the evidence for his position is strong.

Next time, I'll take a look at Jim Haught's rebuttal.

---

1. Flynn is also executive director of the Council for Secular Humanism, the executive director of the Robert Green Ingersoll Birthplace Museum, author of *The Trouble with Christmas* (1993), *Galactic Rapture* (2000), *Nothing Sacred* (2004), and *The Messiah Game: A Comedy of Terrors, Part One* (2012), and editor of the *New Encyclopedia of Unbelief* (2007). Reference to the articles by Flynn and Haught in the June/July 2013 issue of *Free Inquiry* in this commentary and the subsequent one is by page number.
2. In addition to his role as a senior editor of *Free Inquiry*, Haught is editor of West Virginia's largest newspaper, *The Charleston Gazette*, and author of three books – *Holy Horrors* (1990), *2000 Years of Disbelief* (1996), and *Fading Faith* (2010).
3. Flynn, pp. 4-6.
4. Other examples that Flynn could cite are presidents placing their hand on a Bible when they take the oath of office and adding the phrase "so help me God" which is not part of the oath in the Constitution; prohibition; the singing of "God Bless America" at Memorial Day and Independence Day events; NASCAR races preceded by a prayer by a Christian minister; presidents closing speeches with "May God bless you and may God bless the United States of America"; the fact that after destructive events such as the recent tornado in Moore, Oklahoma, or the massacre of children in Newtown, Connecticut, thousands do not curse God but instead gather in churches to pray and sing; prayer at many public school commencements; the religiosity that pervades much of country music; and the addition of "under God" after "one nation" in the original Pledge of Allegiance.

Jim Haught on the State of Religion in America (June 13, 2013)

Free Inquiry IS A MAGAZINE which serves seculars in the United States and many other nations. Although seculars often disagree, the current issue (June/July 2013) highlights an especially wide gap over the state of religion in America between Tom Flynn, the magazine's chief editor, (1) and Jim Haught, the magazine's senior editor and a frequent contributor. (2) In my last commentary, I discussed Flynn's view that religion is alive and well; in this one, I turn to Haught's view that religion in American is dying. (3)

To make his case, Haught first cites a list of dramatic changes in America since the 1950s. Here are the major ones that he mentions:

- Then, stores didn't open on the Sabbath. Now, in his words, "Sunday is a whopper-shopper-day."
- Then, gays who had sex were arrested and imprisoned in many states for violating sodomy laws. Now, gay sex is no longer a crime.
- Then, blacks were restricted to certain jobs and to segregated neighborhoods, schools, hotels, restaurants, theaters, and swimming pools. Now, civil rights laws prohibit discrimination.
- Then, it was "unthinkable" for unwed couples to live together. Now, millions of unwed couples do so.

- Then, if a single woman had a baby, it was "disgraceful" for her and her family. Now, it is common and it carries no stigma.
- Then, gambling was illegal in many places. Now, governments sponsor it.
- Then, prayer in public schools was mandatory. Now, it is banned by the courts.
- Then, abortion, and in many cases, contraception, were prohibited by law. Now, the courts guarantee access to them.
- Then, writers and photographers who portrayed sex were subject to prosecution. Now, they have remarkable artistic freedom.
- Then, women were blocked from most careers. Now, they can pursue the career paths of their choice.

Next, Haught gives us an interpretation of why these changes occurred. They took place, he opines, because secular humanism has won out over religion. "*Humanism*," he writes, "means striving to improve people's lives – and *secular* means to do so without religion." (Apparently, few among the religious share the commitment to improve lives in the here and now, according to Haught, because they are fixated on the afterlife.) Indeed, he says, religious conservatives have resisted "each step forward." In Haught's words, "throughout history" secular humanists "have been (the) key figures in struggles for human rights and social justice."

In my judgment this interpretation is simplistic. While it is true that religious forces have been on the wrong side of the moral fence in some cases, such as slavery, there are frequent instances when they were and are on the right side. Let me give three examples:

- The principal architect of modern democracy with its components of human rights, government by consent, majority rule, and the separation of powers, is 17th century British philosopher, John Locke, a Christian.

- The civil rights movement in America which transformed life for tens of millions was led and energized by Christian clergy, notably Dr. Martin Luther King, Jr., and their congregations.
- Thousands of religious individuals and groups across the nation seek to improve people's lives daily through their work in hospitals, nursing homes, schools, shelters, and soup kitchens, among others.

So, what do you think? Is religion flourishing in America, as Tom Flynn claims? Or is it dying, as Jim Haught claims?

---

1. Flynn is also the director of the Council for Secular Humanism, the executive director of the Robert Green Ingersoll Birthplace Museum, author of *The Trouble with Christmas* (1993), *Galactic Rapture* (2000), *Nothing Sacred* (2004), *and the Messiah Game: A Comedy of Terrors, Part One* (2012), and editor of the *New Encyclopedia of Unbelief* (2007). Reference to the articles by Flynn and Haught in the June/July 2013 issue of *Free Inquiry* in this commentary and the previous one is by page number.

2. In addition to his role as a senior editor of *Free Inquiry*, Haught is editor of West Virginia's largest newspaper, *The Charleston Gazette*, and author of three books – *Holy Horrors* (1990), *2000 Years of Disbelief* (1996), and *Fading Faith* (2010).

3. Haught writes: "The good news is that religion is dying in America, as it did in Europe, Canada, Australia, Japan, and other advanced democracies." (p. 43)

Sylvia Browne, Psychic (June 27, 2013)

Surveys show that 13% of Americans, or roughly 40 million people, believe that a gifted few called psychics have special powers to predict the future, find missing people, solve crimes, and communicate with the dead. Sylvia Browne is arguably the most popular psychic in the United States. She was born in Kansas City in 1936 and she has been doing public "readings" since 1974. She came to prominence mainly as a weekly guest on *The Montel Williams Show* for seventeen years. (1) Today she does personal appearances to packed houses across the country, she does twenty to thirty minute telephone consultations for $550 per session, reduced recently from $850 per session, she runs a church in California which she founded called the *Society of Novus Spiritus*, she maintains an immensely popular website, and she publishes books on the spiritual and the paranormal. (2)

Along the way Sylvia has encountered bumps in the road. She has had five marriages, she was sentenced to one year probation and 300 hours of community service in 1992 after being convicted of security fraud in a gold-mining venture in California, she is a frequent target of skeptics such as James Randi who charge that she is a con artist, (3) and a few years ago she suffered a heart attack.

Despite her huge following, Browne has made mistakes galore. Indeed, one published study of 115 criminal cases that she addressed (4) concluded that she failed to solve a single one. (5) Here are some errors which her critics often cite:

- Browne said that during the Sago mining disaster that the miners were alive when they were dead;
- She said that a missing child in Texas had been abducted and taken to Japan as a slave. It turned out that the child had been kidnapped and murdered in Texas;
- She told a family in 2002 that their missing daughter, Holly Krewson, was a drug addict working at a strip club in Los Angeles. Detectives eventually found that the woman had been murdered six years earlier;
- She said that Bill Clinton was innocent of any wrongdoing with Monica Lewinsky;
- She predicted that breast cancer would be cured by 1999; and
- In 2004 on *The Montel Williams Show*, she assured Louwana Miller, Amanda Berry's mother, that her missing daughter was dead while Amanda and two other young women were being held captive by Ariel Castro in his house in Cleveland. (6)

The last case caused Sylvia Browne great embarrassment. It was obvious that the failure of her psychic powers enabled a captor to confine, beat, and rape three women for a decade. Once the women were rescued on May 6 of this year, a war took place online between Browne's supporters and detractors. The traffic was so intense that Browne shut down her *Facebook* page. Ironically, one of Browne's supporters was Sherry Cole, Amanda Berry's cousin, who gave a statement on behalf of the family because Amanda's mother had died during her ordeal. Cole said: "Our family in no way blames Sylvia. This changes nothing. We still love her and believe in her."

In my judgment, psychics and their fans teach us an important lesson: gullibility, wishful thinking, and loyalty often trump critical thinking.

---

1. According to *Wikipedia*, Browne's appearances on *The Montel Williams Show*, taped in advance, were edited before airing "to show only apparent hits and to remove anything that does not reflect well on the medium." Brown also made repeat appearances on *Larry King Live*.

2. Several years ago Browne's business manager said that Browne's annual earnings were $3 million.

3. On September 3, 2001, in a joint appearance with Randi on *Larry King Live*, Browne agreed to accept Randi's $1 Million Challenge in which she would win the prize if she could successfully demonstrate her paranormal powers in a controlled scientific test. She has since declined to take the test. For other criticisms of Browne, see StopSylvia.com.

4. Ryan Shaffer and Agatha Jadwiszczok, "Psychic Detective: Sylvia Browne's History of Failure," *Skeptical Inquirer*, March/April 2010. A previous study of Browne's failures appeared in *Brill's Content*.

5. The authors claim that of the 115 cases, she had zero correct, twenty-five incorrect, and that the other ninety are unsolved so that we cannot yet tell if she was correct or incorrect on them. (However, see the Amanda Berry case below.) Nevertheless, Browne stubbornly insists that she scores an 87 percent to 89 percent success rate with her pronouncements about missing persons and criminal cases.

6. After the show, Amanda's mother returned to Cleveland, cleaned out her daughter's room, took down her pictures, and gave away her computer. See *The Plain Dealer*, November 18, 2004. Other cases cited by Browne's critics include these: she told an audience that a missing man – Richard Kneebone – was alive in Canada; a few days later his decomposed body was found in California; soon after she assured the family of a 9/11 firefighter that he was alive, his body was found buried deep under the rubble at the World Trade Center; she said that Michael Jackson would be found guilty of child molestation; and she predicted that Bill Bradley would be elected President of the United States of America.

Dr. Carl Hart (August 1, 2013)

CARL HART WAS BORN INTO a poor black family in Miami in 1966. His parents had an abusive relationship and eventually divorced. (1) In the hood, young Carl learned the honor code, stole, carried a gun, slept around, (2) used and sold drugs, and stayed in high school only to play sports. (3)

Fast forward to 2013. Now in his late forties, Carl Hart is married, a father of two boys, a Ph.D. in neuroscience, and a tenured professor at Columbia University where he does cutting edge research on drugs, behavior, and the brain. (4) Indeed, the story of his journey from the hood to an Ivy League campus is grist for a film or a TV series.

How did he do it? How did he turn his life around? In a new book, *High Price*, (5) Hart attributes his success to many factors – encouragement by "Big Mama," his paternal grandmother, nurturing by his older sisters, persistence by his high school guidance counselor, opportunities provided in the U.S. Air Force, mentoring by a handful of higher education faculty and staff, and…*luck*!

In *High Price*, Hart also makes the case that we need to reeducate the nation about drugs and reform the nation's drug laws. The war on drugs, he argues, is based on myths. These are beliefs which have been discredited but which persist. Here are four of them:

- Myth: We can remove virtually all illegal drugs from circulation. Fact: More Americans than ever – twenty million plus – use illegal drugs today despite the fact that since the war on drugs began in the 1970s, we have spent untold billions of dollars, built dozens of new jails and prisons, and incarcerated millions of people. (6) For Hart, the prohibition of drugs has been as successful as the prohibition of alcohol. (7)

- Myth: Regular drug use leads to addiction. (8) Fact: Seventy-five percent of regular drug users aren't addicts. (9)
- Myth: Crack cocaine is far more harmful than powder cocaine and therefore the penalties for the use of crack should be far more serious than those for the use of powder. Fact: Crack cocaine and powder cocaine have the same effect on a user so that disparate penalties make no sense. (10)
- Myth: Crack cocaine is the prime cause of the major problems in poor black neighborhoods today. Fact: With the possible exception of violence due to turf wars among dealers, the major problems in poor black neighborhoods today preceded crack. (11)

So, what does Carl Hart propose as an alternative to the failed war on drugs? He proposes the path taken by Portugal – decriminalization – where drugs remain illegal and users are issued a citation – a ticket – but not arrested or jailed as criminals. (12) This is important, especially to the young, Hart contends, because a criminal record can destroy one's prospects in the job market. (13)

Will Hart get a hearing across the nation? He deserves to, as I see it, for two reasons: the status quo isn't working and he brings science to the table. But I won't be shocked if he doesn't because change is difficult and myths are both soothing and stubborn. (14)

---

1. When the parents divorced, both left the children. Where the father went is not clear in the book. The mother went to New York for two years. The two grandmothers assumed responsibility for the eight children.
2. Hart fathered a child when he was sixteen on a one-night stand. He didn't learn about this until many years later when it was revealed to him and his paternity was confirmed by DNA.

3. The college basketball scholarship that he expected never materialized. Since he had bragged all along that he was a shoe-in for one, he joined the Air Force after high school mainly to avoid the embarrassment of having to stay in town.

4. Technically, Hart is a neuropsychopharmacologist.

5. 2013, Harper. The subtitle is: *A Neuroscientist's Journey of Self-Discovery That Challenges Everything You Know About Drugs and Society.* References to this book here are by page number.

6. Hart points out that spending in the war on drugs between 1970 and 2011 increased by 3,500 percent but "had no effect on daily use of marijuana, heroin, or any type of cocaine." (p. 18)

7. Hart contends that there never was and never will be a drug-free society on earth. (p. 210)

8. The definition of addiction which Hart uses is from psychiatry's *Diagnostic and Statistical Manual of Mental Disorders* (or DSM), which is widely accepted. According to DSM, regular use is a necessary but not a sufficient condition for addiction. For addiction, the use must be regular, "must interfere with important life functions like parenting, work, and intimate relationships," and "must continue despite ongoing negative consequences, take up a great deal of time and mental energy, and persist in the face of repeated attempts to stop or cut back." (p. 13)

9. Page 13. Hart says that since the news often features cases involving users who are in trouble with the law, the public assumes that this is the norm for users.

10. The federal Drug Abuse Act of 1986, passed amid hysteria over crack, provided a penalty for use of crack a hundred times more severe than the penalty for use of powder. During the Obama administration, the ratio has been lowered from 100:1 to 18:1 but even this reduced penalty is indefensible. Further, Hart points out that one side effect of this disparity has been the incarceration of huge numbers of blacks for use of crack which is cheap, popular, and accessible in many black neighborhoods, and which is often purchased in locations known by police.

11. The list of such problems includes gangs, teen pregnancy, absentee fathers, poverty, dropping out of school, obesity, reliance on public assistance, and unemployment, among others.

12. In the Portuguese model, however, selling drugs remains a punishable crime. Also, the Portuguese model provides counseling and treatment for users who request them.

13. Page 324. Hart points out that in the U.S. "more than 80 percent of arrests for drug offenses involve only simple possession." (p. 324)

14. And at times myths can be – dare I say it? – addictive.

Academically Adrift (August 29, 2013)

ACCORDING TO SURVEYS, VIRTUALLY ALL faculty members in higher education in the United States believe that helping students become effective thinkers and writers is an essential goal and that their courses meet this goal. (1) But is this confidence justified? According to two sociologists, Richard Arum and Josipa Roksa, it is not. In their book, *Academically Adrift: Limited Learning on College Campuses,* they present research that shows that many students today meet course requirements, produce a good grade average, and earn a degree while making little progress in thinking and writing. (2)

In their research Arum and Roksa used an instrument called the Collegiate Learning Assessment, or CLA, to test 2,322 students at a diverse group of twenty-four four-year institutions scattered across the nation. (3) The CLA tests for critical thinking, complex reasoning, and writing – *general skills.* It does not test for *specific information* gained in particular courses or disciplines. (4) It presents a student with a written statement and a series of questions about it which require written responses. The students in the study took the CLA at the start of their first year and at the end of their second year. By comparing the results, the researchers were able to determine the impact of the college experience on the skills tested. (5)

And what were the results? The average gain in general skills of the more than 2,300 students tested over the two-year period was only seven percentile points (a 0.18 standard deviation). (6) Remarkably, forty-five percent of those tested showed no gain at all. (7) Anticipating a rebuttal that their measurement instrument, which requires written answers, could skew the real picture, the authors cite another study, the Wabash National Study of Liberal Arts Education, which reached the same findings using multiple choice questions. (8)

If Arum and Roksa are on target – and they seem to be – what most graduates take away from college is "subject-specific knowledge," a diploma, an expanded social circle, and plenty of debt – period.

What explains this retreat from general skills? The authors cite these points:

- Firstly, the "college for all" policy which we follow today puts many poorly prepared students on our campuses;
- Secondly, time devoted to study has shrunk from an average of twenty hours a week a generation ago to an average of twelve hours a week today. In fact, nearly two out of five students today study less than five hours a week;
- Thirdly, most students spend more time outside of class in social and recreational activities than they devote to their courses;
- Fourthly, reading and writing expectations for college students are low. One-third never have a single course that requires forty pages or more of reading a week and half never have a single course that requires twenty pages or more of writing during a term; and
- Fifthly, grade inflation is rampant. Even though study time is minimal, 55 percent of college students earn a B plus or higher GPA and 85 percent of them earn a B minus or higher GPA. (9)

Clearly, *Academically Adrift* is a wake-up call to all of us – students, parents, faculty, administrators, trustees, government officials, taxpayers, and benefactors – who care about education and its place in a democracy.

---

1. Richard Arum and Josipa Roksa, *Academically Adrift: Limited Learning on College Campuses*, University of Chicago Press, Chicago and London, 2011, p. 35. References to this book here are by page number.

2. The research project culminating in this book was organized by the Social Science Research Council and the Pathways to College Network and funded by grants from the Lumina Foundation for Education, the Ford Foundation, the Carnegie Corporation of New York, and the Teagle Foundation. (pp. ix-x)

3. The Collegiate Learning Assessment was developed by the Council for Aid to Education. As of 2013, over 700 institutions of higher education in the U.S. and abroad have used it.

4. Website, Council for Aid to Education, and *Academically Adrift*, p. 21.

5. This is a "longitudinal study," one that tracks the change in the subjects over a period of a year or more. (p. 19)

6. Page 35.

7. Page 36.

8. Page 36. Arum and Roksa cite other studies with similar results, including ones that test during the first and fourth year of college. See pp. 36-37. The Arum-Roksa study showed that a high percentage of students who did relatively well on both CLA tests had common characteristic, including college-educated and financially solvent parents, and a history of academic achievement in high school. See pp. 37-50. Nevertheless, among the students who demonstrated "notable gains" from test 1 to test 2 were individuals "from all family backgrounds and racial/ethnic groups" and students with weak high school preparation. (p. 56)

9. Arum and Roksa also cite the following: evidence suggests that college students today, unlike their predecessors, are more interested in financial success than personal growth ("a philosophy of life"), faculty acquiesce in low standards in their courses to free up time for research and publication, and administrators focus on access and graduation rates rather than what students learn because these factors are central to institutional revenue and public image.

Alternative Medicine (October 31, 2013)

RECENTLY A SURGICAL NURSE IN a Toledo hospital discarded as trash a healthy kidney donated by a brother to save the life of a sister. We're all familiar with flaws such as this in conventional medicine. The list is long – misdiagnosis, infections acquired in a hospital, botched surgeries, long waits in a doctor's office, mistakes by lab technicians, ever-rising co-pays and deductibles, cold and arrogant doctors, and so on. This helps to explain why half of the adult population in the United States has turned to alternative medicine which is now a $34 billion a year industry.

As Paul Offit observes in a new book:

> Americans love alternative medicine. They go to their acupuncturist or chiropractor or naturopath to relieve pain. They take ginkgo for memory or homeopathic remedies for the flu or megavitamins for energy or Chinese herbs for potency or Indian spices to boost their immune system. (1)

But is alternative medicine the cure for the shortcomings of conventional medicine? I, for one, am skeptical because of the dramatic differences between them, namely,

1) *conventional medicine rests on scientific testing while alternative medicine does not,* and
2) *conventional medicine is regulated by law while alternative medicine is not.*

Under the law, the Food and Drug Administration requires that medical devices, medications, vaccines, and treatments used in conventional medicine must be proven safe and effective before sale. The FDA also requires disclosure of the side effects and it can recall a product after marketing for public safety. By contrast, alternative medicine gets a free pass. There is no legal mandate for testing, proof, disclosure, or recall.

While many insist that alternative medicine has helped them and they remain fiercely loyal, two serious problems remain. The first is overall effectiveness. Studies show, for example, that contrary to claims, saw palmetto doesn't shrink prostates, glucosamine doesn't relieve joint pain, St. John's wort doesn't cure depression, and vitamin C doesn't cure colds or cancer. The second is that alternative medicine can make a bad situation worse. For example chiropractic manipulation has torn arteries; acupuncture needles have caused infections and ended up in lungs, livers, and hearts; dietary supplements have caused "bleeding, psychosis, liver dysfunction, heart arrhythmias, seizures, and brain swelling;" and, as was likely the case with Steve Jobs, the substitution of unproven alternative treatment for proven conventional treatment has resulted in avoidable death. (2)

One reason for the success of alternative medicine is effective marketing by charismatic celebrities, such as Suzanne Somers and Jenny McCarthy. Defenders of alternative medicine will reply, as they should, that conventional medicine often uses celebrity spokespersons as well, and, of course, they're right. A product or service should stand or fall on proven effectiveness, not celebrity endorsements.

Another reason for the success of alternative medicine is the National Health Federation, the long-time voice of alternative medicine in Washington. The NHF track record is a lobbyist's dream. Thanks to the political clout of the NHF, the prospect of government regulation of alternative medicine, like it or not, is negligible. (3)

---

1. Paul A. Offit, M.D., *Do You Believe in Magic? The Sense and Nonsense of Alternative Medicine*, HarperCollins, 2013, p. 1. Offit also reports that ten percent of Americans use alternative medicine on their children and that due to "patient demand," forty-two percent of U.S.

hospitals provide access to alternative medicine. See Offit, p. 1. Other terms for alternative medicine are complementary medicine, integrative medicine, and holistic medicine.

2. Offit, p. 5, p. 19, p. 48, p. 53, p. 123. The quote is taken from page 5.

3. One of the NHF's strongest allies in Washington is Senator Orrin Hatch of Utah. In 2003 Senator Hatch owned 35,621 shares of Pharmics, a Utah-based nutrition supplement company. Utah is also the home of four of the nation's largest supplement companies and Hatch's son is a lobbyist for the supplement industry. See Offit, pp. 80-81.

Herbal Supplements: a New Study
(November 7, 2013)

IN A RECENT COMMENTARY I argued that we should be skeptical of alternative medicine because, contrary to conventional medicine, its claims are not confirmed by science and it is unregulated by the Food and Drug Administration. New evidence has now surfaced about herbal supplements, a staple in alternative medicine, which underscores the need for such skepticism. The evidence appears in an important research study in Canada which was published last month in the journal *BME Medicine* (1) and reported this month in *The New York Times*. (2)

The study was led by Steven G. Newmaster of the Biodiversity Institute of Ontario at the University of Guelph. He and his colleagues genetically tested forty-four bottles of popular herbal supplements sold by twelve companies in Canada and the United States. Here is what they found:

- The products of only two of the twelve companies contained the ingredients listed on the label while the products of the other ten companies contained substitutions or adulteration with fillers, such as rice, soybean, or wheat, which were not listed on the label. In fact, the products of two of these ten companies contained *none* of the ingredients listed on the label. (3)
- Bottles of Echinacea, a supplement used by millions to prevent or treat colds, were found to include a bitter weed and a plant which has been linked to rashes, nausea, and flatulence. (4)

- Two bottles sold as St. John's wort, a supplement widely used to treat depression, were found to include none of this herb. One bottle contained rice and the other an Egyptian shrub called Alexandrian senna which is a powerful laxative. (5)
- Bottles of ginkdo biloba, a supplement marketed as a memory enhancer, were found to include fillers and black walnut, a hazard to people who are allergic to nuts. (6)
- A bottle sold as black cohosh, a supplement used to treat hot flashes and other problems associated with menopause, turned out to be a bottle of a plant – Actaea asiatica – that can be toxic to humans; (7) and
- One-third of the supplements tested showed "outright substitution," that is, there was no trace of the plant advertised on the bottle." (8)

And what was the reaction to the study? One the one hand, a senior nutritionist at the Center for Science in the Public Interest – David Schardt – concluded that the study shows such a serious lack of quality control that people who recommend herbal supplements should stop doing so. On the other hand, spokespersons for the supplement industry – Stefan Gafner of the American Botanical Council and Duffy McKay of the Council for Responsible Nutrition – insisted that the study exaggerated the problem and that the herbal supplement industry can improve quality control without government interference. (9)

Meanwhile, in the wake of the study, three things seem clear: herbal supplements may be both ineffective *and* dangerous, there are very few safeguards in place to protect supplement users, and given the political clout of the National Health Federation and other organizations which promote the interests of alternative medicine, change is unlikely.

So, to buyers of herbal supplements, I invoke a Latin warning from the 1500s: "Caveat emptor!" "Let the buyer beware!"

1. Steven G. Newmaster et al., "DNA Barcoding Detects Contamination and Substitution in North American Herbal Supplements," *BMC Medicine*, October 2013, 11:22.
2. Anahad O'Connor, "Pills That Aren't What They Seem," *The New York Times*, November 5, 2013, p. D1, p. D5. Referred to here as "O'Connor" with a page number.
3. O'Connor, p. D5.
4. O'Connor, p. D1.
5. O'Connor, p. D1.
6. O'Connor, p. D1, p. D5.
7. O'Connor, p. D5.
8. O'Connor, p. D5.
9. O'Connor, p. D5.

Jennifer Hecht on Suicide
(December 5, 2013)

IN THE UNITED STATES OVER the past decade, the rate of suicide has risen sharply. Although it rose among all age groups during this period, it shot up dramatically in two groups. In the 35-64 age group, suicide increased by 30 percent, and among men in their fifties, it increased 50 percent. Today, deaths per year due to suicide (38,364) exceed deaths per year due to auto accidents (33,687). (1)

These sobering facts have prompted poet, historian, and philosopher, Jennifer Hecht, to call for a national conversation on suicide in a recent book entitled *Stay*. (2) She also proposes that the conversation focus on two key arguments against suicide, one based on hope, the other on community. Let's consider each. (3)

On hope, Hecht cites studies of near-suicide cases which show a clear pattern. Most of those who nearly took their own lives find that their later lives are "full and rich beyond expectation." (4) She sees three lessons in this: a suicidal mood is often temporary, one's situation is likely to improve as time passes, and suicide is a mistake because it closes off the possibility of improvement.

We must learn, Hecht argues, that moments of happiness in our past are likely to return if we show the patience and courage to endure the sorrow-filled moments of the present. (5) Once we grasp this, she reasons, we will not allow ourselves to be victims of the mood of the moment. (6)

On community, Hecht argues that we have a duty to others, near and far, to stay alive. This is because humanity is "profoundly interconnected." (7) Each of us matters. Each of us contributes in some way to helping others, and when we help others, we promote their happiness *and* our own.

For Hecht, the choice to live says that you care about yourself, your family and friends, and others while the choice to die says that you don't. For Hecht, the choice to live is an acceptance of responsibility and a commitment to *help* others while the choice to die is a rejection of responsibility and a commitment to *harm* them.

On the issue of harm, Hecht addresses two specific types.

The first is the sense of loss among those who value or depend on the deceased. A sudden and unexpected death results in sorrow for the survivors in virtually all cases. When the death is self-inflicted, though, the sorrow is much deeper. In most suicides the one who takes his or her life is not the only victim. (8)

The second is the ripple effect. The evidence is strong that one suicide invites others. The reason is that it legitimates suicide as a response to the shocks, troubles, disappointments, and setbacks that are part of the human condition. It serves as a disincentive to endure a storm. (9)

I applaud Hecht for her attempt to bring suicide out of the shadows. Since anti-suicide programs currently offered by government are not well known and haven't had much impact, I hope that *Stay* will be a catalyst for a fuller understanding of suicide among all age groups and for initiatives to reduce suicide across our culture by schools and colleges, religious groups, the private sector, the media, entertainment, sports, and others.

---

1. *The New York Times*, May 2, 2013. Also, many sources report that suicides in the military now exceed combat deaths.

2. Yale University Press, 2013. Hecht is prudent in calling for nation-wide attention to suicide. Here's why: a) The U.S. Government already has a multi-agency program aimed at stemming the trend toward more suicides and that doesn't seem to be working; and

b) Most other nations with much higher suicide rates than the U.S. also have anti-suicide government programs which don't seem to be working. Examples are Greenland, which leads the world with 108.1 suicides per 100,000 population, and South Korea, which is second in the world with 31.7 suicides per 100,000 population. In Greenland, estimates are that one out of four or one out of five people attempts suicide. In South Korea, suicide is the most common form of death for those under 40. The suicide rate in the U.S., which ranks 33rd among the 107 nations for which data are available, is 12.0 per 100,000 population.

3. While Hecht aims to reduce the suicide rate among the general population, she seems to approve of suicide in most cases of dying people who wish to hasten death.

4. *Stay*, p. 175.

5. Hecht quotes talk-show host Phil Donahue as follows: "Suicide is a permanent solution to a temporary problem." *Stay,* p. 192.

6. On this point, Hecht quotes Voltaire: "The man who in a fit of melancholy, kills himself to-day, would have wished to live had he waited a week." *Stay,* p. 176.

7. Here Hecht quotes the poet John Donne:

> No man is an island, entire of itself; every man is a piece of the continent, a part of the main… (A)ny man's death diminishes me, because I am involved in mankind, and therefore never send to know for whom the bell tolls; it tolls for thee. (*Meditation XVII*, 1623, quoted in *Stay*, p. 121.

8. On the harm caused by suicide, Hecht quotes the 17th century French Enlightenment Philosopher Julien Offran de La Mettrie: "What sort of monster is someone who, afflicted with a momentary pain, tears himself away from his family, his friends, and his homeland, and has no other aim but to deliver himself from his most sacred duties."
The quote is from de La Mettrie's "Epicurean System" and it appears in *Stay*, p. 132.

The realization that one's voluntary, premature death can cause significant harm to others can dissuade a person from suicide. For instance, one man whom I know was deterred from an imminent suicide by a friend who convinced him that his death would be a cruel and hateful legacy to his young daughter who loved him dearly. Incidentally, as time passed, the man's situation improved markedly so that today he is a different person from the one on the verge of suicide. This anecdote illustrates the wisdom of Hecht's arguments against suicide.

9. Hecht uses this reasoning to argue that suicide is immoral: as a social being, you may perform an act provided that it is covered by a maxim (rule) that you can wish to universalize (endorse for everyone to follow). The maxim covering suicide is "I may take my life when it becomes too heavy a burden." According to Hecht, you cannot universalize this maxim. Since all humans sooner or later confront heavy burdens in life, doing so would result in the extinction of the human race, an outcome that no rational person could support. This theory, of course, originated with Immanuel Kant in the 18th century. See *Stay*, p. 138.

Religion and the Founders
(December 19, 2013)

In popular culture there are two sharply contrasting views about religion and the founding fathers. One is that the founders were devout Christians who read the Bible and prayed daily. The other is that they were products of the Enlightenment who abandoned religion for reason and science. So, which view is accurate? Neither! If we could take a snapshot of religion in the colonies in 1770, here is what we would find: (1)

- The founders were born into a Christian culture. Nearly all of the 3,000,000 residents of the colonies were Christians, nine of the colonies had an official state church, and nine of the ten existing colleges were founded by religious groups to train their clergy and lay leaders.
- Religious diversity was a fact of life. There were over twenty Christian sects in the colonies with strong differences on issues of faith. (2)
- Religious toleration was more the exception than the rule. Rhode Island, for instance, founded by Roger Williams, and Pennsylvania, founded by William Penn, were the only colonies that welcomed all stripes of Christians and non-Christians. (3)

- Deism, which originated in Europe, had infiltrated colonial culture among the educated class and challenged traditional religion. According to Deists, reason, not faith, is the path to knowledge; the universe was designed by God, a Grand Architect, a First Cause who imbued it with natural laws and then retreated from it; if one wishes to know God, one must study God's complex handiwork, the universe; the Bible is a collection of myths and fables triggered by superstition; Jesus was an inspiring moral teacher but neither a god nor a savior; and contrary to the teachings of Calvin, humans are neither depraved nor predestined.
- Nearly all of the founders modified their Christian beliefs to a greater or lesser extent to accommodate Deism. As a result, the religious views of the founders were scattered across a spectrum with traditional Christianity on one end and Deism on the other. The founders fell into three groups: traditional Christians, Christian Deists, and Non-Christian Deists. The majority were Christian Deists. (4)
- And, despite their absorption of Deism, all of the founders but Benjamin Franklin attended their ancestral church at least occasionally, most of them never abandoned their ancestral church, and the wives and daughters of most of them remained traditional Christians.

Thus, the founders were religious hybrids and their religious views were complex and diverse. Commentators who paint a different picture, according to historian Robert Holmes, "revise history to align the founders' beliefs with their own." (5)

Given this broad range of religious views, it is all the more remarkable that the founders reached a consensus on key issues as the new nation emerged. They prized personal liberty, they opposed religious dogmatism, intolerance, and coercion, they valued civic virtue, they opposed compulsory support of churches, they sought to separate government from the churches, and they embraced the doctrines of natural rights, government by consent, limited government, the separation of powers, and majority rule. (6)

---

1. I rely here mainly on David L. Holmes, *The Faiths of Our Founding Fathers*, Oxford University Press, 2006. Holmes is Walter G. Mason Professor of Religious Studies, Emeritus, at the College of William and Mary. Holmes spent 46 years at William and Mary. Among his other books are *A Brief History of the Episcopal Church* (1993), and *The Faith of the Postwar Presidents: From Truman to Obama* (2012). The latter has won praise among historians but has gotten little notice outside of academe.
2. Among the sects were Anglicans, Calvinists, Congregationalists, Baptists, Dutch Reformed, Quakers, Lutherans, Presbyterians, Roman Catholics, Mennonites, Methodists, Moravians, Anabaptists, the Brethren, Sandemanians, Antinomians, Arminians, Shakers, Universalists, Antisabbatarians, Socinians, and Ranters.
3. For example, Maryland imposed severe penalties by law on anyone who denied the divinity of Jesus, the trinity, or the virgin birth.
4. Traditional Christians included Patrick Henry, Samuel Adams, Elias Boudinot, and John Jay. Christian Deists included John Adams, George Washington, Benjamin Franklin, Thomas Jefferson, and James Monroe. Non-Christian Deists included Tom Paine and Ethan Allen.
5. David L. Holmes, *The Faiths*, p. 17.
6. The founders were all deeply influenced by the writings of John Locke (1632-1704), including his *Letter Concerning Toleration, First Treatise of Government,* and *Second Treatise of Government.*

The Care and Feeding of the Brain
(January 1, 2014)

THE HUMAN BRAIN, WHICH WEIGHS only three pounds, is on duty around the clock whether we're awake or asleep, conscious or unconscious. Electrical and chemical messages fly around it constantly. It regulates all the other organs in our body and makes possible every action that we perform.

Fortunately, there are steps that we can take to make and keep our brain fit. In fact, as science writer Guy P. Harrison points out in his new book entitled *Think*, they are the same steps that benefit our overall health. (1) According to Harrison, here is what we should do for our brain:

One: Eat well. (2) Since the food that we consume is the brain's fuel, the performance of the brain can be helped or hindered by the quality and quantity of its fuel. So, we should eat the right foods in moderation. Specifically, he suggests that we:

- reduce red meat, alcohol, and candy;
- avoid hot dogs, sausage, fried potatoes, and sugary soft drinks; and
- increase wild salmon, baked chicken, green vegetables (especially spinach and broccoli), fruit (especially blueberries and blackberries), nuts, trail mix, and non-sugary soft drinks.

Two: Exercise. (3) Harrison likens the brain to a "three-pound vampire" which craves blood. (4) Exercise stimulates blood flow and delivers nutrients to the brain. It causes the brain to grow new cells and, over the long haul, it helps us cope with "stress, anxiety, depression, and age-related problems such as dementia." (5) Harrison offers these recommendations on exercise:

- Exercise at least twenty minutes a day at least six days a week;
- Select the type of exercise which works for you, whether it is walking, running, swimming, cycling, sit-ups, push-ups, jumping jacks, or a combination;
- Lift weights twice a week to strengthen bones and muscles; and
- Avoid prolonged sitting at home or at work. Stand up and move about regularly. (6)

Three: Get plenty of sleep. (7) According to Harrison, science has shown that a rested brain functions well and a tired one doesn't. Too little sleep reduces alertness and concentration, and diminishes the ability to learn, to solve problems, and to remember. (8)

When it comes to sleep, Harrison concedes, one size doesn't fit all. For some people, six or seven hours may suffice; for others, eight or more may be necessary. Harrison therefore recommends keeping a sleep diary in which you log how many hours you sleep on a given night and how you feel and function the next day. (9) He also recommends brief naps when circumstances permit. (10)

Four: Use it or lose it. (11) Harrison cites studies which show that active brains prosper while inactive ones "wither and weaken." (12) So, it is essential that we keep thinking, learning, and solving problems. According to Harrison, if you want to be good at running, then you must run, and if you want to be good at thinking, then you must think. The secret to a healthy brain, he assures us, lies in reading and writing, learning new skills (especially a second language), exploring nature, studying the universe, travelling (preferably to distant places), and visiting museums. (13)

Harrison challenges us to accept responsibility for the well-being of the most important organ in our body. For those of us who are couch potatoes, the start of a new year gives us a perfect opportunity to take up his challenge.

---

1. Guy P. Harrison, *Think: Why You Should Question Everything*, Prometheus Books, 2013. Although *Think* is a primer on critical thinking that deals with the usual topics found in a book on this subject (see below), it could be subtitled "The Care and Feeding of the Brain" because of the attention which it devotes to the brain. See especially Chapter 2, "Pay a Visit to the Strange Thing That Lives Inside Your Head," pp. 55-85, and Chapter 4, "The Proper Care and Feeding of a Thinking Machine," pp. 167-183. Chapter 2 does a fine job of pointing out the strengths and weaknesses of the brain. On the latter, he notes: "Unfortunately, most people know little or nothing about how the brain operates so they make incorrect assumptions about its reliability. The brutal truth is that human brains do a poor job of separating truth from fiction. This leads to many false beliefs." *Think*, p. 55. Harrison's four main recommendations to promote the efficiency of the brain are given in Chapter 4.

The topics covered in *Think* which are often found in books on critical thinking include the value of skepticism, the importance of science, the need for intellectual self-reliance, our susceptibility to common thinking errors, the gullibility that pervades all strata of society, examples of unproved or discredited beliefs that remain popular, and the rewards of effective thinking.

Harrison's previous books include *50 Reasons People Give for Believing in a God* (2008), *Race and Reality: What Everyone Should Know about Our Biological Diversity* (2010), *50 Popular Beliefs That People Think Are True* (2012), and *50 Simple Questions for Every Christian* (2013). *Think* incorporates some material from his previous books.

2. On food, see pp. 170-173.
3. On exercise, see pp. 173-176.
4. *Think*, p. 173. Although the brain weighs only three pounds, it uses twenty percent of the body's blood.
5. *Think*, p. 173.
6. To those who protest that they don't have the time to exercise, Harrison observes that "the average American spends nearly *forty hours per week* watching television." (pp. 174-175) He adds: "If nothing else, do jumping jacks and push-ups in your living room during one thirty-minute episode of your favorite TV show every evening." (p. 175)
7. On sleep, see pp. 176-178.
8. *Think*, p. 177. Further, Harrison notes that sleep deprivation over extended periods has been linked to "significantly higher risk for heart attack, cancer, diabetes, stroke, and obesity." (p. 177)
9. *Think*, p. 177.
10. *Think*, p. 177.

11. On "Use it or Lose It," see pp. 178-182.
12. *Think*, p. 179.
13. *Think*, pp. 178-182. Harrison recommends combining several of these experiences when possible. He writes:

"One of the best things you can do for your brain on a regular basis is join exercise, thinking, and nature into one outing. The closest thing to a miracle tonic for the brain might be something like a vigorous walk/run on a previously unexplored mountain trail or along a new stretch of beach, during which one notices and photographs an unusual plant or insect to research after returning home. That would be a good day for any brain." (p. 181)

In this same segment of his book, Harrison insists that those who believe that they can help their brain through products sold at a health food store or promoted on infomercials are wasting their time and money.

Jerry DeWitt's Journey (January 9, 2014)

JERRY DEWITT GREW UP IN the 1970s in the heart of the Bible Belt in rural Louisiana where he attended a fire-and-brimstone Pentecostal church. From the day that he watched Jimmy Swaggart mesmerize an audience of over 8,000, he believed that God called him to be a minister. To prepare for his life's work, though still a teen, he started a daily routine of prayer and scripture study, he awoke frequently during the night to pray, and he helped the pastor in his own church.

After high school, DeWitt took his ministry on the road, going from revival to revival, and from church to church. After he married, he and his family moved many times. Since he earned very little, the family faced "grinding poverty." They lived in mobile homes and run-down apartments and houses, they drove a rickety old car, and they relied on relatives and welfare to make ends meet. After a time, they took secular jobs to supplement Jerry's meager income.

Jerry felt that his family's sacrifice was necessary so that he could enhance his knowledge and skills under experienced and successful pastors. His mentors, he expected, would help him, in his words, "get his doctrine straight," and become an inspiring preacher and a competent administrator.

Although many pastors were helpful, many were not. Some, he discovered, were simply entrepreneurs seeking wealth, power, and security; others concealed serious theological doubts. Also, as time passed, he faced intense competition from hundreds of aspiring peers, making a call from a large, prosperous church less and less likely. Not surprisingly, the frequent moves, the poverty, and DeWitt's dim prospects put great stress on his marriage.

And whom did he blame for his misfortune? He blamed himself. His problems were a sign, he was certain, that he wasn't as devoted to God as he should be.

As the years passed, however, DeWitt found it increasingly difficult to bring solace to his parishioners when their world turned upside down. He couldn't reconcile debilitating illnesses, untimely deaths, tragic accidents, financial crises, and devastating storms with a God whose power and love have no limits. He concluded that the usual responses – we deserve to suffer for our sins or God is testing our faith or God has a plan for us – were cruel excuses. Finally, he did the unthinkable – he left both his ministry and his faith. (1) This brought anger and hostility from the surrounding community. (2) When his wife insisted that they move and DeWitt refused, she packed up her son and her belongings, moved, and filed for divorce. And who could blame her?

Today, nearly three years after his momentous decision, DeWitt is active in two organizations which serve former ministers. He tells his own story in a new book entitled *Hope After Faith*. (3) While the book takes us through DeWitt's fascinating journey, it also illuminates the precarious existence of thousands of ministers who serve the great majority of churches in America – small ones. It shows that the celebrity pastor, with a megachurch, televised services, a mansion, fine clothes, and expensive cars, is the exception to the rule.

---

1. DeWitt found no answer to the central issues of theodicy: How can there be so much suffering and tragedy if there is a God whose power, goodness, and knowledge have no limits? How can a loving God punish sinners for eternity in hell? Why does God fail to respond to so many supplicants who invoke God's help?

2. The DeWitts were variously shunned, harassed, ridiculed, and threatened after Jerry's departure from his ministry and faith. Further, the secular firm for which he worked fired him after complaints from church leaders.

3. Jerry DeWitt with Ethan Brown, De Capo Press, 2013. The subtitle is *An Ex-Pastor's Journey From Belief to Atheism*. DeWitt came to the attention of the publisher after an article about him appeared in the *New York Times*. See Robert F. Worth, "From Bible Belt Pastor to Atheist Leader," *New York Times*, August 22, 2012.

The Odd Couple (January 16, 2014)

IN 2006, JIM HENDERSON, a Christian minister, (1) turned to an unusual source for help with his project to improve churches. He outbid more than a dozen competitors in an eBay auction in which Hemant Mehta, a self-described "friendly atheist," offered to attend churches and evaluate their services and programs. Thus was born a religious version of the odd couple. (2)

Over the next few months, Mehta visited fifteen Christian churches of differing sizes in four states. (3) So, what did an atheist have to say about them? (4) Here are eight of his major findings and recommendations:

* One. There are very few female pastors and speakers. Churches need to do more to identify and recruit gifted women for these roles;
* Two. Some churches overdo music and singing. As a result, many members, by their own admission, show up late or tune out in midstream.
* Three. Common rituals, such as frequent standing and sitting, and scripted group responses, are typically mechanical and meaningless. Some rituals should be phased out; the history, meaning, and value of those that are kept should be fully explained to the congregation;
* Four. Pastors often quote the Bible without giving any indication of its relevance to day-to-day life. A greater effort should be made to show a connection between Bible verses and the actual issues and challenges which people face in their lives; (5)

- Five. Some churches invest significant resources in missionary work in faraway places but do little to help those in need locally. Part of the mission of all churches should be to improve living conditions in their own community for all residents. (6)
- Six. Some pastors tend to attack virtually everything they oppose as part of a war on Christianity. Examples are evolution, gay marriage, and objections to religious displays on public property. This practice demonizes many good people, closes off the possibility of honest dialogue, and needlessly fosters a bunker mentality. Pastors need to tone down the rhetoric and work harder to understand, tolerate, and respect people with whom they differ.
- Seven. Many pastors and other speakers, especially those at megachurches, are very effective communicators. They give instructive *and* entertaining talks, they focus on one central theme, and they use humor. By contrast, some pastors are poor communicators who do none of this. They would benefit from a refresher course in public speaking; (7) and
- Eight. Many churches need an infusion of energy and excitement. To this end, they should institute programming such as inviting "a compelling speaker"; sponsoring debates on critical issues, featuring opposed viewpoints; (8) holding question-and-answer sessions; organizing volunteers for community service; and donating funds to a charity that helps all people, not just Christians. (9)

As the project drew to a close, Henderson and Mehta learned that Mehta's reports resonated with many of the congregations that Mehta visited and many others. Thus, the eBay collaboration was a win-win venture for this odd couple. (10)

---

1. Henderson is also author of *Evangelism Without Additives*, WaterBrook Press, 2005.
2. Eventually Mehta wrote a book about his project entitled *I Sold My Soul on eBay*, WaterBrook Press, 2007. The forward is by Rob Bell, a well-known evangelist. WaterBrook Press serves the Christian book market. Subsequently, Mehta published two books: *Friendly Atheist*, which

is available from Amazon in a kindle edition, and *The Young Atheist's Survival Guide*, Patheos Press, 2012. Also, see his website – FriendlyAtheist.com. Money was not the reason that Mehta opted for the eBay auction. In fact, he donated his proceeds to a secular organization, the Secular Student Alliance, "an umbrella organization for atheist and agnostic college groups." *I Sold My Soul on eBay*, p. 49. His primary motivation was to learn more about Christianity. Although he grew up in Chicago, Mehta's exposure to Christianity was minimal because his family was part of a "committed Jain community"; his secondary motivation was to promote dialogue between believers and non-believers.

3. At each site, Mehta looked and listened, used a tape recorder, took notes, and in many cases talked with pastors and church members.

4. Mehta submitted his reports online on off-the-map.org.

5. See p. 146. On scriptural relevance, Mehta writes: "One thing I always found effective in the churches I visited was that certain pastors followed their retelling of a Bible story with a variety of current applications: Here's how we can be like Joseph at our workplace. Here's how we can emulate Jesus in our relationships. Are you having trouble handling the amount of your school work? Let me point you to a relevant passage in the Bible." (p. 147)

6. Mehta gives high marks in this regard to the Windsor Village United Methodist Church, an African American church, which has brought "social services, commercial enterprises, health services, educational opportunities, job skills assistance, and much more to an underserved area in Houston." (p. 95) On the other hand, Mehta is critical of churches which establish "Christian" schools "in parts of town where students are struggling," allegedly to improve education. He opines that the same goal can be accomplished by "pitching in to help improve the work being done at existing (public) schools in the neighborhood." (p. 142) Overall, Mehta says that "the churches that made a big impact on me were the ones that knew their 'church' was not limited to a building. They made it a priority to spread the *values* of Christianity by serving the *real* needs of people around them. In this case, actions speak louder than words." (p. 143)

7. Mehta has a fascinating suggestion for pastors to gauge their effectiveness as speakers. They should videotape their sermons with the camera directed not at them but at the audience. When they review the tape, they should ask "Are the people attentive? Are they taking notes? Are they smiling? Or are they staring at the same page in the day's program for extended periods of time?" (pp. 140-141) This technique is likely to work, however, only if the audience does not know about it.

8. See pp. 143-144. On the need for speakers who differ with many Christians, Mehta writes: "If the church has the correct stance on, say, Intelligent Design, then there should be no problem with bringing in a credible evolutionary biologist who can explain the scientific view. Bring in someone from the gay community when gay marriage issues arise. Bring in a leader from the Muslim community when you're discussing Islam. Bring in a pacifist when you're considering issues of war, national defense, and militarism." (p. 145)

9. Mehta submitted many other findings and recommendations beyond these eight. Among the others are these two: a) Some pastors urge congregants to seek forgiveness from God when they mistreat people. Pastors should also urge them to seek forgiveness from the people whom they mistreated; b) Some pastors condemn the distribution of condoms to young people despite the fact that they impede the spread of STDs and AIDS and despite the fact that calls for abstinence don't work. Pastors need to be more practical and realistic.

10. Henderson was so pleased with Mehta's work that he hired another atheist, Matt Casper, and together they visited and evaluated twelve more churches. This later collaboration resulted in two books: Jim Henderson and Matt Casper, *Jim and Casper Go to Church*, Tyndale House Publishers, 2007, and *Saving Casper*, Tyndale House Publishers, 2013.

Ted Williams (January 24, 2014)

WHO IS THE GREATEST HITTER in the history of professional baseball? My nominee is Ted Williams. Let's take a look at his career and life.

Although the career of Ted Williams spanned the period from 1939 to 1960, he lost five seasons during his prime to military service (1) and parts of two others to injuries. Despite the lost years, his career statistics are staggering. His lifetime batting average was .344. He hit 541 home runs, placing him tenth on the all-time list. (2) He hit twenty or more home runs in sixteen seasons, an American League record that he holds with Babe Ruth and Reggie Jackson. He is the last batter to hit .400 for a season. That was in 1941. He won the American League batting championship six times, including 1957 when he was thirty-eight, and 1958 when he was thirty-nine. He won the Triple Crown twice and he was named American League MVP twice. (3) He led the American League in both home runs and RBIs four times, and he led the majors in runs scored four times. Further, Williams made seventeen All-Star Game appearances and he set a dozen All-Star Game records. (4) To no one's surprise, he was voted into the Hall of Fame in 1966 in his first year of eligibility. (5)

As for his personal life, Williams grew up in San Diego, the son of a Mexican-American mother and an American father. (6) Though he lived in a poor neighborhood, it had one important asset, a lighted playground, where he practiced hitting late into nearly every night and bragged to his friends that he would be "the greatest hitter who ever lived." (7) He struggled in school but, as he aged, he developed a love for history and biography.

After high school, he played one year in the minor leagues, (8) then moved on to Boston where he formed a love/hate relationship with the media and the fans. He married three times and fathered two daughters and a son. His marriages suffered from his foul mouth and extended absences for road trips or fishing. He had an arm's length relationship to his children until late in his life. (9) After his third marriage collapsed, he lived happily with Louise Kaufman, a divorced woman.

When it came to money, Ted Williams was an enigma. On the one hand, he would boycott expensive restaurants and pay his tab at many others with a check in the hope that the proprietor would display it rather than cash it. On the other hand, when he found out that a former major leaguer was destitute, he quietly deposited $10,000 into his bank account. And he did this many times! (10) What's more, he raised millions of dollars over the years for the Boston-based Jimmy Fund, which serves children with cancer and their families, and he helped players with drug and alcohol problems, such as Daryl Strawberry, who lived with Ted and Louise during his recovery. Further, he went out of his way to welcome and encourage the first black players, Larry Doby among them. (11)

We have to take Ted Williams warts and all. Despite the failure of his marriages and his personality quirks, he was as gifted an athlete and as generous a person as we're likely to find.

---

1. Initially Williams applied for a military deferment. When it was denied, he enlisted. He turned down opportunities to play on military baseball teams and, after training, served as a pilot and instructor in two wars. In Korea Williams flew in a unit with John Glenn who described Williams as one of the best pilots he knew. Williams flew as Glenn's wingman for roughly the last half of his missions in Korea.
2. Most sports historians are confident that Williams would have broken Babe Ruth's home run record had he not spent five years in the military.
3. The fact that he was league MVP only two times is due almost certainly to his sour relationship with a number of baseball writers.
4. Williams is tied for most All-Star Game appearances by an American League player with Brooks Robinson and Cal Ripken. He leads the American League in career All-Star Game hits, runs scored, extra-base hits, total bases, home runs, RBIs, and walks. Also, he holds single game All-Star Game records for both leagues in hits, runs scored, home runs, and RBIs.

5. Williams was also named to the Major League Baseball All-Century Team and All-Time Team. He and Babe Ruth are the only two players honored with a statue in Cooperstown.

6. Fearful that his Mexican heritage could harm his career, he kept it a secret as much as he could.

7. See Richard Ben Cramer, *What Do You Think of Ted Williams Now? A Remembrance*, Simon & Schuster, 2007, p. 85.

8. During his one year in the minors, Williams led the league in batting average, home runs, and RBIs.

9. Sadly, his son, John Henry Williams, exploited his father's change of heart to promote John Henry's company which sold various items with Ted's autograph. Even after Ted had a stroke, he would sign autographs many hours a day at his son's insistence. John Henry and one of Ted's daughters also arranged for Ted's head to be cryogenically preserved despite the fact that Ted's will provided for cremation.

10. Richard Ben Cramer, *What Do You Think...*, p. 9. According to Cramer, to get the bank account number, Williams phoned the person on the pretext of soliciting a contribution to the Jimmy Fund, and after hearing his story about falling on hard times, Williams said, "OK, send me a check for $10. Don't tell me you can't afford that!" Once he got the check, Williams contacted the bank and made a $10,000 deposit.

11. Doby, the first black player in the American League, reported that on his first visit to Fenway Park, Williams congratulated him and wished him good luck. See Richard Ben Cramer, *What Do You Think...*, p. 96. Also, at his induction into the Hall of Fame in 1966, Williams made special mention in his talk that Satchel Paige, Josh Gibson, and other great black players should be voted into the Hall.

Larry Doby (March 6, 2014)

ELEVEN WEEKS AFTER JACKIE ROBINSON suited up as a Brooklyn Dodger, Larry Doby joined the Cleveland Indians. These two remarkable athletes broke the color barrier in major league baseball, Robinson in the National League and Doby in the American. Let's focus here on Doby. (1).

Larry Doby was born in 1923 in South Carolina. His parents, who left him in the care of relatives when they moved north to work, later divorced. After the eighth grade, Doby moved to New Jersey to join his mother. In high school he was an outstanding athlete, winning all-state honors in three sports – football, basketball, and baseball. (2) As he grew up, Doby developed the personality that stayed with him over the long haul. He was a quiet, patient, determined loner. Although racism offended and angered him, he was never a militant.

World War II took Doby out of college for two and a half years of service in the Navy. After his discharge, he played baseball for the Newark Eagles in the Negro League. At mid-season in 1947, when Doby was batting .451 with 14 home runs for Newark, Bill Veeck of the Cleveland Indians identified him as the best young black player in the nation and signed him to an Indians contract.

As was the case with Jackie Robinson, Doby encountered racism daily. When he was introduced to his teammates, three players refused to shake his hand. When he attempted to dine with his teammates in a restaurant, he was often refused service. When he sought entry to a stadium at the players gate, he was sometimes turned away. Also, when he took a road trip, he had to stay in segregated hotels. (3)

Doby's first full season, 1948, was one of his best. That year he hit .301 as the Indians won the pennant and the World Series. Player-manager Lou Boudreau publicly credited the Indians success that year to the extraordinary contributions of two players – catcher Jim Hegan and center fielder Larry Doby.

Over his thirteen year career, Doby batted .283 with 253 home runs and 970 RBIs, and he was named to seven All-Star teams. He led the American League in home runs twice and in 1952 he led the league with a .541 slugging average. He was also one of the premier outfielders in baseball. In 1953, for instance, in a game in Cleveland, he made a catch in center field which Hall-of-Famer Dizzy Dean said was "the greatest catch I ever saw..." Also, in 1955, he set the league record of 164 consecutive games by an outfielder without an error. (4)

Doby finished his playing career after stints with the Chicago White Sox, the Baltimore Orioles, the Detroit Tigers, and a team in Japan. In 1977, the White Sox made him the second black manager in the majors. Eventually Doby won dozens of honors, among them induction into the Hall of Fame in Cooperstown. He died at age 79 in 2003, two years after his beloved wife Helyn.

With his humility and courage, Larry Doby paved the way for thousands of black athletes in baseball and other sports. As we celebrate Jackie Robinson, Rosa Parks, Dr. Martin Luther King, Jr., and other icons of civil rights, let us not forget Larry Doby.

---

1. Most of the information in this commentary is taken from John Thomas Moore, *Larry Doby*, Dover Publications, 2011.
2. During summers in high school, he also played for semi-professional all-black basketball and baseball teams under the name "Larry Walker."
3. Racist hecklers were also a constant problem.
4. This record held up for seventeen seasons until Al Kaline broke it.

Casinos and Seniors (March 13, 2014)

A RACINO IS A CASINO which features slot machines and horse races. Hollywood Gaming at Mahoning Valley Race Course, a racino owned and operated by Penn National Gaming, is scheduled to open later this year west of Youngstown in Austintown on Route 46 near I-80. The facility will have a 100,000 square feet casino with up to 1,500 slot machines and a one-mile track. It will also have the potential to expand if business thrives.

If the Austintown facility follows the pattern of others across the nation, it will offer special inducements to one group of gamblers – senior citizens. Casinos attempt to build loyalty among seniors for three reasons: (1)

- Older Americans gamble a lot. In 2012, more than half of the more than 100 million customers of U.S. casinos were over fifty;
- The great majority of seniors – seventy-five percent over the age of 65 – prefer slot machines over other forms of gambling, such as table games (roulette, poker, and black jack), and slots are very profitable. For example, at nearby Thistle Down Racino, slots brought in an average of over $300 per machine per day after payouts in 2013 (2) and in Atlantic City, slots have outperformed table games since 1984; (3) and
- Seniors tend to patronize casinos on weekday mornings and afternoons when business is slow. Thanks to seniors, rows and rows of slot machines are kept busy during these off-peak hours.

Since our region has a huge and growing population of older people and the new racino will have thousands of slots but no table games, at least initially, it is a virtual certainty that it will sink or swim based on patronage by seniors.

So, what inducements can we expect the Austintown racino to offer to seniors? At a minimum, we can expect the following:

- The racino will cater to seniors' mobility and health problems with wheelchairs, scooters, and adult diapers, and possibly free transportation and discounts on medication; (4)
- The racino will provide free coffee, pop, and snacks, and low-cost breakfasts and luncheons for seniors; (5) and
- The racino will sponsor special senior clubs which award "free play" and extra player points to frequent customers. (6)

While the racino will create hundreds of jobs, generate significant revenue for government, help local businesses, and produce profits for investors, it is a mixed blessing according to many. Critics point to the side effects, especially addiction. They argue that the racino will attract lonely seniors on fixed incomes, particularly women, who are mesmerized by slots for hours a day as they spend far more than they can afford. Also, critics see racinos and casinos as the new senior centers, the emerging institutions for eldercare, "a refuge where (seniors) will be safely transported, fed, and occupied during the day," (7) or, in the words of journalist Jeremy Rivlin, "day care for the elderly." (8)

Perhaps the critics have a point. Nevertheless, given government's need for revenue and the fascination of older Americans with gambling, I'm confident that the racino in Austintown will be around for a long time. In fact, I'll bet on it.

---

1. Most of the information in this commentary is taken from Amy Zeitlow, *Seniors in Casino Land: Tough Luck for Older Americans*, Institute for American Values, 2014. References to this volume here are by the author and page number.

2. See John Kasich, newsnet5.com, August 8, 2013.
3. See UNLV Center for Gaming Research, January 2014, gaming.univ.edu.
4. Zeitlow, p. 26. One casino featured by Zeitlow actually operated an in-house pharmacy where 8000 club points cover the copay for certain prescriptions.
5. Zeitlow, p. 26. The casinos featured by Zeitlow offered a $2.99 buffet for seniors.
6. Zeitlow, p. 26. Many casinos have a "third-of-the-month club" for seniors who patronize casinos after they receive their Social Security checks.
7. Zeitlow, p. 28.
8. Zeitlow, p. 29.

The Cost of Higher Education: the Problem (March 27, 2014)

LET'S BEGIN WITH A QUESTION. Which of the following rose in cost the most over the past thirty years: housing, medical care, or higher education? The correct answer is higher education. (1) Over this period, housing went up 375%, medical care 600%, and higher education an astonishing 1,120%. (2) At the same time, financial aid provided by the federal government and institutions of higher education also shot up but so did "net cost," that is, what students and their families must pay after grants, scholarships, and tax credits are subtracted. (3)

The rise in net cost also explains the student loan debt picture. Institutions of higher education enroll more than twenty million students a year and two-thirds of them supplement financial aid with loans from Uncle Sam or banks. Student loan debt now hovers around $1 *trillion* and the average student leaves college with a loan debt of $27,000. Among bachelor degree recipients, borrowers in a recent year included 62% at public institutions, such as Youngstown State University, 72% at private non-profit institutions, such as Hiram College, and 96% at private for-profit institutions, such as the University of Phoenix. Today there are 37,000,000 student loan borrowers with outstanding student loan debt. The average debt balance for all borrowers from all types of schools is over $24,000. Moreover, the delinquency and default rates are very high (4) but borrowers can find no relief in bankruptcy because the U.S. bankruptcy code exempts nearly all cases of student loan debt from discharge. (5)

75% of the college students in the U.S. attend public institutions, so let's focus on them. A major reason that cost has skyrocketed in the public sector is the steady decline in state support. In Ohio, for instance, state support has dropped from more than 70% of the operating costs of the public universities in 1970 to less than 20% today. In this regard, Ohio is a microcosm of the nation. All states have reduced spending in higher education to cover mushrooming costs, especially Medicaid and prisons. On a national basis, state support per student at public universities, adjusted for inflation, dropped from $8,500 in 1987 to $5,900 in 2013. (6)

Understandably, public institutions across the nation have turned to tuition increases to compensate for declining state support. Consider these facts:

- In 1987 tuition provided 23% of the revenue of public institutions. Today it provides 47% - nearly half;
- From 2008 to 2012, as state support per student shrunk 27%, average tuition rose 20%; and
- In the year 2000, the average family spent 25% of its income to cover the cost of college for a family member. Today it spends 40%.

Two obvious questions remain: "Is college worth it?" and "What can we do to contain the cost of college?" I'll address these in my next commentary.

---

1. This commentary draws information from many sources, including the following: Davis Educational Foundation, "An Inquiry into the Rising Cost of Higher Education: Summary of Responses from Seventy College and University Presidents," 2012; Helen Li, "The Rising Cost of Higher Education: A Supply and Demand Analysis," Bachelor Thesis, New York University, 2013; William Trombley, "The Rising Price of Higher Education: College Affordability in Jeopardy," 2003; Allie Bidwell, "The Rise in Tuition Is Slowing, But College Still Costs More," *U.S. News & World Report*, online edition, October 24, 2013; Beckie Supiano, "Evaluating the Payoff of a College Degree," *The Chronicle of Higher Education*, February 24, 2014; Pew

Research, Social & Demographic Trends, "The Rising Cost of Not Going to College," February 11, 2014; and American Student Assistance (asa.org/policy/resources/stats).

2. Over the past decade, college tuition has risen three times as fast as the Consumer Price Index and twice as fast as medical care.

3. See Allie Bidwell, "The Rise..." The actual average in-state tuition at four-year public institutions in 2012-2013 was $8,893 while the average net cost of tuition was $3,120, and the actual average tuition at four-year private institutions in 2012-2013 was $30,090 while the average net cost of tuition was $12,460. The federal government currently spends about $40 billion a year for Pell Grants. One estimate is that financial aid has gone up since 1970 fifty-fold.

4. For instance, among students from non-profit institutions and public two-year institutions, the delinquency and default rate is about 50%.

5. See Kayla Webley, "Why You Can't Discharge Student Loans in Bankruptcy," *Time*, February 9, 2012.

6. State support in actual dollars has gone up typically in the states annually in recent decades but support measured by percentage of operating costs and in real dollars per student, however, has declined sharply. Real dollars are dollars adjusted for inflation. A slight exaggeration by one public university president summarizes the national subsidy trend nicely. He said, "When I came here, my school was state-supported, then it was state-assisted, and now it's state-located."

The Cost of Higher Education: the Solution (April 3, 2014)

IN MY LAST COMMENTARY, I tracked the skyrocketing cost of going to college. (1) In this one I'll deal with two questions: Is college worth it? And what can be done to contain the cost of college?

I judge the "worth" of college on two criteria – personal and economic.

College is worth it on the first criterion if college helps a student to think, write, and speak well; to value science, history, literature, and the arts; and to grasp the problems facing the world today. On this criterion, college is worth it for some graduates but not worth it for others. (2)

College is worth it on the second criterion if college enhances a student's prospects in the marketplace. On this criterion, college is indeed worth it! The earnings gap between non-graduates and graduates is significant and widening. A decade ago the income of non-graduates was 77% of graduates; today it is only 62%. (3)

Next, to make college more affordable, we first need to understand the causes of the ballooning cost. They include:

- severe cuts in support by states to public institutions in real dollars;
- mission creep, that is, an increase in the tasks undertaken by institutions of higher education;
- a huge increase in the ranks of administrators and professional staff;
- the proliferation of academic departments, centers, and institutes;

- the expansion of services to students, including remediation, advisement, tutoring, counseling, health care, physical fitness, and entertainment;
- study overseas programs;
- a reduction in faculty teaching loads;
- expansion of opportunities for research and professional development for faculty;
- enhancement in compensation for employees, especially presidents and vice presidents;
- participation by employees of public institutions in state pension programs;
- subsidy of intercollegiate athletics programs which operate at a loss on most campuses;
- the mistaken perception by the general public that there is a direct correlation between the cost and the quality of an institution; (4)
- upgrading technology for faculty, staff, and students; and
- construction of new and expanded facilities, ranging from impressive office and classroom buildings, to presidential residences, to upscale inns for campus guests and visitors, to luxurious student unions and student housing, to hospitals and research centers, to costly indoor and outdoor venues for athletics. (5)

Can colleges bring these causes under control? Although some are trying, they've had little success. (6) For the 3,800 colleges across the nation to adopt the reforms that are necessary to drive down cost significantly, I believe that coercion is required. Here is my plan:

1. A group of approximately twenty-five institutions, including some that are endowment-rich, such as Ivy League institutions, and some that are tuition-dependent, such as public institutions, must simultaneously reduce cost well below the current private and public national average and challenge all other institutions across the nation to follow suit;

2. Boycotts, facilitated by social media, must be launched against schools which refuse to follow the lead of these cost-cutters, and, if necessary;
3. Congress must pass a law prohibiting federal financial aid and loans to students and federal research grants to faculty at institutions whose tuition exceeds a prescribed ceiling.

Absent these initiatives, U.S. families will continue to hand the higher education industry a blank check.

---

1. It costs eleven times more to go to college today than it did thirty years ago and student loan debt has exploded to $1 trillion.

2. For example, on this criterion, college has not been worth it for a graduate who says: "I seen her..." instead of "I saw her..." or "Me and him went..." instead of "He and I went..." or who doesn't know that the term "theory" in science means a well-established explanation and not a mere hunch or guess or who doesn't know who wrote *Macbeth* or who doesn't know whether Adam Smith or Karl Marx advocated the free market theory of economics.

3. Consider millennials – those born after 1980. 34% of millennials are college graduates. Millennials with degrees are far better off than millennials without them: they earn $17,500 a year more ($45,000 v. $28,000), they report higher job satisfaction, they are more likely to work full-time, and they are less likely to be out of work (3.8% v. 12.2%). Degreed millennials recognize these facts; they're satisfied customers. Nine-in-ten of them give college, despite its cost, a resounding thumbs-up. Nevertheless, in the current economy, it often takes new graduates longer to land a position than it did in the past. See the Pew Research Center, "The Rising Cost of Not Going to College," February 11, 2014.

4. According to *The New York Times*, December 12, 2006, there is a strong sentiment that "if the college costs more, it must be better." This helps to explain a type of tuition arms race, according to the *Times*, wherein colleges jack up their tuition "to match colleges they consider their rivals."

5. At most institutions, construction of costly, new buildings – which has been called "the edifice complex" – is funded mainly through bonds, resulting in huge bonded indebtedness, payment of which figures into the calculation of tuition, room and board, and fees. Avoidance of further bonded indebtedness has prompted some institutions to authorize private companies to build and own student housing on campus. According to one source, the bonded indebtedness of Ohio's public universities tripled between 2003 and 2013 and in 2003 it stood at $5 billion. See "Ohio State Universities Increase Indebtedness," *Tribune-Chronicle*, February 3, 2013. This article also reported that Moody's Investment Services "downgraded the outlook for the higher education sector (in Ohio) to negative because of such concerns."

6. Cost-reduction steps taken by some institutions include online courses and programs, "blended" courses (a mix of traditional classroom and online instruction), use of part-time

instead of full-time faculty, conversion of tenure-track positions to multi-year, renewable positions, a three-year bachelor's degree, tuition freezes for an incoming class for a set period, usually four years, and partial tuition reimbursements for those who graduate on time.

Domestic or Foreign? (May 8, 2014)

As a teenager in the 1950s, I worked part-time at a gas station. When a vehicle pulled in, I took the driver's order, pumped the gas, cleaned the windshield, checked the oil, and, if requested, checked the tire pressure.

My, how things have changed! The gas station attendant has gone the way of the milkman and the auto industry today bears little resemblance to its former self. Let's consider some of the changes.

In the 1950s the "Big Three" – General Motors, Ford, and Chrysler – led the world in the production of motor vehicles. Here are today's top ten: Toyota, GM, Volkswagen, Hyundai, Ford, Nissan, Honda, Peugeot, Suzuki, and Renault. Chrysler is eleventh.

The popularity of pick-up trucks continues to grow. In 2013, the Ford F-150, which has been the top-selling vehicle in the U.S. for 32 consecutive years, outsold the Toyota Camry, the top-selling passenger car, nearly two to one. (1) Further, in the first quarter of 2014, three pick-up trucks – the Ford F-series, the Dodge Ram, and the Chevrolet Silverado – all outsold the Camry, the #1 car.

Another change in the auto world is the emergence of SUVs – sport utility vehicles – in the 1990s. Seen by many as the successor to the station wagon, more than eighty models of SUVs are produced today in a variety of sizes, some on passenger car frames, others on truck frames, and two SUVs ranked in the top ten in U.S. sales in October, 2013. The Honda CR-V ranked 8th and the Ford Escape ranked 9th. Also, the market share of SUVs continues to grow. About one of every three vehicles sold today in the U.S. is an SUV.

Finally, the line between domestic and foreign is no longer clear. Here's why:

- Firstly, many models which are top sellers in the U.S. but which many people consider "foreign," such as Toyota and Honda, are assembled in U.S. plants by American workers. For instance, the Toyota Camry is built in Georgetown, Kentucky, and the Honda Accord in Marysville, Ohio. In fact, Toyota and Honda produce more vehicles in the U.S. than Chrysler.
- Secondly, auto makers are relying more and more on parts suppliers outside the U.S. The domestic parts content as defined by federal law (2) is declining across the board. In 2007, there were thirty-nine models with a domestic parts content of 85%; in 2014 there are none! Further, many popular models made by GM, Ford, and Chrysler have a' lower domestic parts content than popular models made by Toyota or Honda. For instance, the domestic parts content of the Chevrolet Cruze is 50%. (3) By contrast, four Toyota models and three Honda models have a domestic parts content of 75%; (4) and
- Thirdly, Chrysler is owned by Fiat, an Italian company, and GM and Ford own parts of a variety of auto companies overseas. (6)

In conclusion, one fact stands out. The auto industry has gone global – permanently! (5)

---

1. In 2013, Ford sold 763,402 F-150s and Toyota sold 404,484 Camrys.
2. I refer to the American Automobile Labeling Act which was enacted in 1992. Under this law, vehicles assembled in Canada and the U.S. qualify as "domestic" and parts suppliers in Canada and the U.S. qualify as "domestic."
3. The Cruze's engine is from the U.S., Mexico, and South Korea. The Cruze's transmission is from the U.S., Australia, and Japan.
4. Kelsey Mays, "The 2013 American-Made Index," cars.com, lists the following as the top "domestic" vehicles: Ford F-150, Toyota Camry, Dodge Avenger, Honda Odyssey, Toyota Sienna, Chevrolet Traverse, Toyota Tundra, GMC Acadia, Buick Enclave, and Toyota Avalon. Note that only five are products of GM, Ford, and Chrysler. Toyota has four and Honda one.

5. Another indicator of the globalization of the auto industry is this. In the past, the U.S. has been the world's largest passenger vehicle market. In 2012, for instance, there were over 254 million registered passenger vehicles in the U.S. In the same year, however, there were over 240 million passenger vehicles in China and experts predict that the Chinese market will soon surpass the U.S. market.

6. For a list of companies owned by the major auto makers around the world as of the end of 2013, see "Car Brands: Who Owns What? A Road Map to the Auto Industry Partnerships," consumerreports.org, December 23, 2013.

Faith (December 17, 2015)

RELIGIOUS PEOPLE OFTEN REFER TO faith as a precious gift from God which they cherish. (1) But what exactly is this gift called faith? And is it really precious? According to *Webster's* dictionary, faith is "firm belief in something for which there is no proof." (2) By contrast, knowledge is belief in something for which there is proof. Thus, if you believe in the parting of the Red Sea, the virgin birth, the miracle of the loaves and fishes, the resurrection, and heaven and hell, you have faith, and if you believe that water boils at 212 degrees Fahrenheit, that smoking cigarettes is harmful to a person, that regular exercise is helpful to a person, that there are over seven billion humans today on Earth, and that you should stop when a traffic signal is red, you have knowledge. Faith is the foundation of religion while reason and science are the foundation of knowledge.

Having said this, let's acknowledge, however, that faith does play a role in science. A scientist often embraces a belief without proof tentatively as a hypothesis, sometimes based on a mere hunch, to test whether it is supported by evidence. If the hypothesis turns out to be confirmed by the evidence, he or she then publishes the results of the research to peers so that they can evaluate the validity of the test and duplicate its findings. This type of provisional "faith" is markedly different from that exhibited in religion where believers typically embrace a belief as a certainty with no intent (or even possibility) to test it as scientists do.

While faith is held in high regard by tens of millions of Americans, the fact is that once we endorse faith, once we authorize people to believe without proof, we open a Pandora's Box, (3) for faith takes people down many different paths. On the one hand, there are benign paths where the faithful perform socially beneficial acts. They volunteer at a food bank, give to a charity, rescue abandoned and abused animals, or donate an organ. On the other hand, there are not so benign paths where the faithful perform socially harmful acts such as the following: (4)

- Some Christians, following a passage in the Epistle of James (5:14), rely exclusively on prayer and never on doctors, to heal the sick. This results in the avoidable death of hundreds, if not thousands, in the U.S. every year, especially children;
- Some Christians, believing that God directs them to stop abortions at any cost, murder medical staff, patients, and volunteers at women's clinics; (5)
- Some Muslims, following passages in the Quran (Sura 4:76 and Sura 8:12) and the Hadith (Muslim 1:20), the teachings and deeds of the prophet Muhammed, seek to murder non-Muslims – infidels – even at the cost of their own lives, resulting in violent attacks around the world; (6) and
- In many majority-Muslim nations, Sharia, a legal system based on the Quran and the Hadith, provides that the rape of a woman can be proven only by admission of the rapist or the testimony of four male witnesses. (Needless to say, if four men witnessed the rape without seeking to prevent or stop it, they were complicit in it.) The victim's testimony is inadmissible. (7)

As bad as these expressions of faith are, the situation could be worse. This is because the faithful often cherry-pick scriptures and religious teachings. For instance, if Christians followed the Bible to the letter,

- They would own slaves (Leviticus 25:44-46, Ephesians 6:5); (8)
- They would murder homosexuals (Leviticus 20:13), unruly children (Exodus, 21:15, Exodus 21:17), non-virgin brides (Deuteronomy 22:20-21), and adulterers (Deuteronomy 22:22-24); (9) and
- They would condemn divorce (Mark 10:2-12, Luke 16:18) and tattoos (Leviticus 19:28). (10)

So, what is the lesson here? It's the same lesson taught in the 19th century by W.K. Clifford, a British mathematician. (11) Recognizing that our beliefs translate into actions which can cause harm to ourselves and others, Clifford insisted that we acquire proof – what he called "sufficient evidence" – before we embrace and act upon a belief. For Clifford, this requires the path of reason and science, not the path of faith. In essence, Clifford warns that the path of faith is a dead end – literally and figuratively.

I have little hope that a majority of humans near or far will heed Clifford's warning any time soon. Those who believe that they speak and act on the commands of Christianity's God or Islam's Allah or some other god, or their messenger, will obey those commands at any cost. The proof that reason demands is irrelevant to them.

---

1. Many believers insist that faith in divine justice in the hereafter is essential to a moral life on earth. On this issue, see Phil Zuckerman, *Society without God: What the Least Religious Nations Can Tell Us About Contentment*, New York University Press, 2008. This study of Denmark and Sweden, where most people are atheist or agnostic, shows that violent crime is very low, altruistic behavior is very high, and overall societal health is superior to religious nations such as the United States.

2. *Webster's Tenth New Collegiate Dictionary*, p. 418.

3. According to an ancient Greek myth, the gods bestowed gifts upon the beautiful Pandora in a box but instructed her never to open it. When her curiosity won out, however, she opened the box only to discover to her shock that she unleashed illnesses and hardships galore upon the human race.

4. The focus here is contemporary faith-based beliefs among Christians and Muslims. Poignant examples are available from the past, including the Crusades, the Inquisition, witch hunts, persecution of the Jews by Christians in Europe, human sacrifice in South America, etc.

5. Other examples from Christianity include these. Some Christians, following Proverbs 22:15 beat their children, and in many Christian families, following Ephesians 5:22-24, wives are subservient to their husbands.

6. The Quran says: "I will cast terror into the hearts of those who disbelieve. Therefore strike off their heads and strike off every fingertip of them" (Sura 8:12) and "The true believers fight for the cause of God, but the infidels fight for the devil. Fight then against the friends of Satan." (Sura 4:76) Also, the Hadith says: "The Messenger of Allah said: I have been commanded to fight against people so long as they do not declare that there is no God but Allah." (Muslim 1:30)

7. Further, Sharia also provides that a man determined to be a rapist need only pay his victim a fee and, remarkably, that a woman whose claim of rape is not corroborated by the rapist or four witnesses is subject to punishment as a fornicator or adulterer. Other examples from Islam include the following: In many majority-Muslim nations, Sharia forbids criticism of Islam, and calls for jail, torture, or death for those deemed apostates or heretics; Saudi Arabia, a wealthy Muslim nation, promotes Wahhabism, an extreme form of Islam, and sponsors madrassas around the world, "schools" which often exclude girls and where the curriculum consists mainly of memorizing the Quran and studying Islam; and violence periodically breaks out in the Middle East between Sunni and Shia Muslims who consider one another heretics.

8. The Quran also permits the owning of slaves. See Sura 5:89 and Sura 23:1.

9. Thus, the Christian county official in Kentucky who refused to sign marriage permits for same-sex couples in 2015 violated Biblical commands by doing too little.

10. Examples of faith-based nonsense in other countries include these: In at least three nations in Africa – Sierra Leone, Liberia, and Guinea – the spread of Ebola is fueled by family members and friends washing and dressing the body of the deceased and mourners at the funeral touching it to make sure that the dead don't return to haunt the living; in India, where believers take their own religion as superior to others, violence regularly breaks out among Hindus, Christians, and Muslims; and following Hindu tradition, some women whose husbands die choose to immolate themselves on their husband's funeral pyre even if they have young children.

11. See W.K. Clifford, "The Ethics of Belief," *Contemporary Review*, 1877. (This is reprinted in many places.)

ABOUT THE AUTHOR

TOM SHIPKA RECEIVED HIS PH.D. in philosophy from Boston College in 1969. That same year he joined the faculty at Youngstown State University. Early in his YSU career he spearheaded the unionization of the faculty and served as a leader of the faculty union for many years. Later, he served as chair of the Department of Philosophy and Religious Studies, chair of the Academic Senate, and a member of fund-raising committees for both the academic and athletic divisions. Off campus he served as chair of the higher education councils of the Ohio Education Association and the National Education Association as well as chair of the Ohio Faculty Council. He was inducted into the YSU Heritage Society and the YSU Athletics Hall of Fame as a contributor. He retired from full-time service at YSU in 2006 and stayed on for nine more years teaching philosophy part-time. A speakers series at the university is named in honor of him and his deceased father, a labor leader and YSU trustee.

He has also served on the boards of public organizations, including the Western Reserve Transit Authority, the Public Library of Youngstown and Mahoning County, and the Mill Creek MetroParks.

His publications include two books - *Philosophy: Paradox and Discovery*, Fifth Edition, 2004, and *Beliefs and Practices: Taking A Fresh Look*, 2016 - and dozens of articles in social and political thought, critical thinking, and higher education labor relations.

Made in the USA
Columbia, SC
17 March 2019